Businessmen, Clientelism, and Authoritarianism in Egypt

Businessmen, Clientelism, and Authoritarianism in Egypt

Safinaz El Tarouty

BUSINESSMEN, CLIENTELISM, AND AUTHORITARIANISM IN EGYPT
Copyright © Safinaz El Tarouty, 2015

First published in 2015 by PALGRAVE MACMILLAN® in the United States—a division of St. Martin's Press LLC, 175 Fifth Avenue, New York, NY 10010.

Where this book is distributed in the UK, Europe and the rest of the world, this is by Palgrave Macmillan, a division of Macmillan Publishers Limited, registered in England, company number 785998, of Houndmills, Basingstoke, Hampshire RG21 6XS.

Palgrave Macmillan is the global academic imprint of the above companies and has companies and representatives throughout the world.

Palgrave® and Macmillan® are registered trademarks in the United States, the United Kingdom, Europe and other countries.

ISBN: 978-1-137-49337-8

Library of Congress Cataloging-in-Publication Data

El Tarouty, Safinaz, 1974-
    Businessmen, clientelism, and authoritarianism in Egypt / Safinaz El Tarouty.
        pages cm
    Summary: "After the ousting of former Egyptian president Hosni Mubarak in February 2011, there was much debate about the reasons for the former regime's longevity and its collapse. Here, Safinaz El Tarouty provides an original contribution to the study of authoritarianism in Egypt by focusing on the role of businessmen in authoritarian survival. As the regime intensified neo-liberal economic reforms that led to social deprivation and frustration amongst increasing numbers of Egyptian citizens, they co-opted businessmen in order to defuse challenges and buttress the regime, constructing a new political economy of authoritarianism. Extending the existing literature on clientelism, El Tarouty creates a typology of regime-businessmen relations to describe the multiple mechanisms of co-option in the context of economic liberalization. Ultimately, though, these businessmen proved too narrow a constituency to provide legitimacy to the regime and in fact formed one of the reasons for its collapse"—Provided by publisher.
    Includes bibliographical references and index.
    ISBN 978-1-137-49337-8 (hardback)
    1. Businessmen—Political activity—Egypt. 2. Business and politics—Egypt. 3. Authoritarianism—Egypt. 4. Patron and client—Egypt. 5. Egypt—Politics and government—1981- 6. Egypt—History—Protests, 2011- I. Title.

    JQ3869.P7E5 2015
    322'.30962—dc23   2015010843

A catalogue record of the book is available from the British Library.

Design by Scribe Inc.

First edition: September 2015

10 9 8 7 6 5 4 3 2 1

To my daughter
Farida Emara

Contents

Acknowledgments

This book is the result of four and a half years of PhD research conducted at the University of East Anglia (UEA). During the course of my study at UEA, I have benefited greatly from the help of many people. I am particularly indebted to Nicola Pratt, who supervised my dissertation and whose advice and suggestions have been invaluable. I am immensely grateful to her for having given me so much of her time and effort in reading and discussing my work. Her encouragement and support have seen me through many difficult times.

I would like to thank John Greenaway and Alan Finlayson for their useful feedback on my work during the writing stage. I am also thankful to Ray Bush and Lee Marsden for their thoughtful comments, which helped me revise my work and, hopefully, improve it.

I would like to thank all the interviewees whom I met in Cairo and London during my fieldwork. Through their gracious support, generosity with their time, and candor in answering my questions, I was able to see the light at the end of the tunnel.

I would like to thank my close friend Lisa Blaydes of Stanford University for her support. I am grateful to Adel Beshai and his wife Magda Barsoum for their friendship and support, which I will always cherish. I am very thankful to my friends Hossein Mahdavy and his wife Nevine Mahdavy for taking the time to discuss some of the ideas contained in this book. My dear friend Aida Yehia also deserves special thanks for providing me with online articles whenever I could not access them.

During my studies at the American University in Cairo for my bachelor of arts and my master of arts, I was lucky to be taught by professors who came from different political backgrounds: Saad Eddin Ibrahim, Mustapha Kamel El Sayyid, Emad Shahin, and Maye Kassem. Even though they are not directly related to this work, they helped shape my understanding of Egyptian politics.

Very special thanks go to Ali El Din Hillal, whose unconditional care and support during this journey will make me forever grateful to him.

My family is owed particular thanks. I would like to thank my father and my mother, who supported me financially and morally. My late brother *become engaged in politics? (3) What was the relationship between the regime and those businessmen who did not engage in politics? (4) Did all businessmen support the regime? If not, how did the regime deal with businessmen opposing the regime?*

This research finds that businessmen's support for or opposition to authoritarianism is not always contingent on their economic interests. It could be contingent on other factors that include the nature of their relations with the regime and their personal or ideological beliefs or values. This book uncovers the diversity of relations between businessmen and politics.

Why Businessmen and Authoritarianism? Situating the Research Questions

The answers to these research questions are important for understanding the role of businessmen in sustaining or opposing authoritarianism, particularly in the context of a shift from a state-led to a market-led economy. This shift created new challenges for Egypt's authoritarian regime, as its control of a large public sector had enabled it to provide socioeconomic benefits to Egypt's citizens in return for their obedience to the regime.[4] Egypt began its economic transition in 1991, with an increase in neoliberaleconomic reforms after 2004. On the one hand, economic liberalization increased the wealth of Egypt's business class, potentially constituting an economically powerful opposition to the regime as business classes had done in other developing countries. For instance, in the Philippines under Marcos (1965–86), Filipino businessmen in 1984 filled the ranks of the demonstrations against Marcos.[5] Simultaneously, as the Egyptian regime sped up neoliberal economic reforms, it created more social deprivation. For instance, during the period from 2003 to 2007, there was a decrease in public spending on social services like health care, education, and social security. In health care, public spending fell by 25 percent, and in education, it fell from 16.2 percent to 12.6 percent of total government expenditure.[6] This reduction in social services negatively affecting the majority of citizens weakened the relationship between the state and the citizenry and threatened the regime's legitimacy.

I argue that in order to defuse the challenges of economic liberalization, the regime deepened its ties to some businessmen in order to create a new political economy of authoritarianism. However, this was too narrow of a constituency to provide legitimacy to the regime. An indicator of this was the outbreak of the revolution on January 25, 2011.

This study attempts to go beyond the representation of businessmen as supportive to authoritarianism and of democratization depending on their economic interests.[7] It also attempts to go beyond the representation of businessmen as unable to shape laws and policies for their own economic benefit.[8] While accepting some of the arguments put forward by Eva Bellin[9] and Amr Adly,[10] this work argues for a less black-and-white understanding of the role of businessmen under authoritarianism. This book attempts to provide a framework for understanding the different roles of businessmen in either opposing or supporting authoritarianism.

This work has emerged in an attempt to find answers to some of the questions raised in the course of my political and professional background. Since the late 1990s, I have been interested in understanding why authoritarianism has persisted in Egypt. In order to deepen my understanding of the situation, I decided to join the NDP. A few years later, I was one of a handful of young females who were appointed to the newly established Policies Secretariat, headed by the president's son Gamal Mubarak. The Policies Secretariat has included a number of business tycoons in addition to academics and intellectuals. At the beginnings of the monthly meetings of the Policies Secretariat, members would rush to greet the young Mubarak and exchange brief words with him. The regular presence of businessmen in the meetings raised questions for me about what led them to engage in politics. Are they looking out for their own business interests or the interest of the country? Is their presence in this Secretariat to support Mubarak's regime and the project of hereditary succession?[11]

On an independent level, I participated in two research projects that examined the Muslim Brothers (MB) in elections and parliament. Through these projects, I conducted several interviews with members of the MB and visited their offices many times during the period from 2005 to 2009. During my interactions with the MB, I had in mind several questions: Why do they engage in politics by joining the MB organization despite their constant detention and arrest by the regime? Is their opposition to the regime for the benefit of the country? Or does their opposition aim to challenge the regime and replace it with an Islamic one?

During my professional career, I worked from 2005 to 2008 in an Egyptian think tank, which allowed me to meet with different opposition activists. My interactions with them led me to raise questions about whether they wanted democracy for the country or whether they were playing the role of a "loyal" opposition that actually supported rather than opposed Mubarak's regime. Do we have different types of opposition? And why is the opposition divided and not united against the regime?

To sum up, through my various professional experiences, I was confronted with conflicting evidence about the role of different political actors in either opposing or supporting authoritarianism. I chose to examine the role of businessmen from different political backgrounds in an attempt to understand the different roles they played in Egypt under Mubarak and if they were agents of democratization or supportive to authoritarianism.

Original Contribution

This book seeks to make an original contribution in a number of ways. First, it attempts to go beyond the concept of co-option as dyadic and static. By examining how—in light of Egypt's economic liberalization—co-option was flexible and took a variety of forms, I seek to add to the Middle East literature on clientelism.

Second, this book seeks to fill the gap in the existing literature on clientelism, which does not discuss what would happen if the opposition were to refuse to be co-opted. I also seek to add to the literature by examining how the regime used divide-and-rule tactics among an opposition that refused to be co-opted. Building on Ellen Lust-Okar,[12] who argues that the regime created a divided political environment among the political parties in the legal and illegal opposition, this book seeks to argue that the division among parties in the opposition took other forms as well. The regime created a division inside the legalized opposition parties that turned radical, which resulted in two parties: one legal and one illegal. Then the regime created division among the political parties and movements in the illegal opposition.

By providing a detailed examination of case studies on businessmen from different political backgrounds, I make an original, empirical contribution to the study of businessmen in Egypt. This study also seeks to make a contribution to understanding the role of businessmen in comparative politics.

Methodology and the Process of Doing Fieldwork

I selected the role of Egyptian businessmen in Egyptian politics and their relationship to authoritarian survival and collapse under Mubarak as a case study through which to explore my research questions. The time period for this study is 1990 to February 2011. In this research, I examine relatively large-scale businessmen whose scale of activity tied them to the regime. Their business activities cover different sectors, including trading, investment, industrialization, agriculture, tourism, telecommunication, or in some cases, multisectoral activities. I also examine bureaucrats who turned into businessmen.

The reason for choosing this period is that implementation of the structural adjustment program in Egypt started in the early 1990s, heralding a new period in Egypt's political economy. The end date of this study has been chosen because this was when Mubarak's regime was overthrown. The fieldwork for this research started about a year before the Twenty-Fifth of January Revolution (in December 2009) and ended in September 2010. I have used qualitative research methods to answer my research questions on the role of businessmen in authoritarian survival. Through interviews, newspaper articles, secondary sources, and interpellations submitted to parliament, I was able to construct case studies about different types of businessmen and their relationships with the regime (for example, authoritarian clientelism, semiclientelism, mutual dependency, and patron-broker-client relationships versus radical opposition that refuses to be co-opted). Through these case studies, I analyze the role of businessmen in authoritarian survival and renewal.

I selected the interviewees after making a short list of large-scale businessmen who come from different political backgrounds: NDP businessmen, independent businessmen, and businessmen from opposition organizations and movements. I have chosen a case study approach to allow for an in-depth understanding and analysis of businessmen's relationships with the authoritarian regime. For instance, Robert Yin defines the case study research method as "an empirical inquiry that investigates a contemporary phenomenon within its real-life context; when the boundaries between phenomenon and context are not clearly evident; and in which multiple sources of evidence are used."[13] Businessmen who were examined in this research entered into clientelistic relations with the regime, and they have been classified based on the institutional tool by which the regime co-opted them: (1) businessmen who were co-opted by running for parliament as NDP members or independents, (2) other businessmen who did not engage in politics and were co-opted through social-network relations with Mubarak and his family, and (3) other businessmen who were co-opted by joining the loyal opposition parties. This is why I examine these three categories of businessmen in three different chapters: "Parliamentary Businessmen," "The Social Networks of the Mubarak Family and Businessmen," and "Businessmen in the Opposition." I believe that these classifications provide a comprehensive examination of samples of different types of large-scale businessmen who were co-opted by the regime through different institutional mechanisms. In order to complement my case study approach to businessmen and authoritarianism, I examine in each of these classification examples of the businessmen who refused to be co-opted by the regime.

The data I have collected were triangulated by information from different sources to confirm their accuracy. For instance, I conducted more than sixty interviews with NDP businessmen, opposition businessmen, opposition parliamentarians, political activists, economists, bankers, members of business associations, and journalists. During the interviews, I presented myself as a PhD student, without revealing my party affiliation, in order to gain the credibility of the interviewee; however, in very rare cases, I revealed my membership in the ruling party to the interviewees with whom I had met several times and developed a friendship outside of the fieldwork project. When dealing with the data collected through interviews, it was important to check the information. So I triangulated the data from interviews with other sources, including other interviews, newspaper articles, court rulings, interpellations, and other secondary sources. I faced some problems in triangulating the data. For instance, I looked for data about the corruption of businessmen, since the mechanisms of their corruption could reveal their relationships to the regime. But under authoritarianism, the collection of these data presents certain challenges for the researcher. The data that I have collected include court rulings about specific cases of businessmen's corruption. I requested permission from the Centre of Legal Studies in the Ministry of Justice to get copies of some court rulings; however, the center refused to give me permission. This is a common practice by authoritarian regimes, which are usually suspicious of anyone looking for information, especially PhD students enrolled at foreign universities abroad. To solve this problem, I got the court rulings from either the businessmen or the lawyers who were involved in these cases.

Another type of data that helped triangulate my data was the interpellations submitted to parliament by opposition parliamentarians. These interpellations were important because they present direct accusations against the government regarding its involvement in the corruption of businessmen and enabled me to identify those businessmen implicated in corruption and the role of the regime in it. Attached to the interpellations are firsthand documents about business-government relations and corruption in Egypt (for example, contracts about selling state-owned lands and factories). But these interpellations were not available in the Library of Parliament following a fire in parliament in the summer of 2008 when these documents were burned. So I had to meet with the opposition parliamentarians independently to obtain these interpellations. The topics of the interpellations I have collected include the corruption of businessmen in the steel industry, the monopoly in telecommunications, and corruption in the selling of state-owned lands and in privatization.

Other data I have collected for this research that have helped me triangulate my information include newspaper archives from semiofficial newspapers, such as *Al-Ahram Daily*, *Al-Akhbar*, and *Rose Al-Youssef*. Despite these newspapers being progovernment in their coverage, they are useful because they cover government policies. Moreover, these newspapers provided in-depth interviews with regime elites, including former President Mubarak, the then ministers, the leading members of the NDP, and NDP businessmen. I have analyzed and quoted from these interviews. Then, after the revolution, these newspapers started to cover the corruption of Mubarak's regime, his family, and NDP businessmen.

I have used opposition newspapers, like *Al-Destour*, *Al-Masry Al-Youm*, *Al-Wafd*, *Al-Youm Al-Sabae*, *Sout Al-Oma*, *Al-Usbu'*, and more independent newspapers, like *Al-Ahram Weekly*. These newspapers were useful in covering the corruption of businessmen. But when it comes to former President Mubarak, his wife, and his sons, their business corruption was never covered. However, after the collapse of Mubarak's regime, more information became available in these newspapers about the business corruption of the Mubarak family.

In triangulating my data, I have also used secondary literature in English and Arabic on Egypt's political economy. This secondary literature is based on empirical data gathered through interviews, newspaper archives, minutes of meetings of the People's Assembly, reports from the Central Agency for Public Mobilization and Statistics, reports from human rights organizations, reports from the Central Bank, and copies of police investigations (of businessmen). After the revolution, more books were published in Arabic that included empirical data about Egypt's political economy and the corruption of businessmen co-opted by the regime.

Finally, the process of triangulating the data was sometimes faced with obstacles. For instance, when I met with NDP steel tycoon Ahmed Ezz and asked him about accusations concerning his illegal acquisition of the Al Dekheila Steel Company, he denied them and then refused to continue the interview. So I met with his competitors and workers in the steel industry, and I relied on parliamentary interpellations and information from different newspapers. An example of another challenge in triangulating the data was when I met with Egyptian businessmen living in London. These businessmen have fled Egypt because of financial or political problems with the regime. In order to avoid being misled by the information they provided me, I had more interviews in Cairo with senior bankers who provided me with oral information about the irregularities of these businessmen. So in each case study that I wrote, I used a cross-checking method by triangulating my data with information from different sources, newspapers articles, other interviews, court rulings, interpellations, and empirical data published in books.

Organization of This Book

The following chapters examine the role of businessmen in the survival of Mubarak's authoritarianism. I demonstrate how the regime created new relationships with businessmen by co-opting some of them while excluding others. After the introduction of economic liberalization, the co-option of businessmen took a variety of forms. This included the continuous subordination of businessmen to the regime based on credible threats of coercion or a form of political bargaining between businessmen and the regime due to the increase in their structural and financial power. In exceptional cases, the power of businessmen could increase to the extent that they were able to threaten the regime. In other cases, the regime delegated its role in the provision of social services to businessmen, which led to a triadic, clientelistic relationship composed of the regime, the businessmen, and the clients. On the other hand, there are businessmen from the radical opposition who refused to be co-opted by the regime, which led them to be excluded from participating in the formal political process; also, the regime created a division among them. The different varieties and flexibilities of co-option and the regime's exclusion of the radical opposition and the divisions created among them promoted a new political economy of authoritarianism.

This book is divided into five chapters in addition to a conclusion. The first chapter surveys the literature on authoritarian survival or renewal. The literature is classified into two groups: the political economy approach and the institutional approach. The aim is to create a framework to analyze businessmen in Egypt under Mubarak.

The second chapter starts with a historical background about the rise of modern Egyptian capitalism in the 1920s until the overthrow of the monarchy in 1952. The chapter then examines businessmen under Nasser, Sadat, and Mubarak in the 1980s. The aim is to argue that the political economy of authoritarianism relied on co-opting the loyal businessmen while excluding those who represented a challenge to the regime.

Chapter 3 demonstrates the growing political role of businessmen in Mubarak's Egypt after 1991, and particularly after 2004, when neoliberal economic reforms were accelerated. The chapter examines the role of businessmen in the People's Assembly and the ruling party. It demonstrates the change in the relationship between businessmen and the regime and how they contributed to the reshaping of authoritarianism. The chapter documents how NDP businessmen and independent businessmen were co-opted by the regime through existing institutions (elections, parliament, and the ruling party). This co-option was flexible and took different forms that varied from authoritarian clientelism, semiclientelism, mutual dependency, and patron-broker-client relationships.

The fourth chapter examines empirical cases of businessmen who were not engaged in politics but who created personal relationships with the Mubarak family. The aim is to show that the regime not only co-opted businessmen through existing political institutions but also created social institutions through informal alliances and social networks with businessmen not involved in politics, through which the regime helped these businessmen grow successfully in return for their loyalty to the regime. These businessmen also played a role in helping the enrichment of the Mubarak family.

The fifth chapter focuses specifically on businessmen in the loyal and radical opposition, like the Ghad Party, the Wafd Party, the illegal MB organization, and the Kefaya (Enough) political movement. The relationship between the regime and opposition businessmen is discussed to illustrate how the regime selectively co-opted the loyal opposition while it harassed and excluded the radical opposition. The chapter also argues that the regime has weakened the opposition by creating division on different levels: among the political parties in the legal and illegal opposition; inside the political parties in the opposition that turned radical, which resulted in a legal wing and an illegal wing; and among the political parties and movements in the illegal opposition.

In the concluding chapter, the consequences of Mubarak's new political economy of authoritarianism are assessed. The regime's predation and co-option of businessmen may appear to be a useful instrument for the maintenance of the political status quo; however, the chapter reflects on how the Twenty-Fifth of January Revolution proved the failure of the new political economy of authoritarianism. The chapter also examines the role of businessmen in the post-Mubarak period and the role of businessmen in the overthrow of the MB president Mohammed Morsi (2012–13) when they found that their economic interests did not coincide with those of his regime. Finally, the chapter concludes with a brief assessment of current President Abdel Fattah El-Sisi's relationship with the businessmen and their role in either maintaining or threatening his rule.

I

The Uprising, Authoritarianism, and Political Transformation

Introduction

By the beginning of 2011, the economic and political climate in Egypt was highly charged. On the economic level, the economic reforms that started in the early 1990s produced some success, like an increase in the growth rate of the gross domestic product (GDP) by an average of 4.5 percent over the previous two decades.[1] In 2007, foreign direct investment increased to $11 billion compared to $400 million in 2004, and Egypt's exports increased by 20 percent.[2] However, the majority of the population was hurt by the economic reforms. For example, economic growth failed to translate into providing an adequate amount of jobs. During the last years of Mubarak's rule, unemployment among university graduates reached 40 percent for men and 50 percent for women.[3] The proportion of the population living below the national poverty line rose from 16.7 percent in 2000 to 22 percent in 2008.[4] The number of shanty towns increased to more than one thousand, spread around twenty governorates, with a total population of 17.7 million.[5]

On the political level, the previous decade witnessed protests and demonstrations from different segments of Egyptian society. As Mona El-Ghobashy writes,

Egypt's streets had become parliaments, negotiating tables and battlegrounds rolled into one. To compel unresponsive officials to enact or revoke specific policies, citizens blockaded major roads with tree branches and burning tires, organized sit-ins in factory plants or outside ministry buildings, and blocked the motorcades of governors and ministers. Take this small event in the logbook of popular politics from January 2001, one of forty-nine protest events that year recorded by just one newspaper. Workers at the new

Health Insurance Hospital in Suez held a sit-in to protest the halt of their entitlement pay. State security officers and local officials intervened, prevailing upon the authorities to reinstate the pay and fire the hospital director. By 2008, there were hundreds of such protests every year, big and small. In June 2008, thousands of residents in the fishing town of Burg al-Burullus blocked a major highway for seven hours to protest the governor's abrupt decision to halt the direct distribution of flour to households. Police used tear gas and batons to disperse demonstrators, and ninety people were arrested.[6]

In parallel, since 2000, Gamal, the son of President Mubarak, became visible in the political scene. His grooming in the ruling party over the previous decade confirmed that he had been prepared to inherit the presidency. In 2010, the parliamentary elections were rigged in favor of the ruling party. This led the opposition to unite and establish a shadow parliament. Mubarak criticized the opposition by saying, "Let them have fun," which highly outraged the population, especially that the next presidential election was scheduled one year later and that the most likely candidates were either Mubarak or his son Gamal. As political scientist Emad Shahin explains, "Fraudulent elections have been a common trigger factor in many prodemocracy revolutions, and Egypt was no exception. Its political and economic elites have grown completely isolated from society and were even more determined to push for the succession of Gamal Mubarak, despite growing popular opposition to this plan. Ahmed Ezz, a business tycoon, top NDP [National Democratic Party] official and close associate of Gamal, wanted to make sure his friend's path to the presidency was secure and smooth, and as a result, he oversaw one of the most tainted parliamentary elections in the country's recent history."[7]

By the time January 25, 2011, arrived, the protestors went to the streets with economic and political grievances. They complained about the emergency law, police torture, the rigging of elections, the low minimum wage, inflation, and unemployment. These complaints were reflected in their slogan: "bread, freedom, social justice, and dignity."[8]

Mubarak's three decades of authoritarian rule collapsed after an 18-day popular mass uprising. Those who participated in the uprising were the youth of the middle and the upper classes, the poor, the upper classes, the workers, the peasants, women, Copts, old people, and urban and rural residents.[9] As journalist Hossam el-Hamalawy wrote on his blog one day after the collapse of Mubarak's regime, "In Tahrir square you found sons and daughters of the Egyptian elites together with the workers, middle class citizens and the urban poor. Mubarak has managed to alienate all social classes in society including [a] wide section of the bourgeoisie."[10]

The breadth of opposition to Mubarak illustrates how his regime alienated the majority of the population, relying for its survival on the co-option of a small constituency of businessmen who benefitted from economic liberalization to accumulate wealth illegally and who, in return, provided support to the regime. We can consider Egypt to be a "predatory state" in the sense of Peter Evans, who argues that "those who control the state apparatus seem to plunder without any more regard for the welfare of citizenry than a predator has for the welfare of its prey."[11] This means that businessmen co-opted by the Mubarak regime were looting for their own interests at the expense of the interests of the rest of Egyptian society.

This chapter discusses the existing literature on authoritarian regime survival in light of this book's research question: to what degree do businessmen challenge or support authoritarianism? I have classified the literature on authoritarian survival and renewal into two groups: the political economy approach and the institutional approach. The former looks at how changes in the relationship between the state and the market, or the state and the nature of the economy, impact political outcomes. From this approach, I build on Eberhard Kienle's argument that economic liberalization has increased authoritarianism.[12] In addition, I discuss Amr Adly's argument that businessmen in Egypt under Mubarak were not able to capture the state, and in light of my empirical findings, I question the validity of his argument.[13] I also discuss Eva Bellin's argument that businessmen's support of authoritarianism is contingent on their economic interests, and I question the validity of generalizing this argument to businessmen in Egypt.[14] I also examine the variety of relationships developed by authoritarian regimes with businessmen to maintain their regimes' survival.

However, the political economy approach does not explain how businessmen became dependent upon and subordinate to the regime. This is why, in addition to the political economy approach, this research includes elements from the institutional explanations of authoritarianism. From this approach, I build on the work of Maye Kassem,[15] Jason Brownlee,[16] Lisa Blaydes,[17] and John Sfakianakis,[18] who argue for the important role of institutions as tools for co-option to maintain the survival of authoritarian regimes. However, my empirical findings question the validity of co-option as the static concept presented in the literature on authoritarian renewal, especially after the introduction of economic liberalization.

Having reviewed this literature, I combine both approaches in order to create a framework for examining the case of Egypt. I argue that it is necessary to consider both the institutional mechanisms for co-opting businessmen as regime allies and excluding businessmen who are regime opponents as well as the structural power of businessmen in different historical eras as a result of political-economic processes.

Before discussing the literature on authoritarian survival and renewal, the following section examines state-society relations and authoritarianism in Egypt under the Nasser and Sadat regimes and the Mubarak regime in the 1980s.

Authoritarianism and State-Society Relations in Egypt

This section aims to provide a context for the reasons for the regime's co-option of businessmen in Egypt. To understand this, it is important to provide a brief historical overview of Egypt's political economy and authoritarianism before discussing it in more detail in the following historical chapter. Moving from Nasser to Sadat, we find that each president has used his economic policies (socialist or liberal) in ways that created a constituency that supported him and helped in maintaining his regime, as the following section will discuss.

Nasser (1956–70) maintained his regime by providing benefits and welfare services to co-opt the popular forces (the workers, peasants, and middle-class citizens) into the state; in return, they provided support to the regime.[19] For instance, Nasser's land reform legislation in the 1950s and the 1960s redistributed 12 percent of the country's land. The aim of the land reform was to give land to the landless peasants.[20] In addition to land reform, the rents of agricultural land and real estate were fixed at very low levels. Rent contracts became inheritable, which made the tenants almost half owners. If the owner wanted to sell his or her agricultural land or real estate, he or she would have had to get the approval of the tenant, who would have obtained half of the amount of the sale in return for vacating the property.[21] Also, the workers benefited from Nasser's socialist policies. Import substitution industrialization (ISI) was successful in its early years. During the period of 1960–65, industry grew annually at 9 percent, and total GDP growth reached 5.5 percent. The number of those in the labor force increased during this period from 6 million workers to 7.3 million workers, which is a total increase of 22 percent.[22] The increase in growth rate enabled the state to extend social services like health care, food subsidies, education, and so on. For instance, during the period from 1952 to 1966, the number of schools built averaged one a day, and the number of individuals receiving free primary education rose by 1.3 million to 3.4 million.[23] This is how Nasser created a constituency (composed of middle class citizens, workers, and peasants) that supported his policies and benefited from them.[24]

Unlike Nasser, Sadat (1970–81), upon coming to power, shifted away from socialist policies. For instance, in the early 1970s, Sadat returned the sequestrated properties (for example, the land taken from the landowners during Nasser's land reform) to their owners.[25] Moreover, in 1974, Sadat introduced the open-door economic policy called "the *Infitah*," which gave the private sector a greater role in investment. The *Infitah* provided an opportunity for businessmen to engage in parasitic activities. For instance, they made quick profits and benefited from shady deals at the expense of society. This suggests how the experience of economic liberalization in the 1970s resulted in a predatory state, as Nadia Farah argues.[26] Farah used Peter Evans's definition of "predatory" to formulate one of her own, in which the state is dominated by narrow special interests. Farah here refers to the parasitic businessmen who seemed to plunder and fulfill their own interests at the expense of society's interests.[27]

Unlike Sadat, who initiated the *Infitah*, Mubarak, upon coming to power in 1981, announced the return to central planning and the major economic role of the state.[28] During the 1980s, the regime appealed to the lower-class segment of society for its support. Mubarak's speeches in the 1980s stated that he was against selling the public sector. For instance, in a speech in 1985, Mubarak said, "To start with, we don't sell the public sector . . . we don't dissolve it, and this should be clear for all."[29] Mubarak was also critical of economic reforms. On the occasion of Farmers Day on September 8, 1988, he criticized the International Monetary Fund (IMF):

> The IMF acts like someone in the rural areas in the past who made himself a wiseman—a doctor. He is not a doctor or anything. A patient, for example, needs a treatment for one month. Instead of this doctor telling the patient to take the medicine daily for one month, he tells him to take all the medicine today and tomorrow and that he will recover the day after. Of course, he will take the medicine to go to sleep at night and will not wake up in the morning. He dies. This is the IMF. It writes a prescription for those who require prolonged treatment, just as for those who require short treatment . . . I tell the IMF that economic reform should proceed according to the social and economic situation and according to the people's standard of living. One should not come and say increase the price by 40 percent. Surely, no one will be able to live. This will not be an IMF process: it will be a slaughter.[30]

The economic policies of the 1980s led to a decline in real income and an increase in unemployment, which "threatened to produce exactly what some feared would be the result of orthodox economic reforms: riots and political instability."[31] At the international level, in the early 1990s, the total external debt amounted to $49 billion,[32] and Egypt was "turning into an eternal beggar for debt forgiveness and emergency loans."[33] This situation was further aggravated by the 1991 Gulf War, after which more than a million workers returned to Egypt from Kuwait. The war negatively affected the amount of worker remittances and also led to a reduction in tourism.[34] The total cost of the war to Egypt was estimated by the World Bank at $4.5 billion.[35]

Due to these unsustainable economic conditions, Egypt entered into negotiations with the IMF and the World Bank. According to Youssef Boutros Ghali, the then minister of economy and a member of the Egyptian negotiating team, "the overriding instruction from President Hosni Mubarak to the team was to reach an agreement that would quickly trigger the debt relief arrangements offered by the Paris club."[36] In fact, Egypt's role in the Gulf War through military and political help, as one author noted, "had inclined the donors to look favourably on attempts to resuscitate the economy. They not only seconded the efforts of international organizations, but also undertook bilateral actions, especially in the forms of write-offs and rescheduling of Egypt's debt."[37]

In May 1991, Egypt signed an agreement with the IMF, and in November 1991, it signed an agreement with the World Bank.[38] This arrangement, the Economic Reform and Structural Adjustment Program, aimed at stabilizing the economy and starting structural reform. The reforms included an improvement in the balance of payments, the lifting of price controls, a reduction in government subsidies, the imposition of new taxes, and privatization by selling the public enterprises. The economic reform represented a significant change in Egypt's political economy, which until then had been based on state-led development and treating the state as the most important economic actor.

The regime's new stance regarding economic reform was reflected in Mubarak's speeches. Unlike his speeches in the 1980s that likened the IMF to someone who pretends to be a doctor and prescribes the wrong medicines, his speeches after the implementation of the structural adjustment program supported economic reform. For instance, "He has characterized subsidies as social injustice, since the rich also benefited, asked why the public should bear the burden of losing state companies and argued that socialist countries which fixed prices destroyed their economies."[39]

Those who were particularly negatively affected by the economic reform were the poor, like the peasants and workers. For instance, Mubarak's Law 96 of 1992 ended the legal rights of tenants, which were introduced by Nasser in the 1950s and the 1960s This meant that landlords were allowed to retake their lands from their tenants and also charge them a market-based rent, which increased the rent by around 400 percent.[40] As Ray Bush comments, "The ruling NDP managed to achieve two significant aims: demonstrating to the international community its serious intent to 'modernise' tenure, and providing enhanced security for landowners, a social class closely aligned to Mubarak's party."[41]

Moreover, by the mid-1990s, several state-owned firms were privatized; however, this has not improved the working and living conditions of workers. For instance, while textile workers in the private sector earn double the salary of the public-sector workers, the former work 12-hour shifts compared to the latter's 8 hours. Also, textile workers in the private sector seldom receive the health and social benefits that they are supposed to receive. There was also no security that protected their jobs in private-sector companies. This is because before starting a new job in private-sector companies, workers are asked to sign an undated resignation letter, which means they can get dismissed at any time by the employer.[42] This explains why liberal economic policies were unpopular with a large number of citizens and were met with a lot of resistance, particularly among workers and peasants.

So how did Mubarak and other authoritarian rulers renew their authoritarianism after the introduction of neoliberal economic policies that undermined their legitimacy among significant constituencies? To answer this question, I examine the existing literature on the renewal of authoritarianism, dividing it into two categories: the political economy approach and the institutional approach. The next section will review the political economy approach to explain the renewal of authoritarianism.

The Political Economy Approach

Some authors have sought to explain the survival of authoritarianism in terms of the political economy. In particular, they focus on the transition from state-led to market-led economies, which—rather than leading to greater political liberalization, as predicted by modernization theories—has led to the maintenance of authoritarianism.

For instance, Nazih Ayubi argued that economic liberalization will not directly lead to political liberalization, but to a more complex picture of multiplicity of interests. He explained, "The state bourgeoisie wants some expansion in the private sector but not the disappearance of the public sector. The private sector calls for economic liberalization but wants to continue to make use of patronage and asks for state support and protection. This prevents political-economic relations from becoming transparent: only 'transparency' would delineate the political from the economic, the public from the private, the employer from the employee—thus expanding the political arena in which politics of individuals, groups, parties and classes can take place."[43]

Indeed, Eberhard Kienle argues that economic liberalization necessitates greater authoritarianism. He writes, "The economic evolution affected the evolution of liberties because the regime lost, or was afraid to lose, control over a number of activities and actors previously directly dependent upon it. Those measures which led to a redistribution of resources limited the exercise of such control through patronage. And those measures which sought to liberalize the economy limited the influence of the regime over the running of part of the economy. In both cases, it seems the regime sought to compensate for this loss of control by new restrictions on liberties."[44] However, authoritarian regimes were not able to rely on restrictive measures alone to maintain their rule. As Stephen King argues, in reference to Egypt, Syria, Algeria, and Tunisia,

> Economic reform policies created and favoured a rent-seeking urban and rural elite supportive of authoritarian rule and took resources away from the workers and peasants who increasingly had the most to gain from democratization. Thus, the privatization of state assets provided rulers with the patronage resources to form a new ruling coalition from groups that would be pivotal in any capitalist economy: private-sector capitalists, landed elites, the military officer corps, and top state officials, many of whom moved into the private sector and took substantial state assets with them. At the same time, ruling parties maintained elite consensus and contained the dissatisfaction of the lower strata in the new multiparty arena by offering them a dwindling share of state resources. In the end, political openings in the four countries culminated in transformed authoritarian rule.[45]

Other authors argue that even though this new constituency benefited from economic liberalization, they could not influence the policies for their own benefit. For instance, by focusing on postliberal Egypt, Adly argues that even though the regime created rent havens and cronyism in favor of its new constituency of businessmen, it could not capture the state. He writes,

> Given the rampant corruption State-business relations developed in postliberal Egypt, there is a wide consensus that Egyptian business has never gained significant capacity to shape public policies, [laws and regulations] ... There are ample examples that reveal limited business influence on law making: the transfer of public property into private hands has been quite slow and went according to the pace determined by the ruling regime that often considered the interests of unionized labour. Moreover, the State could pursue public policies that run against big business through signing unilateral trade liberalization measures exposing uncompetitive domestic sectors to foreign competition, joining the TRIPS (Trade-related Intellectual Property Rights Agreement) with its negative prospects on pharmaceutical firms, and last but not least the gradual removal of tariff barriers on automobiles in

the context of the Euro-Egyptian associational agreement which is expected to squeeze big Egyptian firms out of the market.[46]

Different authors have conceptualized the relationship between authoritarian regimes and businessmen in different ways: dependency of businessmen on regimes, dependency of regimes on businessmen, or bargaining between regimes and businessmen. Yet in all cases, authors argue that regime-business relations result in authoritarianism. For instance, critiquing the modernization paradigm, Eva Bellin argues that in Tunisia, under former President Ben Ali, industrial capitalists enjoyed the benefits of state sponsorship and became dependent upon the regime, which led them to have less interest in challenging authoritarianism:

> In the case of capital, state sponsorship has spelled compromised autonomy for the private sector and, hence, political timidity. Beyond owing their origins to state largesse, delivered in the form of subsidized start-up capital, subsidized infrastructure, and protected markets, many private sector industrialists find that their economic well-being continues to be beholden to the goodwill of the state. Trade protection and fiscal concessions still buoy the profitability of many firms, and spot subsidies and support programs distributed by the state on a discretionary basis have helped many firms restructure to face foreign competition on a firmer footing. The state's adoption of a more market-driven strategy of development has diminished the role of discretion in the provision of state support to the private sector but has not yet eliminated it. Friendly collaboration with state elites, not public contestation, continues to be important to private sector success. Entrepreneurs have good reason to remain aloof from campaigns for democratization, since their embrace would be interpreted by regime elites as provocative and confrontational.[47]

Bellin confirms her argument that businessmen's political leanings were contingent on their business interests by examining businessmen's dependency on and independence from the state in other countries. For instance, in South Korea during the postwar era, the state was extensively sponsoring the private sector, which made it "diffident about democratization." However, the worldwide recession in the 1980s caused by the oil crisis led the Chun regime (1980–88) to adopt a structural reform program that reduced state support to the private sector in credit supplies and protection of the domestic market, and policy loans were eliminated. But by the mid-1980s, Korean industry became competitive and did not need state protection from foreign competitors, which explains why businessmen became sympathetic toward democratization. The same situation, the author continues, was evident in Brazil. During the 1960s, its emerging industry was dependent on different forms of state support. As a result, private-sector capitalists were keen to support the authoritarian regime since it prioritized their interests. However, by the late 1980s, the state reduced its support to businessmen, which made them support a democratic transition.[48] A similar pattern is also described with regard to Turkey by Ziya Onis and Umut Turem.[49]

In other cases, the regime became dependent on businessmen because of their structural or collective power. For instance, in South Korea under Park (1961–79), *chaebols*—which are large, diversified conglomerates that cover different sectors of the economy—originated and expanded. The regime provided them with protection, cheap loans, preferential tax treatment, and export subsidies.[50] In return for the regime's illegal assistance in expanding *chaebols*, businessmen were paying political funds for the presidency and the ruling party.[51]

However, Beatrice Hibou argues that with the increase in the financial power of businessmen, their relationship with the regime took the form of bargaining. In reference to the Tunisian businessmen's donation to the National Solidarity Fund (NSF) established in 1992 by former President Ben Ali, she writes that the NSF is

> a system of taxation because of the obligatory nature of the contributions; "private" due to the absence of any public controls and in terms of the methods of gathering and distributing funds in the name of a single personality ... Even if [the NSF] is not included in the national budget nor subject to parliamentary control, and even though the fund belongs personally to the president of the Republic ... nonetheless, we cannot say that the [NSF] constitutes simply a process of extraction. We cannot reduce this mechanism to the simple capture of wealth, albeit used for social welfare purposes. Rather, these funds constitute a form of "exchange" in which real services are traded for control and other political benefits ... Contributors are listed and receive a receipt for their contribution, even those living abroad. Entrepreneurs and other influential businessmen who fail to make their voluntary contributions find themselves excluded from public markets and other economic opportunities, and run the risk of an audit or other administrative scrutiny.[52]

Other authors examined the relationship between authoritarianism and businessmen in the context of rentier states in the Arab Gulf countries.[53] For example, in the Arab Gulf countries, oil revenues were redirected from the ruler to the population. In Kuwait, the ruling family, al-Sabah, purchased substantive areas of urban lands from merchants at artificially high prices and then resold them at low prices to the richest merchants.[54] Moreover, the existing laws in the Arab Gulf countries has given privileges to merchants by allowing foreign companies to sell their products only through local agents or by partnering with local merchants. This explains how rich families in the Gulf made their wealth by partnering with brand names—for example, in Kuwait, the Alghanim family with GM; in Saudi Arabia, the Juffali family with Mercedes; in Dubai, both the Futtaim family with Toyata and the Galadari family with Mazda; and so on.[55] When rentier states distribute benefits and favors to the population, they are likely to tax their citizens very little or not at all. In return, the citizens are less likely to demand accountability from their governments. As a result, these governments are more likely to be authoritarian.[56] As Hazem Beblawi explains, in rentier states, the government budget is one sided, with only expenditures (for example, distributing benefits to the citizens, including the merchants) and not revenues (for example, from taxes). Beblawi continues his argument that without taxes, citizens are less likely to demand political participation. On the other hand, countries that derive their revenues through taxes are more likely to be democratic.[57]

Samer Soliman criticized the rentier theory because it implies that the decline of the rentier revenues and the growth of taxation are conducive to democratization; however, Egypt's authoritarian regime refutes this argument. This is because Soliman argued that in the case of Egypt, the decline of rentier revenues since the mid-1980s did not lead to a democratic transformation; instead, the state has been transformed from a rentier to a predatory one.[58] Soliman used Margaret Levi's definition of a "predatory state," which defines it as a state that sets income generation above any other consideration and will do anything to collect more money from society, even by unconstitutional means or by ruining the economy.[59] Here Soliman refers to how the Egyptian predatory state extracted money from the population by force to compensate for the decline in its revenues. This included imposing an unconstitutional tax on Egyptian public- and private-sector employees working abroad[60] and an appeal to businessmen to engage in philanthropic activities. In other words, instead of the businessmen paying taxes to the state for the construction of schools, hospitals, and so on, they would directly finance these activities themselves. For example, as Soliman wrote,

> The regime may have turned more and more to the private sector for help in the 1990s, but it ensured that this help remained under its control and came from quarters it felt it could trust . . . In the wake of the [1992] earthquake, the president's wife championed a campaign to collect donations to repair the schools that had been destroyed and to build new ones. The appeal was directed primarily to the regime's loyal base in the business community. As part of the campaign, the names of donors were announced on television immediately after they had made their contribution—the state paid its debt of recognition upon receipt.[61]

Within the literature that adopts the political economy approach, there are different understandings of the relationship between businessmen and authoritarianism. Bellin argues that it is in the economic interest of businessmen to support authoritarianism in contexts of state-led development and economic protectionism.[62] Beblawi argues that in the context of the rentier state in the Arab Gulf countries, businessmen have been granted favors in their businesses, without paying taxes, that make them less likely to demand democratization.[63] Soliman argued that in the case of Egypt, the decline of rentier revenues led to the transformation of the state from a rentier to a predatory one that extracted money from the population, including the businessmen, in a way that served authoritarianism.[64] In the case of South Korea, the increase in the structural and financial power of *chaebols* led the regime to become dependent on their financial funding;[65] however, Hibou argues that the increase in the power of businessmen has led to the development of a bargaining relationship between them and the regime.[66]

The political economy approach explained the different relations that developed between the businessmen and authoritarianism, ranging from coercion to dependency to bargaining to predation; however, this approach could not explain the institutions in which these relations occurred. This is why I complement the gap in the political economy approach by using the institutional approach. I argue that the Egyptian authoritarian regime used different institutional tools to co-opt and subordinate businessmen. The following section reviews the literature on the different institutional tools used by authoritarian rulers to maintain their rule through co-option.

The Institutional Approach

Several authors have discussed the use of co-option by authoritarian regimes in the Middle East to maintain their rule. This section reviews this literature in order to identify and disaggregate the different institutional mechanisms (both formal and informal) of co-option. I start by discussing the definition of co-option. Then I review the literature on the different institutional mechanisms for regimes' co-option of supporters and containment of opponents. I argue that there are gaps in the literature on authoritarian renewal regarding co-option. Finally, the last subsection examines the regime's divide-and-rule tactics against an opposition that refused to be co-opted.

Definition of Co-option

Co-option is a process of incorporating individuals into the state's institutional framework. It functions within a system of clientelism, which is characterized by patron-client structure. Carl H. Lande defined clientelism as "a vertical dyadic alliance: an alliance between two persons of unequal status, power or resources each of whom find it useful to have an ally superior or inferior to himself."[67] Other authors have provided a more detailed and clarified definition of clientelism. For instance James C. Scott explains that "the patron-client relationship—an exchange relationship between roles—may be defined as special case of dyadic (two person) ties involving a largely instrumental friendship in which an individual of higher socioeconomic status (patron) use his own influence and resources to provide protection of benefits, or both, for a person of lower status (client) who, for his part, reciprocates by offering general support and assistance, including personal services, to the patron."[68]

While in a clientelistic relationship the balance of power is in favor of the patron, the process of reciprocity distinguishes patron-client ties from other relationships. Scott writes, "A patron may have some coercive power and he may also hold an official position of authority. But if the force and authority at his command are alone sufficient to ensure the compliance of another, he has no need of patron-client ties which require some reciprocity. Typically then, the patron operates in a context in which the community norms and the need for clients require at least a minimum of bargaining and reciprocity."[69]

Within this unequal reciprocal relationship, the patron subordinates the client by making credible threats of coercion. As Jonathan Fox writes, "The focus here is on specifically *authoritarian* clientelism, where imbalanced bargaining relations require the enduring political subordination of clients and are reinforced by the threat of coercion. Such subordination can take various forms, ranging from vote buying by political machines, as under semi competitive electoral regimes, to a strict prohibition on collective action, as under most military regimes, to controlled mass mobilization, as in communist or authoritarian populist systems."[70]

Different Institutional Mechanisms for Co-option

This section examines the different institutions (formal and informal) used by authoritarian regimes as tools for co-option to maintain their survival. These institutions are the elections, the parliament, the ruling party, corporatist groups, and social networks. The aim of this section is to show

how these different institutions co-opted the regime's supporters and loyal opponents into a patron-client structure.

Samuel Huntington argued that during the third wave of democratization (from 1974 to 1990), some elections kept incumbents in power but that these cases were exceptional and in the general trend, elections removed autocrats.[71] Contrary to Huntington's arguments, holding elections seems to be one of the institutional mechanisms that authoritarian rulers use to maintain their survival. For instance, a decade after Huntington's third wave of democratization, Brownlee observed that multiparty elections backfired on some rulers, but others maintained their authoritarian rule.[72] The type of political system that includes noncompetitive multiparty elections and limited pluralism seems to conform to Juan Linz's earlier definition of authoritarianism: "Authoritarian regimes are political systems with limited, not responsible, political pluralism; without elaborate and guiding ideology (but with distinctive mentalities); without intensive nor extensive political mobilization (except at some points in their development); and in which a leader (or occasionally a small group) exercises power within formally ill-defined limits but actually quite predictable ones."[73]

Since the transition to democracy did not happen in all countries, a number of authors have tried to explain why elections do not lead to democratic transition but, instead, to authoritarian survival. The conventional argument for why authoritarian leaders hold multiparty elections is that they enhance the legitimacy of the autocrat. As Huntington wrote, "When their performance legitimacy declined, authoritarian rulers often came under increasing pressure and had increasing incentives to attempt to renew their legitimacy through elections. Rulers sponsored elections believing they would either prolong the regime of their rule or that of their associates."[74] However, some authors argued that there are other functions to elections than providing legitimacy to the ruler. For instance, Blaydes argues for the important role of elections in the distribution of spoils to co-opt the regime supporters. She writes,

> The authoritarian leadership needs a mechanism to provide members of the political elite with continued "payment" in exchange for their support. One strategy to accomplish this might have been to appoint individuals to parliament or some other body and distribute benefits on this basis. However, those that would have been excluded from the distribution of spoils could have become embittered and sought strategies of overthrow the leadership. In addition, the regime would continually face the challenge of picking the right people. Through elections, on the other hand, the regime distributes access to state resources in what is perceived be to a fairly free and competitive basis.[75]

Authoritarian regimes were not able to rely on co-opting only the regime supporters to maintain their rule. Kassem argues that the role of elections is to co-opt both the regime supporters and the non-extremist opposition. In explaining why Mubarak held multiparty parliamentary elections, she writes,

> Egypt's democratization efforts as reflected in its contemporary electoral framework functions predominantly as a mechanism for reaffirming and, more importantly perhaps, expanding the regime's informal grip on political participation so as to include political opponents and their supporters. This strategy is based on the logic that, within a specific setting, a multiparty electoral arena could be utilised by the regime as a means of providing, at various levels of the political and social structure, the opportunity to participate in the existing political system and, in most cases, to gain access to a share of the resources it commands. In this way, disparate political activists and their potential supporters would be recruited into the regime's informal system of containment and control.[76]

However, gaining access to a share of the state's resources through elections could not be a useful tool for co-option when the regime faces strong opposition. For instance, Jennifer Gandhi and Adam Przeworski argue that when the opposition is strong, it is co-opted through its participation in elections and thus in legislatures that influence policy. Dictators make more extensive policy compromises to keep the opposition from rebelling. Gandhi and Przeworski write, "Policy compromises require an institutional forum, access to which can be controlled, where demands can be revealed without appearing as acts of resistance, where compromises can be hammered out without undue public scrutiny, and where the resulting agreements can be dressed in a legalistic form and publicized as such. Legislatures are ideally suited for these purposes."[77] This argument does not seem to conform with the attitudes of most authoritarian regimes, since the main job of parliamentarians under authoritarianism is to provide services to their constituents rather than to legislate.[78]

Other authors argue that in order to understand authoritarian survival, we should turn our attention to the institution of the ruling party. For instance, Brownlee argues for the important role of the ruling party in co-opting the regime's coalitions and containing their contestation. In reference to regime survival in Egypt under Mubarak and Malaysia under Mahatir, Brownlee writes, "Both rulers entered their positions in control of parties, and those organizations continue to lay the groundwork for what will follow them. For the past fifty years, the NDP (and its forebears) and UMNO (the United Malays National Organisation) have dominated electoral politics and kept their opponents from power. By providing opportunities for long term advancement and political influence, these parties have curbed elites' incentives to exit the regimes or push for change from the outside. Motivations to defect have been dulled, if not eliminated, and public dissent from the party has been confined to localized rebellions."[79] Unlike the process of co-optation that incorporates individuals or small groups (for example, through election, the parliament, or the ruling party), in corporatism, co-option is based on socioeconomic classes and targets larger social groups. Corporatized groups include trade unions, professional syndicates, business associations, and other interest groups, and they receive economic benefits as well as inclusion in policy making in return for their support for the regime.[80] In Egypt, different types of corporatist institutions have been either included or excluded depending on their support for or opposition to the regime. For instance, Nasser reinforced the economic power of the trade union "through far-reaching redistributive reforms, including codetermination and profit sharing in the nationalized and state-run enterprises."[81] In fact, Nasser's support of the workers corresponds with his economic policy of state-led development that depended on workers as one of the constituencies that provided support to his regime. On the other hand, when Sadat faced resistance from the peasants' corporatist agricultural cooperatives due to his economic policy, he abolished its national confederation and shifted its resources to village banks controlled by allies of the ruling party. As a result, the cooperative movement "was powerless to prevent Sadat's reversion to openly, inegalitarian, neocapitalist policies."[82]

However, after the introduction of economic liberalization, Egyptian regimes did not have the type of state resources to sustain corporatist relations that previously existed. For instance, Ninette Fahmy argues that under Mubarak, a new and tighter form of corporatism replaced the classical corporatism, which Fahmy labels "cointegrationism." She argues that it is "a strategy of co-option of top group leaders into the system and integrating their interests with that of the state using special privileges, patronage networks, and institutionalized corruption."[83]

Sfakianakis argues that the economic liberalization allowed for the emergence of networks in which the regime's coalitions were co-opted. In this clientelistic relation, the network of beneficiaries (businessmen and bureaucrats) provided support to the regime in return for their self-enrichment. He writes,

> The wealth that these businessmen amassed over the course of the decade could not have been accumulated without their crony ties to the state . . . As such, their fortunes depended on an economic system that rewarded those

closest to the state and not necessarily the most innovative or efficient. And not surprisingly, this type of accumulation benefited state officials as well as bureaucrats-turned-businessmen. Privatizing the state became a process by which wealth was generated for both . . . The composition of this network was hybrid, and included high state officials that had developed important accumulative and investment interests in Egyptian business, as well as those emanating from the ranks of the business elite. These groups formed an alliance not only because some had joint projects in the formal sector of the economy, but also because business was conducted on the basis of the transfer of contracts in return for money.[84]

In other cases, the regime formed particular patron-client relationships with specific businessmen in return for their substantial funding to the regime and the enrichment of important figures in the regime. This was evident in Indonesia under Suharto. When Suharto came to power in 1965, the most immediate coercive threat to him was the military, so he created personal relations with ethnic Chinese businessmen and granted them exclusive parts of the Indonesian market. In return, these businessmen had to share funds that personally enriched the generals, and they also had to provide provisions for troops.[85] For instance, Liem Bogasari was "among the circle of trusted ethnic Chinese businessmen with whom Suharto established close connections. [Liem Bogasari used his contacts with the regime and] acquired several export licenses and held import monopolies on cloves."[86] Jeffrey Winters explains, "Liem and other similarly positioned businessmen profited handsomely, but it was always understood from the beginning that in exchange for lucrative deals, Suharto could direct key military officers or elite political figures to Liem and others to be taken care of in generous [spoils sharing]. Sometimes this only meant envelopes stuffed with $100 bills, or sometimes it meant meeting operational needs for troops or building barracks."[87]

Other authoritarian rulers created particular patron-client relationships with specific businessmen to implement development goals that aimed to legitimize their regime. For instance, in South Korea, Park (1961–79), developed personal relationships with Chung Ju-Yung of Hyundai and Cho Chung-hun of Hanjin. In return, they helped Park achieve his development goals. For instance, Chung fulfilled Park's goal of developing the ship-building industry, and Cho privatized the government-owned airline.[88]

In other cases, network relations could be used as a tool for co-option and exclusion. For instance, in Syria, under Hafez al-Assad, informal networks served to exclude the opposition and co-opt loyal businessmen. For instance, Bassam Haddad argues that following the populist authoritarian unraveling, the regime thought of bringing the private sector back in. However, the regime feared a resurgence of businessmen who had strong roots and relationships with the traditional market (of manufacturers and artisans) from which members of the Muslim Brothers (MB) were recruited. So out of security concerns, the regime established informal networks with particular loyal businessmen.[89] As Haddad writes, "The showdown between the state and the [Islamists] between 1979 and 1982 further catalyzed selective rapprochement between state and business in the form of informal networks. The civil unrest, very much tied to the power of the then-weakened traditional business community, accelerated the formation and consolidation of economic networks."[90]

The different institutions examined previously (elections, parliament, political parties, corporate institutions, and social networks) have been created by dictators to co-opt potential clients. The dictator, who is the patron in this clientelistic relationship, can change the results of elections, reverse legislations to be in his favor, and dissolve the parliament, political parties, or networks that he created. For instance, King Hussein of Jordan opened and closed the legislature twice. In Algeria, after the Islamic Salvation Front was about to win the majority of seats in the 1992 election, the military suspended the second round of elections and dissolved the parliament. This means that the dictator always has the power to threaten the use of force,[91] which suggests how, in authoritarian clientelism, the patron can subordinate the client by making credible threats of coercion.

Gap in the Literature on Authoritarian Renewal Regarding Different Forms of Co-option

The literature discussed previously does not explain that authoritarian clientelism is flexible and can take different forms. For instance, as mentioned in the section on the political economy approach, the introduction of economic liberalization increased the financial and structural power of businessmen, which in turn developed a new bargaining relationship between them and the regime. Businessmen thus became less subordinate to the regime—a change that leads to semiclientelism. This means that the patron (for example, the regime) uses less coercion and only threatens the clients (for example, businessmen) with the removal of benefits. As Fox writes, "If the authoritarian-clientelistic combination of material inducements and coercive threats is to be effective, elites need to appear to be able to enforce compliance. If instead they lack the means to uncover, oversee, and punish noncompliance, then the deals they strike with their subordinates are much less enforceable. Semiclientelistic power relations induce compliance more by the threat of the withdrawal of carrots than by the use of sticks. Semiclientelism differs from authoritarian clientelism because it relies on unenforceable deals."[92]

Moreover, the client may become as strong as the patron, which makes the relationship change from semiclientelism to mutual dependency. Patterns of mutual dependency between the regime and businessmen were evident in Russia under Boris Yeltsin. For instance, before Yeltsin's 1996 reelection, the polls showed that his communist opponent was far ahead.[93] At the same time, Yeltsin's communist opponent was considered a threat to the wealth and political connections of businessmen.[94] This meant that it was in the interest of both the businessmen and Yeltsin for him to be reelected for a second term. In this context, a relationship of mutual dependency developed between Yeltsin and businessmen. On the one hand, Yeltsin allowed key firms to be sold off at bargain prices to politically favored businessmen, which led to the rise of oligarchs. On the other hand, in return for amassing huge fortunes from privatization, the oligarchs helped Yeltsin in his political campaign through their financial support and by providing sympathetic coverage through their media outlets: the press and television empires.[95]

It seemed that Yeltsin also depended on oligarchs for the enrichment of his family. For instance, Yeltsin's son-in-law headed the Russian airline Aeroflot, owned by Boris Berezovsky, one of the oligarchs who became wealthy during privatization. In the late 1990s, an arrest warrant was issued for Berezovsky for profit skimming at Aeroflot; however, the charge was dropped.[96] This was because, as one author put it, "while the president had to publicly denounce corruption, any action taken against Berezovsky would implicate him as well."[97] This situation reinforced the mutual dependency between Yeltsin and Berezovsky.

Other patterns of mutual dependency between the regime and businessmen are evident in South Korea. For instance, as mentioned earlier, in South Korea, under Park (1961–79), *chaebols* were established and grew through the support of the regime. But over time, the regime's legitimacy became dependent on the success of *chaebols*. As one author writes, "Over the course of Park's rule, the regime's legitimacy became inextricably tied to the fate of the economy, and the fate of the economy increasingly depended on the burgeoning chaebol. While maintaining the upper hand over business, subsequent regimes have all reneged on early promises of taming the chaebol and have pursued pro-growth strategies relying on the chaebol as the engines of that growth."[98]

Consequently, despite the precarious financial position of the *chaebols*, their importance in the economy "limit[s] state leverage and force[s] the state 'into the role of lender of last resort' because the bankruptcy of a chaebol 'would threaten not only the financial but the economic stability of the country.'"[99] This suggests that the relationship between the regime and *chaebols* had transformed from mere co-option to a mutual dependency in which each one of them needed the other for survival.

However, by the 1980s the symbiotic relations between the regime and businessmen changed in favor of the latter. Businessmen did not need to rely on the regime for support, and "many of the *chaebols* were sufficiently large to provide on an in-house basis many of the financial services that the state had previously supplied."[100] This has encouraged businessmen to convert their economic power into political power in order to challenge the regime. For instance, in 1991 Chung Ju-Yung, founder of Hyundai (which is the largest industrial *chaebol* in South Korea), established a new political party, the Unification National Party, which aimed to challenge the ruling Democratic Justice Party. In 1992, Chung's party got 17 percent of the popular vote in the general elections. In the same year, Chung made a bid for presidency.[101]

The literature on authoritarian renewal with respect to clientelism has discussed the role of elections, parliament, and the ruling party in co-opting the regime supporters and the non-extremist opponents in the regime's patron client structure. This means that clientelism has been examined as a static and dyadic relationship that links the client (for example, the regime supporters or opponents) to its patron (the regime) in a clientelistic chain. However, clientelistic relations are flexible and can take a triadic form that includes the patron, the broker, and the client.[102] This research demonstrates that in Egypt, after the implementation of economic liberalization and after the state reduced its role in the provision of social services, we find the emergence of triadic relations that include the patron (the regime), the broker (subpatron), and the client. This means that the previously examined institutions of elections, the parliament, and the ruling party have provided an opportunity for the regime supporters and the non-extremist opponents to gain access to a share of state resources, but in turn, the regime supporters act as brokers to distribute some of these spoils to the clients in their constituencies.

Paying attention to the varieties and flexibility of clientelism furthers understanding of how authoritarian regimes renew their authoritarianism through different forms of co-opting businessmen, thus preventing them from playing a democratizing role in politics.

Opposition Refuses Co-option

Despite the varieties and flexibility of co-option, it is not always a successful mechanism for authoritarian regimes, since the opposition may refuse to be co-opted. As long as the opposition is not willing to be recruited into the regime's clientelistic chain, it is less likely to win elections or even expand its private businesses. However, the literature on clientelism is not sufficient to explain how authoritarian regimes can survive in the face of an opposition that refuses to be co-opted. This is because the non-co-opted groups can ally with other members of the opposition, which can constitute a challenge to the regime. This is why authoritarian regimes depend not only on co-option but also on divide-and-rule tactics among the opposition to ensure their survival. For instance, overcoming divisions among parties and movements in the opposition could result in authoritarian collapse, as it did in Iran after the Shah eliminated all opposition parties, leading to a broad coalition of opposition forces that succeeded in overthrowing the Shah.[103]

Sydney Tarrow argues that instead of repressing all the opposition, most authoritarian regimes rely on selective repression to divide their opponents and perpetuate their rule: "By negotiating with some elements among the spectrum of contenders, governments encourage moderation and split off the moderates from their radical allies . . . especially when it coincides with the decline of mass support and with factionalization inside the movement, this policy of facilitation and selective repression pushes radicals into more sectarian forms of organization and more violent forms of action and encourages moderates to defect."[104]

In Morocco, King Hassan II divided opposition groups into loyalist and radical factions. This division, as Ellen Lust-Okar argues, prevented political unrest, despite the economic crises in the 1980s. She writes,

> In Morocco, political party elites were sharply divided from groups left out the political system. The palace controlled the loyalist opposition's participation in the political arena and limited its demands. Loyalist opposition elites were required to accept the king's supremacy and support Morocco's bid for the Western Sahara. Within these constraints, however, they acted as the king's "spokesmen of demands," providing an important channel of communication between the masses and the palace. In return, they enjoyed government subsidies and privileged access to the palace. Illegal opposition, mainly religious based-societies, remained outside this system. Many questioned the legitimacy of the king and the political system, including the role of the included parties. Despite their potential for antiregime activity, however, King Hassan II allowed the growth of Islamic opposition in the early 1980s, attempting to counter his secular opponents. He thus fostered a divided political environment.[105]

In Egypt, the divided environment between the secularists and the Islamists created by the Mubarak regime weakened the opposition. As

Dina Shehata writes, "Divisions between Islamists and non-Islamists in the Egyptian opposition have weakened the ability of the opposition parties and movements to build broad-based alliances that are capable of effectively challenging the hegemony of the authoritarian regime . . . The Egyptian regime for its part has successfully manipulated and deepened these divisions and asymmetries to ensure its continued survival and the continued weakness and fragmentation of its challengers."[106]

The divided environment was not only among the Islamist and non-Islamist opposition groups. For instance, Prime Minister Ali Lofty (1985–86) formed a joint committee between the government and the businessmen that aimed for better understandings between them. But the composition of the members in the committee showed the regime's attempt to create division among the businessmen. This was manifested in the regime's inclination toward more representation from the Egyptian Business Association (EBA) and against the chambers of commerce and of industry. While this resulted in conflict among the different business groups, the regime continued to defend the committee and the EBA.[107] As Fahmy writes, "In creating such conflicts among the business community . . . the state ensures the fragmentation of the business community and keeps the power of the wealthiest among them within check, thus preventing their evolution into a strong autonomous pressure group."[108]

The regime has used formal and informal institutions to co-opt potential allies. However, the literature we examined is not sufficient to explain the different varieties and flexibility of clientelism. In addition, what would the regime do when the opposition refused to be co-opted by the regime? What consequences would their refusal to be co-opted have on the regime's survival? Since these questions are not answered in the literature on co-option, this research will fill this gap by focusing on how the regime uses clientelism in a variety of ways to co-opt its supporters and also the tactics used to divide and rule among the opposition and within the groups that could challenge the regime.

Research Questions Emerging from the Gap in the Literature Review and the Framework for Analysis

In Egypt, authoritarian regimes have used their control of the economy to promote their survival. In the post-1952 revolution, the regime utilized populist rhetoric and policies to co-opt the lower classes of society. However, after Mubarak committed himself to economic liberalization in the early 1990s, he had to reduce populist policies, threatening the loss of support from the lower classes of society. As a result, the regime's new political economy of authoritarianism had to look for a new constituency that could support Mubarak's regime and later, the project of hereditary succession. In order to understand how Mubarak maintained his survival for almost three decades, especially after the introduction of economic liberalization, this research uses both the political economy approach and the institutional approach.

From the political economy approach, this research builds on the work of Kienle,[109] who argues that economic reform has been accompanied by more authoritarianism. I also build on the work of King,[110] who argues that authoritarian regimes renew their authoritarianism by creating a new constituency that provides support to the regime.

I agree with Adly's[111] argument that economic liberalization has resulted in uneven distribution of property rights for businessmen close to the regime; however, I do not agree with the rest of his argument that businessmen under economic liberalization were not able to capture the state and shape laws for their own economic benefit. This is because this research demonstrates that with Egypt's economic liberalization, there has been an increase in the structural and financial power of businessmen, which allowed them, in few cases, to influence laws to enhance their profits. Relevant examples to be discussed in this book are the case of Ahmed Ezz and the amendment of the monopoly law in Chapter 3 and the 1997 investment incentive law tailored for the Sawiris family in Chapter 4. In other cases, the increase in the power of businessmen allowed them to have some bargaining relationships with the regime. Relevant examples to be discussed are the cases of the loan MPs (members of parliament) in Chapter 3 and the case of a businessman named Wagih Siag in Chapter 4.

Also, while I agree with Bellin's[112] argument that businessmen were supporting authoritarianism for their own business interests, since they were economically dependent on the regime, this research argues that businessmen may also oppose authoritarianism and sacrifice their wealth and private business. This is not because they are agents of democratization but because of their ideological stances. A relevant example will be discussed in the case of the MB businessmen in Chapter 5.

From the formal and informal institutional approach, this research builds on the work of Kassem,[113] Blaydes,[114] Brownlee,[115] and Sfakianakis,[116] who argue for the importance of institutions as tools for co-option to strengthen authoritarianism. I also build on the argument of Sfakianakis[117] on how network relations between the regime and its coalitions helped enrich bureaucrats who turned into businessmen. However, this research further argues that the regime allowed bureaucrats to accumulate wealth— through their own network relations—not only to provide support for the regime but also in return for their help in the enrichment of the Mubarak family and their associates. A relevant example will be discussed in the case of the minister of housing, Ibrahim Soliman, in Chapter 4.

Moreover, the literature on authoritarian renewal regarding co-option (through parliament, elections, the ruling party, and social networks) did not discuss clientelism's flexibility and variable forms. The literature also did not discuss the fact that despite the varieties and flexibility of clientelism, not all businessmen agreed to be recruited into the regime's clientelistic chain. For instance, businessmen who were members of radical opposition parties or organizations like the MB refused to be co-opted by the regime. This is why this research builds on the work of Lust-Okar,[118] who argues for the importance of creating a divided environment among the legal and illegal opposition. While I build on Lust-Okar's argument, my research further argues that authoritarian regimes created a divided environment not only among the political parties in the legal and illegal opposition but also inside the legalized opposition by particularly targeting businessmen, like in the case of the Ghad Party, which resulted in two wings—one legal and another illegal—as discussed in Chapter 5. The regime has also created a division among the political parties and movements in the illegalized opposition like the MB and Kefaya (Enough) movement discussed in Chapter 5.

This research fills the gaps in the literature, in both the political economy approach and the institutional approach, by answering the following questions: What is the role of businessmen in authoritarian renewal and survival? Other subquestions emerge from this question: How far were businessmen able to capture the state and influence policies for their own benefit? Why did some businessmen refuse to support Mubarak's authoritarianism to the extent that they sacrificed their wealth and private business? What are the varieties of clientelistic relations used by the regime to co-opt businessmen, especially after the introduction of economic liberalization? How did the regime weaken the opposition that refused to be co-opted? Why would the authoritarian regime allow bureaucrats to turn into businessmen and accumulate wealth in illegal ways?

This research argues that after the introduction of neoliberal economic policies, Mubarak's regime co-opted a large number of businessmen (supporters and loyal opponents) through formal and informal institutions. Businessmen from the ruling party, members of the loyal opposition, or those affiliated with the regime through network ties agreed to be co-opted into the regime's clientelistic chain because their business interests coincided with the survival of Mubarak. On the other hand, members of the radical opposition, like those in the illegal MB, refused to continue in their co-option by the regime and opposed Mubarak's authoritarianism. Their opposition to the regime was at the expense of sacrificing their wealth and private businesses because of their ideological stance.

In order to weaken the opposition that refused to be co-opted, the regime created a divided environment between the legal opposition that was loyal and agreed to be co-opted and the illegal opposition like the MB. This divided political environment further increased when the regime created division between the different illegal opposition groups, like the MB and the Kefaya movement, and within the legalized parties, like the Ghad Party. These different levels of division prevented all opposition groups from playing an important role in either supporting or opposing the regime in the Twenty-Fifth of January Revolution. Rather, it was the people and the mobilizing efforts of youth groups and social movements that sustained the protests. The opposition political parties, including the MB, came late to the protests and also tried to hedge their bets by negotiating with the regime. The Twenty-Fifth of January Revolution illustrates how Mubarak's policies and the political economy of authoritarianism undermined the possibility of opposition parties forming a coalition either for or against the regime.

2

Egyptian Businessmen in a Historical Perspective

Introduction

This chapter starts by providing a background on the relations between Egyptian landowners/capitalists and the British during the period of British occupation (1882–1952). I argue that Egyptian capitalists like Talaat Harb refused foreign interference in the economy and established local industries and companies. Then the chapter examines businessmen under Nasser, Sadat, and Mubarak during the 1980s. I argue that the political economy of authoritarianism from Nasser to Mubarak relied on co-opting businessmen. As mentioned in the previous chapter, Nasser introduced land reform to redistribute the land, and at the same time, he created a new constituency composed of middle class citizens, workers, and peasants, who supported and benefited from his socialist policies. However, while Nasser's regime excluded the big landowners of the old regime from political and economic life, he did not turn against all of them. Nasser co-opted members of the upper class from the old regime, as well as the state bourgeoisie, for the purpose of implementing his national development plan.

This chapter also argues that Sadat co-opted the bourgeoisie of the *Infitah* (open door) policy, who were linked to foreign capitalism through trade and foreign franchises for the purpose of allying with the West. I argue that Sadat's economic liberalization provided an opportunity for the *Infitah* bourgeoisie to be co-opted at different levels (by the foreign capital and by the regime through high-level government officials). In an exceptional case, a businessman named Osman Ahmed Osman entered into a clientelistic relationship with President Sadat. At each of these levels of co-option, the *Infitah* bourgeoisie engaged in parasitic activities that relied on quick and high profits.

Mubarak started his rule by excluding the parasitic bourgeoisie associated with Sadat by dismissing them from the ruling party; however, to ensure survival of his regime, he co-opted other members of the *Infitah* bourgeoisie, such as the owners of the Islamic investment companies. But when their economic power increased to the extent that they could threaten the regime, he then prevented them from continuing in business.

Businessmen under the Monarchy and the British Occupation

The formation of the new class of big landowners started under the rule of Mohamed Ali Pasha (1805–49). He co-opted members of his own family, army commanders, bureaucratic cadres, and local notables by granting them large plots of land in return for their loyalty.[1] The big landowners were later able to expand on land ownership due to international factors that included the American Civil War in the 1860s, which led to an increased demand for cotton. The profits made from selling cotton were reinvested in buying or reclaiming more land. Another factor that contributed to land concentration was the British occupation of Egypt in 1882. From 1882 until Egypt's modicum of independence in 1922, the British encouraged the export of cotton by co-opting the big landowners and giving them credit facilities through Egyptian banks that were only extensions of London banks. Bank loans helped the landowners fund their agriculture or purchase more land.[2] Also, big landowners made a lot of profit from exporting cotton; however, the British co-option of the big landowners did not help improve Egyptian industry. Cotton exported to England was exported back to Egypt in the form of finished textile goods, which is why Egyptian capitalists like Talaat Harb sought investment opportunities outside the agricultural sector by developing local industry. In 1910, Harb started writing a series of articles asking Egyptians to gather their economic resources for a national economic struggle against the British. Harb's campaign led to the founding of Misr Bank in 1920.[3] The bank was established with start-up capital of eighty thousand Egyptian pounds (EGP). Harb raised funds for Misr Bank by relying on the support of large landowners, who contributed 92 percent of this capital. Then, after the establishment of Misr Bank, Harb used its funds to develop industry by establishing the Misr Group, which depended only on Egyptian capital. The companies established by the Misr group in the 1920s included Misr Printing Company, Misr Ginning Company, Misr Transport Company, and Studio Misr.[4]

In 1930, the tariff system was amended, reducing taxes to 5 percent on essentials and raising them to as high as 50 percent on luxury items and products that have an equivalent which is produced locally.[5] This resulted in an 11-fold increase in the production of local textiles from 1930 to 1937, while it was a loss to the British in one of their most valuable markets. Calico Printers and Bradford Dyers are two British factories that were affected by the decline in the export market. They sought to establish British factories in Egypt; however, they were only allowed to create joint business ventures with leading Egyptian companies. Calico Printers entered Egypt in 1933 in an arrangement with a local firm, the Filature National D'Egypt. In 1938, Bradford Dyers entered into a joint venture with the Misr Spinning and Weaving Company, which is one of the ventures of Talaat Harb's Misr Group. Both companies were obliged to work as subordinate affiliates with local Egyptian companies.[6] In his annual message to Misr Bank, Harb said to the shareholders that "the Misr firms blocked Bradford's original intention to enter the country as an independent producer and had captured its technical and managerial skills for itself."[7]

By the time the Second World War erupted, import substitute industrialization was almost complete, and Egypt was advanced and self-sufficient in a number of industries. By 1939, Egypt was able to produce consumer goods like sugar, alcohol, cigarettes, shoes, soap, boots, cotton cloth, and so on. Chemical and pharmaceutical industries started in 1940. It is worth mentioning that Egypt did not go beyond producing consumer goods until the Nasser period, which will be discussed later. Even though, during the period from 1920 to 1950, Egypt witnessed development and structural changes, there was no increase in gross national product per person, and it is even estimated that it fell.[8] By the late 1940s, neither the free market economy nor the partnership with foreign capital helped the economy create jobs for the growing number of the young and the poor.[9] In addition, the Second World War had worsened economic conditions in the country. Recession and high inflation had increased income inequalities. In 1950, wages represented 38 percent of the gross domestic product (GDP), while profits absorbed 62 percent of the GDP. By the end of World War II, unrestricted foreign trade had resumed, which increased competition among cheap foreign imports compared to local industry. British troops were still in Egypt and would have stopped any attempts to control free trade, since it was beneficial for them.[10] The political and economic turmoil in the country ended in July 1952 when a military coup by the Free Officers, led by Gamal Abdel Nasser, overthrew the monarchy.

The next section will discuss how Nasser's political economy of authoritarianism relied on excluding landowners of the old regime from economic and political life; at the same time, it co-opted members from the upper class of the old regime, as well as the state bourgeoisie, for the purpose of implementing Nasser's national development plan.

Businessmen under Nasser

As mentioned in the previous chapter, Nasser created a new constituency of workers, peasants, and middle class citizens that supported his socialist policies. He also introduced land reform to abolish large landownership. The first reform law was issued in September 1952 and put a two-hundred-feddan (one feddan equivalent to 1.038 acres) ceiling on land ownership. Two other reform laws were implemented in 1961 and 1969. The laws reduced landownership to one hundred feddans per person, and then restricted ownership, to fifty feddans per person. This is how Nasser's regime eliminated the economic base of the power of the landed elites.[11] As a result of land reform, nine hundred thousand feddans were taken from big landowners (about two thousand families), many of whom were politically isolated, and redistributed to small farmers and deprived peasants.[12]

After the 1952 revolution, Nasser's regime showed its commitment to industrialization. In 1956, the Ministry of Industry was established. One year later, it prepared its five-year industrial development plan (1960–65). The plan aimed to increase the annual growth rate of production from 6 percent to 16 percent. In order to achieve this goal, private capital had to contribute 55 percent of total investments.[13] But the capitalists refused to engage in the state's industrial plans, and their refusal can be explained as follows: First, the Free Officers wrongly distinguished between the landowners and the capitalists. It seems that they had not understood that both the landowners and the capitalists were fractions of the same class.[14] Second, during the late 1950s, Nasser used vague concepts in describing capitalists, which made them unwilling to engage in his industrial plans. For instance, while he assured businessmen that the government supported patriotic capitalists, at the same time, he threatened exploitive capitalists. The reluctance of capitalists to implement the government industrial plan encouraged Nasser in 1960 to nationalize all capitalists' industrial and commercial assets. By 1964, all banks and large companies in every field of the economy had been nationalized.[15]

Even though Nasser eliminated from the old regime the economic and political power of the landowners, who could have represented a challenge to his rule, and threatened the exploitive capitalists, he did not turn against all businessmen from the old regime. Laws issued during the 1950s suggest that the regime was not against all Egyptian capitalists. For instance, in the late 1950s, British and French companies were sequestrated, and a number of laws were issued in 1957 to end foreign control over the economy. Law 22 required all banking and business to be run by only Egyptian joint stock companies. Law 23 required the same for insurance companies. Law 24 stated that commercial agents in import/export companies must be Egyptian.[16] This law allowed for an increased number of millionaires who worked as commercial agents for foreign companies during the 1950s.[17] For instance, according to a businessman, the son of a pasha and large landowner, who worked as a commercial agent for a foreign company in the late 1950s, he said, "[It] was thanks to Nasser that the Egyptianization process took place and so allowed [me] to take the place of previously foreign-owned companies and set up [my] own business ... those who had begun business during this epoch had been able to build on an extremely strong basis, which meant they could continue their business and in time dominate the market."[18] The number of registered agents of foreign companies from 1957 to 1961 was 1,284 Egyptians, and they included members of the landed elite from the old regime, like the Serag El Din and Younes families, who were two of Egypt's largest land-owning families.[19] Nasser seems to have encouraged the creation of a new class of commercial bourgeoisie that engaged in trade, since the state needed large amounts of imports to implement its first five-year industrial development plan (1960–65).[20] At the same time, this type of business activity seemed to have been convenient for the upper class from the old regime, who were looking for areas for investment that had high and secure profits.[21] As Malak Zaalouk explains, the agents of this class "would have to find individual means of integrating and surviving [and] the path that offered the most secure, inconspicuous shelter was the whole area of trade."[22] This suggests that a clientelistic relationship had developed between the regime and the traders. In return for providing the regime with the imports it needed for implementing the industrial development plan, traders were allowed to accumulate money, despite Nasser's socialist goals, which aimed for social justice and redistribution of wealth.

The private-sector capitalists working in contracting were also co-opted by Nasser's regime. During this period, the public sector had a shortage of personnel, so a large number of contracts were given to private subcontractors to engage in the first five-year plan (1960–65). As a result, many small and medium capitalists accumulated substantial wealth by doing what the public sector was supposed to do.[23] For instance, during the five-year industrial development plan (1960–65), the private sector took up to 70 percent of the contracts compared with the public sector, which dealt with the 30 percent that was left.[24]

Nasser's regime also co-opted a new class that emerged in society: the state bourgeoisie.[25] The rise of this class occurred because there was a shortage of qualified personnel to work as a managerial elite upon the formation of the public sector. So a large number of the pre-1952 businessmen were recruited by the state to work as administrators and civil servants. Other members of the state bourgeoisie were recruited from the civil service, and a smaller number came from the army and the universities.[26] Since the new class of state bourgeoisie fulfilled the regime's aim of filling the required positions in the public sector, this then infers the formation of a clientelistic relationship between them and the regime. Evidence suggests that in this exchange relationship, members of the state bourgeoisie doubled their incomes through either legal or illegal means. High-ranking state bourgeoisie received compensations, extra salaries, and bonuses that they did not deserve. For instance, in 1964, bonuses that were paid to the state bourgeoisie included 37 bonuses that went by different names for only one type of bonus. The state bourgeoisie also engaged in illegal means to accumulate wealth through commissions, brokerage, and bribes.[27]

One of the private capitalists who made a fortune during Nasser's socialism is Osman Ahmed Osman. This was possible because he entered into a clientelistic relationship with Nasser himself. In the late 1940s, Osman founded a small engineering office, which in few years grew to into the Arab Contractor Company. In 1950, Osman went to Saudi Arabia and took advantage of the oil boom. Within a short time, Osman's company was bidding on multimillion-dollar projects in several Arab countries. In the mid-1950s, Osman returned to Egypt, and his company won a $48 million contract to construct part of the Aswan High Dam.[28] In the middle of the project, Nasser initiated the nationalization of major industries, including Osman's Arab Contractor Company. Despite the nationalization of Osman's company, evidence suggests that he was co-opted by Nasser. For instance, while Osman's domestic operations were nationalized, Nasser signed a law tailored for Osman that exempted firms that did a substantial part of their business abroad from public-sector recruitment and wages. Nasser's tailored law allowed Osman to relate salaries and job tenure to productivity rather than to government regulation.[29] While Osman was theoretically like any other public-sector manager, this tailored law allowed him to run his foreign business as a private company and to maintain foreign exchange accounts abroad.[30] Osman benefited from this tailored law by transferring some of the profit from his Egyptian operations to foreign subsidiaries while shifting expenses like depreciated machinery to his public company in Egypt.[31] In return, Osman's companies in the Gulf provided service to Egyptian intelligence by carrying intelligence equipment back and forth with their shipments.[32] Moreover, Osman built private villas for the Nasser family, demanding only a symbolic price for his work.[33]

This discussion suggests that Nasser's political economy of authoritarianism co-opted members of the upper class from the old regime and the state bourgeoisie for the purpose of implementing his national development plan, and in return, they were allowed to accumulate wealth either legally or illegally. This may explain why Nasser's socialism did not produce redistribution. For instance, the income gap between rural and urban areas increased in favor of the latter.[34] The economic crisis worsened when Egypt became involved in two wars: the Yemen War (1963–67) and the 1967 Arab-Israeli War. Both wars were funded by reducing investments rather than consumption.[35] The 1967 defeat obstructed economic growth, since the annual military expenditure from 1967 to 1973 rose to 25 percent of the GDP. From 1965 to 1970, Nasser's foreign borrowings caused Egypt's external debt to increase five times.[36]

The following section will examine President Sadat, Nasser's successor, and his political economy of authoritarianism, which created the *Infitah* bourgeoisie. I will then discuss how President Mubarak dealt with the *Infitah* bourgeoisie during the 1980s.

Businessmen under Sadat and Mubarak

When Sadat came to power in 1970, there was little expectation for foreign or Arab investment as long as Egypt was approaching a war. In October 1973, Sadat went to war against Israel; however, one year after the war, economic conditions had not yet improved. As Sadat explained,

> So that I can give you an idea of what the opening is all about, I must go back to the fourth of Ramadan of last year [October 1, 1973], six days before the battle. I invited to this same house in which we are now seated the members of the National Security Council . . . and I laid before them the situation and asked them to advance their own opinions . . . There were some who advocated fighting, and others who said we were not ready . . . At the end I wanted to tell them one thing only, that as of that day we had reached the "zero stage" economically (*marhalat al-sifr*) in every sense of the term. What this meant in concrete terms was that I could not have paid a penny toward our debt installments falling due on January 1 [1974]; nor could I have brought a grain of wheat in 1974. There wouldn't have been bread for the people, that's the least one can say . . . But as soon as the battle of October 6 was over, our Arab Brethren came to our aid with $500 million . . . and this sum would never have come had we not taken effective action in regards to the battle. But despite these dollars, we are now in the same situation we were in a year ago, perhaps worse.[37]

Sadat thought that in order to attract foreign investments, Egypt had to ally itself with the West, and especially the United States.[38] In 1974, Egypt resumed its diplomatic relations with the United States and started receiving aid. By the late 1970s, Egypt became the second largest recipient of aid from the US Agency for International Development (USAID) after Israel.[39]

USAID aimed to strengthen industry, raise exports, improve productivity, and help in expanding employment.[40] Moreover, the United States believed that economic assistance through USAID would produce new entrepreneurs who would demand more political liberalization.[41]

To encourage foreign and Arab investors to invest in Egypt, it was important to provide legal motivations.[42] As mentioned in the previous chapter, in 1974, Sadat introduced the open door policy *Infitah*, which gave the private sector a big role in investment. For instance, Law 43 of 1974, amended by Law 32 of 1977, allowed foreign investment in Egypt in all fields, provided guarantees against nationalization, and exempted new investments from tariffs and taxes for a minimum of five years (and for no fixed period in the free zones). Egyptian private investors were also guaranteed against confiscations and were granted the same tax and customs exemptions. Also, Law 93 of 1974 allowed Egyptians to import goods and act as agents of foreign firms.[43]

This explains why the political economy of authoritarianism under Sadat "created a new social force linked with world capitalism through trade and foreign franchises."[44] This was evident in the case of commercial agents of foreign firms, who—because of the *Infitah* laws—became linked to Western capitalist countries. For instance, Decree 247 of 1976 of the Ministry of Commerce stated that purchasing committees in the public sector were not allowed to accept offers from foreigners or foreign companies, except through an Egyptian commercial agent.[45] This means that commercial agents were allowed to sell their goods to the public sector, since it was the country's largest importer and purchaser of foreign commodities and their payments were secured. The capital of the majority of agents ranged from 1,000 EGP to 30,000 EGP, and the average was around 11,352 EGP. This is considered a very small amount compared to the profits they made. For instance, one owner of a commercial firm obtained adjudication among several others from the railway authority worth twenty million EGP for one year, and his formal commission was 2 percent. Another commercial agent obtained a tender for the Alexandria Port Authority for the sale of cranes worth $8 million, and he got a commission of 10 percent.[46] The quick profits that the commercial agents were making suggest how members of this *Infitah* bourgeoisie were engaging in parasitic[47] activities that were unproductive.[48] On several occasions, Sadat admitted that he knew about their parasitic activities; however, the leadership chose to provide them with protection on the pretext that turning against them was contrary to the Western model of economic liberalization.[49] Evidence suggests that different segments of the bourgeoisie benefited from the *Infitah*. For instance, the background of the commercial agents for foreign firms included remnants from the bourgeoisie of the pre–1952 revolution, including members of El Badrawi Ashour and Serag El Din families (many of them began with the Egyptianization movement in 1957), the state bourgeoisie who emerged under Nasser, and traditional trading and industrial bourgeoisie families.[50]

The increase in the financial power of the commercial agents through the excessive commissions they were receiving suggests that they entered into clientelistic relationships with foreign capital. The Al Amereya project is a case in point. In 1977, Misr Bank, a public-sector bank, asked for permission from the General Investment Authority to establish the Al Amereya project: a complete industrial textile complex with a total cost of 530 million EGP. The project included foreign participation in the form of imported technology. It was hastily accepted by the investment authority in only four days.[51] The foreign partners in the project were Chemtex of the United States and the Misr Iran Textile Company.[52] There was a large opposition campaign against this project, which was led by the General Industrial Organization, the Misr Company for Synthetic Silk, and the Ministry of Industry. They argued that the project was a duplication of other existing industrial textile projects. A media campaign in the weekly *Rose Al-Youssef* magazine revealed that five commercial agents involved in this project had received excessive commissions for the supply of textile equipment from abroad.[53] The case of the Al Amereya project suggests that the political economy of authoritarianism under Sadat provided an opportunity for Western capitalist countries to co-opt these commercial agents. Through the excessive commissions they received, they were able to influence the outcome of government decision making. Zaalouk explains the dependency of commercial agents on foreign capital:

> Although local commercial agents extract their profits from the national economy, namely the public sector, their primary customer, they are nonetheless dependent upon and subservient to their multinational principals. On one level they are dependent upon them for paying and transferring undeclared part of the commission abroad and for obtaining a formal agency contract in order to fulfil registration requirements. On a broader level, they are dependent upon foreign capital loans and the foreign productive market exporting its goods to the local market. It might be argued that multinationals are in turn dependent upon their local agents for the sale of goods. This is not totally incorrect, but one must ask who is the dominant in this interdependent relationship. Local commercial agents, who desperately compete for agency contracts among themselves, are not protected by law for any breach of the contract; they do not hold a very secure position since contracts are made on a yearly basis; and they are restricted by the exclusivity clause in the contract, while foreign firms may have more than one representative for a single commodity, thus giving them a privilege position.[54]

Another segment of the bourgeoisie who benefited from *Infitah* was the new arrivistes, who found an opportunity for making quick profits.[55] An example of this type of person is Rashad Osman, a famous member of the People's Assembly from the National Democratic Party (NDP) representing the Alexandria district. Rashad was illiterate and, in 1975, smuggled a large quantity of hashish into the country. From the profit he made, he started an import/export business and accumulated a fortune estimated at several hundred million EGP.[56] Evidence suggested that Rashad made his fortune from illegal transactions and that he bribed a number of ministers.[57] In return for these bribes, he seems to have been protected by the regime in his corrupt business practices. Rashad's case suggests how the *Infitah* policy led to the emergence of patron-client relations between high-level government officials and businessmen. This is another level of co-opting the *Infitah* bourgeoisie.

The previous discussion suggests that Sadat's political economy of authoritarianism provided an opportunity to co-opt the *Infitah* bourgeoisie on different levels: first, through co-option of the *Infitah* bourgeoisie by the Western capitalist countries that gave excessive commissions to the commercial agents (for example, the case of the Al Amereya project) and, second, through high-level government officials who helped the *Infitah* bourgeoisie accumulate wealth illegally in return for bribes (for example, the case of Rashad Osman).

But in an exceptional case, businessman Osman Ahmed Osman entered into a clientelistic relationship with President Sadat himself, which allowed him to influence policies for his own benefit. Osman had had relations with the Muslim Brothers (MB) since the 1950s, when he left Egypt to work in Saudi Arabia. Through Osman's connection, in 1971, Sadat promised the MB a safe return to Egypt. Sadat needed the MB to counterbalance the influence of the Nasserites and the leftists. This was the first official service that Osman made for Sadat.[58] In this clientelistic relationship, in 1974, Osman was appointed the minister of housing and reconstruction. Evidence suggests that Osman used his position in the cabinet to serve his own private business. For instance, a special law, Law 62 of 1974, allowed him to import materials and equipment required for reconstruction without going through the process of general procurement. This law gave him the right to import a large amount of Spanish construction steel in 1976. Members of the People's Assembly questioned the high prices of construction steel, and a special parliamentary committee made a list of accusations that included nepotism, conflicts of interest, and receiving foreign kickbacks.[59] Osman's clientelistic relationship with Sadat was reinforced when one of his sons married one of Sadat's daughters.[60]

By the late 1970s, *Infitah* did not succeed in attracting the foreign investment aimed at enhancing development. About one-tenth of new investments in the late 1970s could be directly linked to *Infitah*. But many of these investments were not in productive sectors, like industry and agriculture, that could help the economy recover. During the 1970s, only one-half of the *Infitah*'s investments were in manufacturing; the rest were in banking and housing, and 25 percent of its investments were in tourism. Its investment in manufacturing was in light consumer industries, which competed with existing Egyptian industry. For instance, plants established by foreign investors produced matches and soft drinks; instead of being exported, as the government had expected, the products only competed in the market with those of national industries.[61] Also, the *Infitah* had negative consequences, since it did not lead to equal distribution among citizens. For instance, the liberalization of foreign trade encouraged abuses against the public. Subsidized goods were smuggled for hard currency in order to import luxury goods that were sold at high prices. A number of wholesale traders monopolized the economy. Twenty large merchants controlled the meat trade; 3, the seed trade; 9, the paper market; and 10, the soft drink trade.[62]

On October 6, 1981, Sadat was assassinated by Islamic extremists while watching a military parade on the eighth anniversary of the October victory. Upon coming to power in 1981, Mubarak started by eliminating the power of the *Infitah* parasitic bourgeoisie associated with Sadat.[63] The richest among the parasitic bourgeoisie was Osman Ahmed Osman. In 1980, Osman published a contentious book about Nasser, which caused public anger and obliged Sadat to remove him from the cabinet. Then, when Mubarak came to power, he already had an excuse to remove Osman from the NDP.[64] Also, lesser members of the parasitic bourgeoisie were dismissed from the party under the excuse that the new president would not tolerate corruption. For instance, Rashad Osman was stripped of his parliamentary immunity and was removed from the party because of charges of illegal profiteering from timber sales. Mahmoud Soliman, an NDP deputy from the Rosetta constituency, was also dismissed from the party because of charges of drug trafficking. Salah Abou El Magd, an NDP deputy for Kom Ombo, was another member of the parasitic bourgeoisie who was dismissed from the party on charges of trading in state land.[65] However, Mubarak's exclusion of the *Infitah* parasitic bourgeoisie from the ruling party did not mean that he turned against all businessmen who appeared during Sadat's economic liberalization. It seems that he only eliminated those who were directly associated with Sadat. For instance, among the *Infitah* bourgeoisie whom Sadat allowed to survive under his rule were the owners of the Islamic investment companies. These companies were allowed to emerge due to the 1974 investment law of the *Infitah*. The Islamic investment companies are not mainly Islamic, despite their title. Indeed some of these companies were owned by Christians, or if not, they had Christians who deposited in them.[66] They were investment companies in the sense of inviting deposits; in return, they paid very high rates of return, which reached 24 percent on deposits, compared to banks that gave only 17 percent.[67] This may explain why, by the mid-1980s, the number of these companies reached more than 150, and around one million Egyptians had invested in them by depositing their funds.[68] These companies were accepting deposits as investment banks, but unlike banks, they were not under any controls or regulations. Investors did not have the right to review the activities of the companies or to know about their budgets.[69]

The majority of the owners of these companies came from humble backgrounds and had benefited from Sadat's *Infitah*. For instance, Ashraf El Saad was the son of a low-ranking government official. He migrated to France for couple of months to work as a dish washer but could not save any money, so he returned to Egypt and traded illegally in foreign currency and made millions from these transactions. He then established the El Saad Islamic Investment Company.[70] This situation is nearly similar to the case of Fathi El Rayan, head of El Rayan Group. He also came from a humble background. It is alleged that in 1983, El Rayan's name was included on the minister of interior's list as a well-known illegal currency dealer.[71] He then established the El Rayan Islamic Investment Company, which in few years became the largest one in Egypt. For instance, in 1986, he bought the residence of the US ambassador, a building that the US government had declared unfit for habitation, for $14 million.[72] By 1987, the capital accumulated by all the Islamic investment companies was around 12 billion EGP, including $2 billion in foreign currency.[73] The total amount of foreign currency that these companies had access to was more than the Central Bank.[74] For instance, according to El Saad, "In 1986 then Prime Minister Atef Sidqi asked to meet with the owners of the Islamic companies. El Rayan, me, and many other owners of the Islamic companies attended the meeting. Sidqi told us that the Council of Ministers urgently needed $400 million. El Rayan paid a check with this amount to the Council of Ministers."[75]

This suggests that the Islamic investment companies had entered into a clientelistic relationship with the regime. In such a relationship, these companies were allowed to function and grow. This may also explain why in 1987, one year later, Mubarak allowed himself, for the first time, to appear in advertising campaigns for these companies. Government and opposition newspapers published advertisements in which Mubarak was laughing and was surrounded by the owners of the Islamic investment companies.[76] The increase in the financial power of the owners of the Islamic investment companies allowed them to co-opt high-level government officials by appointing them as consultants in their companies. For instance, former Minister of Interior Nabawi Ismail was appointed to the board of El Rayan.[77] Also, several former ministers were appointed to work as consultants for El Saad's company—for example, Mostafa El Said, former Minister of Economy, and Ali Loutfy former Prime Minister, who earned 25 thousand EGP per month.[78]

Despite the Islamic investment companies' clientelistic relationships at different levels with the regime (either co-opted by the regime or acting as a patron by co-opting high-level government officials), when they began crossing the red line, the regime excluded them from continuing in their business activities. It is argued that the Islamic investment companies tried to start an insurance project and involve members of the armed forces in it. It is also argued that they participated in funding a number of militant Islamic organizations.[79] As a result, the regime issued Law 146 in June 1988 to regulate these companies and open their budgets for official inspection. However, many of these companies were not willing to cooperate and reveal their investment activities, so the government started cracking down on them. In the same year, it seized the assets of El Rayan, and in 1992, the socialist public prosecutor sequestrated the properties of El Saad.[80]

The period of the 1980s under Mubarak also witnessed the continuation of the parasitic activities of a number of members of the *Infitah* bourgeoisie in which they subverted state resources and converted them into private wealth. For instance, government regulations prohibited exporting goods and services produced with subsidized inputs. However, the ZAS airline company made considerable profit by breaking this regulation. It was Egypt's only private air freight carrier and was founded in the early 1980s by the Zorkani brothers, who seem to have entered into clientelistic relations with leading figures in the ruling party.[81] As Robert Springborg explains, "Decisions such as that to award the privilege to ZAS to purchase unlimited quantities of subsidized aviation fuel are made at the very highest levels and require influence, exchange of favors, and/or bribes. Businessmen who have gained access to the resources of the state in this way and those in the state apparatus and/or political elite who have made such access possible have no interest in changing this system. For them, the milking of the state's resources, combined with monopolistic and oligopolistic control of markets, guarantees substantial rewards."[82]

While the *Infitah* introduced in 1974 "granted individual entrepreneurs much greater freedom in the market place, it did not include reforms to increase the independence and flexibility of their traditional associations."[83] For instance, the Federation of Egyptian Industry (FEI) and the General Federation of the Chambers of Commerce that were established pre-1952 remained in the same corporatist structure that was inherited since Nasser's days.[84] Even after the introduction of economic liberalization, no changes were introduced to their structure and mandates. For instance, the FEI remained subject to Decree 1958, according to which the minister of industry appointed its president and one-third of the members of the board. Moreover, the Federation's decisions are subject to the minister's veto.[85] Similarly, in the 25 chambers—the regional bodies—of the General Federation of the Chambers of Commerce, only half of the members were elected, and the other half were appointed by the minister of supply and trade. At the beginning of the 1980s, the presidents of twenty regional chambers were local representatives in the NDP.[86]

The corporatist structure of the FEI and the chambers of commerce led businessmen in the early 1970s to think of establishing private business associations independent of the state.[87] In 1979, the Egyptian Business Association (EBA) was formally registered. During the 1980s, other business associations were established, like the Alexandria Business Association, the Association of Investors of 10th of Ramadan City, and the Association of Investors of 6th of October City. However, all these new associations remained under state control. This is because they function under the umbrella of the Ministry of Social Affairs, which limits their political role. As one author notes, although there were communication channels between the business associations and the government, "associations of this nature have no formal input with regard to the socioeconomic policies of government."[88] However, business associations used informal means to influence policies. As former president of the EBA, Adel Gazarin said, "the influence of the EBA, in reviewing government bills and decisions, depended on personal contacts of its members instead of the power of the association."[89]

There are also joint chambers of commerce, like the Egyptian-American Chamber established by a presidential decree in 1982. It plays the role of the official representative of the private sector during negotiations over aid provided to Egypt.[90] The American chamber provides a variety of services to its members, including the yearly organization of trade fairs in the United States to help its members conduct trade. The chamber's research center publishes information on specific sectors and economic issues. In addition, the chamber's career development center offers training programs to enhance the expertise of member and nonmember companies.[91] While the Egyptian-American and American chambers of commerce are ideologically proeconomic liberalization, there is inconclusive evidence in the existing literature regarding their influence in economic decision making.

After providing a background on the business climate in Egypt during the 1980s, it is worth turning our attention to other actors, like the military, who have benefited from economic liberalization. The military moved into civilian manufacturing in 1986 after negotiating a deal with General Motors to manufacture passenger cars. USAID pledged $200 million from its aid budget to subsidize this project.[92] The military is also making profits from controlling a vast amount of lands. This has been possible due to a law that allows it to seize any public land for "defending the nation." Nevertheless, the military leaders have used this law to acquire public lands to construct real estate projects in different areas in Egypt.[93] The military has also invested in the agriculture sector through the acquisition of reclaimed land and the development of food processing industries, especially in meat, fruit, and vegetables. The food security division of the military is the largest agroindustrial complex in the country. In 1985–86, it produced 488 million EGP, which is nearly one-fifth of the total value of Egyptian food production.[94] The military was able to make profits in food production not because of the superior quality of its products but rather because of its repressive means. The enlisted soldiers were forced by the army to spend their modest salaries on military-produced food products at the army canteens located in faraway areas where nonmilitary products are not sold.[95] The military also played an important role in the construction of bridges, roads, and several infrastructure projects. All these activities allowed for an opportunity for patronage and personal profit making.[96]

While different actors have benefited from the *Infitah*, others were seeking political reform. For instance, since the mid-1980s, there were judges who have been demanding judicial supervision of Egypt's elections. They believed that one of the fundamental components of political and democratic reform is transparent elections; however, the government disregarded their demands until 2000, when the supreme constitutional court ruled for judicial supervision of elections.[97] As will be discussed in the following chapter, even though there was judicial supervision of the elections, security forces arrested opposition activists or prevented their supporters from voting.[98]

In other cases, judges were ordered to change the result of the elections inside the polling station; however, some judges refused. For instance, in 2000, a Wafdist lawyer who ran in an election monitored by judicial supervision in the el Bagour constituency against the then NDP organization secretary, Kamal El Shazly, related a story about a judge who refused to change the result of the election. He said, "After the counting of the votes, I won the election. El Shazly asked the judge to change the result of the election, but he refused. [So to replace this judge with another one who would rig the election], El Shazly asked him to pretend as if he is sick. Then El Shazly called the ambulance, which carried the judge on the stretcher. [This was the only possible way to get the judge out of the polling station]. Then another judge was hired and signed the result in favor of El Shazly."[99]

Against this background of economic and political reform, there were deteriorating economic conditions. In 1986, significant changes happened in the Egyptian Treasury. For instance, the price of petroleum dropped by 50 percent, which caused the revenues of petroleum to fall to $1.2 billion—down from $2.26 billion in 1985. Moreover, Suez Canal revenues fell from $1 billion to $900 million. The economic conditions further deteriorated when Washington refused to give Egypt $265 million in aid until it implemented the economic reforms prescribed by the IMF.[100] In 1987, Egypt signed an agreement with the IMF, but it was only partially implemented.[101] According to the agreement, the government was supposed to reduce public spending, but it increased spending from 54 percent of GDP in 1986–87 to 57.2 percent in 1987–88.[102] The increase in public spending led to the rise of public domestic debts by the end of the 1980s.[103] As a result of deteriorating economic conditions, in 1991, the regime agreed to proceed with the economic and structural reforms as prescribed by the IMF and the World Bank. The 1990s economic reform increased the financial and structural power of businessmen, which also involved them in new types of corruption, as the following chapters discuss.

Conclusion

With the exception of the experience of Egyptian capitalists like Talaat Harb, who resisted co-option by foreign capital, businessmen under Nasser, Sadat, and Mubarak during the 1980s entered into clientelistic relationships with these regimes. The political economy of authoritarianism, moving from Nasser to Sadat to Mubarak, relied on co-opting businessmen but in different ways. Despite Nasser's elimination of the political and economic power of landowners from the old regime, he could not implement his industrial development plan without co-opting members of the upper class from the old regime. They were allowed to work in trade and contracting and to accumulate wealth in return for providing services to Nasser's national development plan.

Sadat wanted to attract foreign investment and ally with the West, which is why his political economy of authoritarianism relied on creating a rich social force linked to foreign capitalism. Sadat's economic liberalization resulted in the co-option of the *Infitah* bourgeoisie at different levels (by foreign capital or by the regime through high-level government officials).

Upon coming to power, Mubarak excluded Sadat's *Infitah* bourgeoisie by dismissing them from the ruling party for corruption charges. At the same time, he co-opted other members of the *Infitah* bourgeoisie, such as the owners of the Islamic investment companies; however, when they became a challenge to the regime, they were prevented from continuing with their businesses, and their companies were closed.

3

Parliamentary Businessmen

Introduction

The primary concern in this chapter is challenging the view that businessmen and liberal economic policies play a democratizing role in politics. For instance, in an analysis of the British House of Commons, Andrew Eggers and Jens Hainmueller argue that members of the Conservative Party used their political influence to obtain lucrative outside employment. Winning a seat doubled a member of parliament's (MP) wealth over the course of a lifetime in comparison to other candidates who lost their elections.[1] In a cross-national study in 47 countries, Maria Faccio estimates that politically connected firms received a cumulative abnormal return of 1.28 percent when their officers became members of parliament. These returns increased in countries with widespread corruption.[2]

In Egypt, the economic liberalization implemented in the 1990s increased the financial and structural power of businessmen. So the regime dealt with the political challenges of economic liberalization through co-opting businessmen, as will be discussed in this chapter, in the case of Ahmed Ezz, the case of the members of parliament known as the case of loan MPs, the case of Ramy Lakah, and the case of Mohamed Abul-Enein.

In this chapter, I build on the work of Maye Kassem,[3] Lisa Blaydes,[4] and Jason Brownlee,[5] who argue for the importance of political institutions as co-option tools for maintaining the survival of authoritarian regimes. However, my findings are distinct from Kassem, Blaydes, and Brownlee, since I argue that the regime's co-option of businessmen, especially after the introduction of economic liberalization, has not been static but took a variety of forms (for example, authoritarian clientelism, semiclientelism, patron-broker-client relationships, and in an exceptional case, mutual dependency). Businessmen who refused to be co-opted, the regime has actively undermined their potential to become a real opposition, as will be discussed in this chapter in the cases of Ibrahim Kamel and Anwar Esmat El Sadat. (To avoid confusion with President Sadat, Anwar Esmat El Sadat will be referred to as El Sadat throughout the text.)

As mentioned in the previous chapter, since the early 1990s, the Egyptian state has been running in debt, so businessmen who were co-opted by the regime were needed to provide direct financial funding to the ruling party, for election campaigns, or to maintain regime legitimacy by providing social services in their constituencies to replace the withdrawal of state services. As Hazem Kandil writes,

> Between 1992 and 2002, domestic debt increased from 67 to 90 percent of GDP. The state was in fact running on debt. And since the ruling party lived off state finances, it too was running on debt. But who were the creditors? Half of the debt lay with public-sector banks, which had little choice but to obey the rulers, even when they went beyond regular deposits and dabbled into the pool of pensions and social security funds. A second source was treasury bills, though raising money through this route was time-consuming and cumbersome. The easiest and most readily available way to keep the political machine solvent was to count on the generosity of regime-friendly capitalists . . . As monopoly capitalists began taking charge of the ruling party and . . . [were elected in the parliament], they assumed financial responsibilities as well. They funded NDP conventions; they launched government media campaigns; they paid bribes to stifle the opposition; they bought votes and organized pro-regime demonstrations; and so on. Reliance on the generosity of friendly capitalists increased systematically. The 27 percent state budget deficit in 2011, an estimated L.E. 140 billion, revealed that the regime was sinking deeper and deeper into debt.[6]

Varieties of strategies for co-opting parliamentary businessmen are used as examples in this chapter. The aim is to substantiate how different types of co-option of parliamentary businessmen prevented them from playing a democratizing role, and thus helped renew Mubarak's authoritarianism.

The Case of Ibrahim Kamel: A Business Tycoon Dismissed from the Ruling Party

Ibrahim Kamel's[7] case suggests how the regime managed to stop an independent business tycoon from becoming a potential challenge to or check on the regime. Kamel is an Egyptian international business tycoon. His business involved the establishment of a number of companies in Switzerland and other countries that worked in diverse economic areas. After living a number of years in Switzerland, he decided to return to Egypt in 1988 in order to retire and help the poor in his hometown, Sirs el-Layan in El Monofeya Governorate. He had no political motive. After Kamel returned to his hometown, he found that the main problem was unemployment, which is why he thought of providing the people in Sirs el-Layan with jobs in a clothing factory, since this is a labor-intensive industry. He then established a clothing factory, which employed around one thousand workers.

Kamel comes from a political family. His paternal uncle was a member of parliament before the 1952 revolution. So in 1989, when the former National Democratic Party (NDP) member of parliament in the Menouf constituency of El Monofeya's governorate died before the end of the parliamentary term in 1990, the governor approached Kamel and asked him to run in the election as an NDP candidate; however, Kamel refused and ran as an independent candidate. He said, "This is because when Sadat changed the system and set up platforms, I visited all the parties like the Wafd, the Tagammu', the NDP. None of these parties had a program . . . and nobody knew what they wanted. I also met with senior members in the NDP, and when I asked them about their program they said: we do what the President tells us to do."

Running as an independent candidate, Kamel got 28,000 votes against the NDP member, who got only 1,600 votes. Then, in the next parliamentary election in 1990, Kamel ran again as an independent and won the election. After joining parliament, Kamel received a phone call from the then presidential advisor, Mostafa El Fekki, who told him that "President Mubarak is asking why you are not attending the party's meeting." However, Kamel did not join the party until a few months later, after he had a meeting with the voters in his constituency, who asked him to join the NDP so that he could help provide them with services. This is because, as Kassem argues, NDP members of parliament have "direct access to a share of the resources that the President and his government command."[8]

While Kamel accepted the offer to join the NDP, he, unlike other NDP businessmen, was less likely to be co-opted by the regime. Kassem explains, in reference to his case, that "the fact that Kamel's primary assets and investments were located in Switzerland meant that his means of livelihood were not subject to government interference, which, in turn, further reinforced his independence . . . Kamel's case is, however, the exception rather than the rule because the majority of NDP [businessmen] who reach public office do not have the same degree of economic independence. Yet, the majority of them do not have the personal wealth to be compared with an international financier such as Kamel."[9]

After Kamel joined the NDP, he managed to recruit ten thousand new members for the party. Based on these new memberships, the then NDP organization secretary, Kamal El Shazly, promised him he would have a role in the nomination of candidates for the local council election. However, Kamel disagreed with El Shazly about the way candidates were nominated for the local council election. After this disagreement, Kamel read in the newspaper that he had been dismissed from the party. After Kamel's dismissal from the NDP, El Shazly told Kamel, "We don't like people like you, who have opinions. We want people who just stamp and accept our orders."

This was not the only disagreement between Kamel and the party. Before his dismissal from the NDP, and during one of the parliamentary sessions, Kamel disagreed with certain economic legislative issues. In fact, it is not common for an NDP member to criticize a policy introduced by the government. For instance, Kamel said that we can introduce real economic reform only if "President Mubarak first took his big red pen to the 40,000-odd laws passed in the last 40 years. Then we'll know where we are."[10]

Before Kamel was dismissed from the NDP, his private business, which aimed to help the poor in his constituency in Sirs el-Layan, was doing well. His clothing factory was exporting clothes, and it had orders from his clients in the United States to make products worth around $1 million every month. But since Kamel refused to be co-opted, he was punished by the regime, both in his political career and in his economic project in Sirs el-Layan, as the following section will discuss.

In order to get raw materials like textiles, buttons, and so on, Kamel's bank in Egypt had to write a letter of credit to the exporting country to import the goods, which came in the name of the bank. Then the bank gave the tariffs department a letter of credit, called a drawback, to guarantee that the raw material would be exported in the form of ready-made clothes. This means that if the imported raw material were not fabricated or exported, Kamel would pay the tariffs. This operation was divided among three different banks: Cairo-Paris Bank, Al Dakahlia Bank, and Misr Bank.

In 1994, Kamel's clothing factory requested that the Misr Bank raise his credit from 1.5 million to 13 million Egyptian pounds (EGP). One year later, the bank's board of trustees issued a letter agreeing to raise the credit of Kamel's clothing factory. After the bank raised the amount of credit, the imported raw materials came to the tariff department based on the new raise.[11] However, El Shazly interfered and caused Kamel trouble after his dismissal from the NDP, and the bank suddenly refused to deal with Kamel. As a result, the bank left the raw material in the tariffs department. Kamel could not get the raw material from the tariffs department, since only the bank had the authority to release the raw material.[12] As a result, Kamel's factory went into debt. Kamel went to meet with the French director of Cairo Paris Bank (this bank was a branch joint venture of Cairo

Bank and Banque de Paris). The director told Kamel, "This is politics . . . I can do nothing . . . I am sorry and embarrassed. This is not our decision. This decision is from the Egyptian side." Then Kamel went to the head of Cairo Bank, Mohamed Abu El Fatah,[13] who told him, "This is a political decision."

Kamel ran for the 1995 parliamentary election as an independent candidate after being dismissed from the NDP. Due to his opposition to the regime, Kamel was denied his seat. During the counting of the votes, Kamel knew that he was going to win the election, since he had many more votes than his competitor. Then, after the votes were counted, a police officer came to Kamel and told him, "We are sorry . . . even though you won the election; we have to change the result in favor of the NDP candidate." Kamel raised a case in the court against the NDP candidate, claiming that the NDP candidate forged the election. In 2000, the court ruled in favor of Kamel, saying that the election was forged by the NDP candidate. However, Kamel could not get his seat in parliament through the court ruling because, according to the constitution, the People's Assembly, which is dominated by a majority of the NDP, is the master of its own decision. Article 93 in the constitution states that

> the People's Assembly shall be competent to decide upon the validity of the membership of its members. The Court of Cassation shall be competent to investigate the validity of contestations on membership presented to the Assembly after referring them to the Court by the Speaker of the Assembly... The result of the investigation and the decision reached by the court shall be submitted to the Assembly to decide upon the validity of the contestation within sixty days from the date of submission of the result of the investigation to the Assembly. Membership shall not be deemed invalid except by a decision taken by a majority of two-thirds of the Assembly members.[14]

Then, in the 2000 parliamentary election, Kamel ran as an independent candidate, and El Shazly told him, "I will bring you an NDP competitor that you can't defeat. He is Ahmed Ezz." This was the first time Kamel had heard of this candidate. Unlike Kamel, Ezz is considered an outsider to El Monofeya Governorate. His presence in this area started only in the 1990s, when he opened a steel factory at Sadat City (which is in the Menouf constituency).

The 2000 parliamentary election was the first election to be held under judicial supervision, which means that it should have been fair. Although it was cleaner than the former elections, it had irregularities. As Mona El-Ghobashy explains, "The management of the 2000 parliamentary elections had more subtle, though no less significant, consequences. Bench judges experienced numerous instances of harassment and obstruction from security agents, and several engaged in verbal and physical confrontations with police as they protested police blockades of roads to polling stations and intimidation of non-NDP voters. Contrary to Law 73's stipulation that it is the prerogative of the supervising judge at the polling station to determine the station's periphery, security agents essentially trapped judges inside polling stations while violence and harassment raged outside."[15]

Similar patterns of irregularities and security interference in the 2000 parliamentary election are evident in the case of Kamel. After the votes were counted, the judge did not announce the result, which was in favor of Kamel. So Kamel went to the polling stations to ask the judge why the result had not been announced. The judge said, "I can't do anything." Then, after a while, a State Security officer went to talk to the judge, and the judge told him that he could not announce a forged result and refused to sign it. Five minutes later, the district chief of police announced the result in favor of Ezz, and the result was not signed. Again, Kamel raised a case in court against this forged result. Kamel won the case; however, he could not get his seat, since as mentioned earlier, parliament is the master of its own decision. The same story was repeated in the 2005 parliamentary election when Kamel ran against Ezz. According to Kamel, before counting the votes, he read in the newspaper that Ezz had won the election. The judge told Kamel, "We had to announce that Ezz won . . . this is a political order."

Kamel made his wealth independently of the state, and his fortune is based abroad,[16] which suggests the reason he refused to enter into a clientelistic relationship with the regime. As a result, he was punished. On the political level, he was dismissed from the ruling party and lost his seat in parliament. On the economic level, Kamel's initial project in his constituency aimed at constructing six clothing factories, each to employ one thousand workers, but he was abandoned by the regime and could not continue his project. In fact, Kamel's case is considered a typical example of the regime's new political economy of authoritarianism, which started in the 1990s when banks were used to control businessmen either by causing them trouble in their businesses or by giving them loans without collateral, as will be discussed later in the section on loan MPs.

The next section will examine the political and economic rise of businessman Ahmed Ezz, who replaced Kamel in his parliamentary seat in the Menouf constituency. Unlike Kamel, who was economically independent of the regime and refused to be co-opted, Ezz depended on the regime to build his fortune. This made him enter into a clientelistic relationship with the regime, as the following case will discuss.

The Case of Parliamentary Steel Tycoon Ahmed Ezz

Unlike Kamel, who made his fortune while living abroad, Ahmed Ezz accumulated his wealth through his co-option by the regime. In the early 1990s, Ezz owned three small factories that made steel and ceramics (El Ezz Steel Rebar, El Ezz for Flat Steel, and El Gawhra for Porcelain and Ceramic Products). But before discussing Ezz's growing role in business and politics, I will provide some background to the political and economic environment at this time.

In 1998, Gamal Mubarak established the Future Generation Foundation (FGF), which is a nongovernmental organization (NGO) that aimed to promote the image of Gamal among the youth. Ahmed Ezz was one of the few businessmen appointed as board members of the FGF.[17] Two years later, Gamal started engaging in politics through his appointment to the General Secretariat of the NDP, which is considered the apex of the ruling party. Gamal aimed to reformulate the foundations of the NDP and make it more convenient to his neoliberal policies, and he needed a new constituency that would support his policies; businessmen were this new constituency. As Mohamed Fahmy Menza noted, "In this case, best fitting with Gamal's persona and affiliations, the suggested power base was the newly flourishing business community of Egypt—mainly . . . comprising prominent businessmen who were on the rise in Egypt's adoption of a more liberal economy."[18]

In order to co-opt these businessmen in the party, in 2002, Gamal headed the newly established Policies Secretariat, and many of the prominent businessmen were appointed to it. Since 2002, the Policies Secretariat has been in charge of formulating the main macroeconomic-level policies adopted by the NDP.[19]

The implementation of neoliberal economic policies after 2000 provided a new opportunity for the regime to renew its authoritarianism by co-opting businessmen. Ezz was one of the businessmen who benefited from this opportunity. For instance, in 2000, he was appointed to the General Secretariat of the NDP. Two years later, he was appointed to the steering office of the newly formed Policies Secretariat. Then, in 2005, he was further promoted in the party as the NDP organization secretary, replacing the party's apparatchik Kamal El Shazly. The regime's political co-option of Ezz seems to have provided him with protection in his business, as he implied by his words when he was asked about his reasons for joining the NDP. He said, "The reason I was attracted to join the NDP is Mubarak's leadership, and not because it is the party in power . . . and because the head of the party [Mubarak] is a guarantee, a leader and a trust."[20]

Moreover, in 2000, Ezz was elected to the parliament as an NDP member in the Menouf constituency in El Monofeya Governorate; this means he replaced Ibrahim Kamel in his parliamentary seat and also headed the Budget and Planning Committee in parliament. Then, a few years after his election to parliament, he was transformed from an owner of small steel and ceramics factories to a steel tycoon who monopolized the steel industry,[21] as the following section will discuss.

The government-controlled Alexandria National Iron and Steel Company[22] (Al Dekheila) had experienced considerable success since its establishment in 1982. Due to this success, the board of directors decided in the late 1990s to expand its activities and to produce steel plate. The new project needed equipment from abroad. In order to delay the payments of tariffs for the new imported equipment, an agreement was made between Al Dekheila and the Ministry of Finance. The agreement was conditional on submitting to the bank a letter of credit for the postponed amount of money; however, on June 20, 1999, the Ministry of Finance broke the agreement and asked the bank to liquidate the letter of credit.[23]

The head of Al Dekheila seemed to have been aware of this obstacle. For instance, Ibrahim Salem Mohamdein, the then chairman of Al Dekheila, sent a petition to Mubarak requesting that he prevent the liquidation of the letter of credit. However, there was no response from the leadership, and the bank liquidated the letter of credit.[24]

Opposition parliamentarian Abu El Ezz El Hariry explained that these obstacles seem to have been tailored by the regime to facilitate Ezz's acquisition of Al Dekheila. For instance, he said,

> There was a conspiracy by the government to cause financial problems for Al Dekheila . . . Why did the Ministry of Finance take possession of the financial deposits—the letter of credit—that were deposited with the customs department for the import of new equipment for the new project? The liquidation of the letter of credit by the Ministry of Finance has caused financial problems for Al Dekheila. At the same time, the Arab fund loan, which was approved by the People's Assembly and allocated to Al Dekheila, was blocked. Both the letter of credit and the Arab fund loan would have been sufficient to overcome any financial deficit coming out of the expansion . . . The reason for all these problems was to move the ownership of Al Dekheila gradually to Ahmed Ezz.[25]

Due to the financial problems that Al Dekheila faced, it had to resort to small loans in order to finish the new project. During this tailored crisis, Ahmed Ezz presented an agreement of intentions in September 1999 to buy assets in Al Dekheila. Even though he had to pay a substantial amount of money, this transaction was not advertised in the newspapers for two consecutive days as the law specifies.[26]

In his first attempt to acquire Al Dekheila,[27] Ezz bought 20 percent of the assets. Even though he had a small percentage of the assets, he became the chairman of the board of Al Dekheila. This is illegal, since his company was represented by only four seats on the board of directors. Then, in his capacity as Al Dekheila's chairman of the board, Ezz reduced the company's steel production. This resulted in a surplus of the billets, which are raw materials used in the production of steel rebar. The excess of billets was bought by Ezz to be used in the production process in his private company, El Ezz Steel Rebar (in Sadat City). Moreover, Ezz prevented steel producers from buying the billets at prices even higher than what he offered.[28] For instance, in 2001, one of the steel producers, whose business had been affected by Ezz's monopolistic practices, filed a complaint to the minister of economy and foreign trade, in which he wrote, "After Ezz headed Al Dekheila, he reduced the production of steel rebar. This had led to a surplus in the billets produced by Al Dekheila, which amount to 45,000/40,000 tons monthly. Ezz bought this extra quantity of billets and then he used it in his own private steel rebar factory to produce the steel rebar. This instead of producing it in Al Dekheila! Our company has submitted several proposals to buy the billets from Al Dekheila with prices higher than what Ezz is paying, but our request has not been considered for more than a year now."[29]

After Ezz became chair of Al Dekheila's board, then Prime Minister Atef Ebeid said in Al-Gomhuriya newspaper on March 30, 2000, that good management made Al Dekheila the second-best factory in the world.[30] In his comments, the former prime minister was praising the management of Ezz, which suggests that Ezz's acquisition of Al Dekheila was supported by the regime.

Despite the government's support for Ezz, his corrupt activity was known to the public. After Ezz's acquisition of Al Dekheila, newspapers widely covered his corrupt practices. For instance, former Editor in Chief Ibrahim Seada wrote on June 16, 2001, in *Akhbar Al-Youm* newspaper (one of the most widely read newspapers) an article on how Ezz prevented local steel factories from buying billets from Al Dekheila with prices even higher than what El Ezz private factories were paying.[31]

Then, in February 2006, in his second attempt to acquire more assets in Al Dekheila, Ezz—in his capacity as chairman of Al Dekheila—exchanged the assets between Al Dekheila and his private company El Ezz Steel Rebar. Independent parliamentarian and journalist Mustafa Bakri accused Ezz of illegally exchanging these assets. In a communication he submitted to the prosecutor general, he wrote,

Although the General Assembly of Al Dekheila approved the exchange of assets, in fact the assets of El Ezz Steel Rebar are much less than the assets of Al Dekheila in productivity and profit . . . this exchange was not between two companies that were owned by one individual. However, the exchange was between El Ezz Steel Rebar (which is owned by Ezz), and Al Dekheila, in which Ezz at this time owned only 20.89% of the assets . . . As a result of the exchange, the assets of Ezz in Al Dekheila jumped from 20.89% to 50.28%. [This is how Ezz became the main shareholder in the company][32]

The press coverage of Ezz's irregularities and his accusation to the prosecutor general (who is appointed by the president)[33] suggest that the leadership was aware of, and perhaps encouraging, the way in which Ezz acquired Al Dekheila; therefore, in return for Ezz's economic protection by the regime, he had to share some of his profits in the form of direct financial support for the ruling party. For instance, after his election to parliament in 2000, Ezz established an NGO called "The National Association for Economic and Political Studies." This NGO started as a consultancy office for Ezz on issues of finance to provide him with assistance for the Committee of Budget and Planning that he was heading, and a number of university professors worked in this NGO to assist Ezz. Then, when the Policies Secretariat was established in 2002, Ezz's NGO became highly involved with this Secretariat. Some of the leading members in the Policies Secretariat were employed in this NGO to perform different tasks in the Secretariat and got substantial monthly salaries. Ezz's NGO also helped prepare annual conferences. For instance, the policy papers of the annual party conferences are prepared by the NGO.[34] Ezz also provided substantial funding for preparations for the annual conferences. For instance, according to the report of the attorney general to the US Congress on the administration of the foreign agents' registration act, Ahmed Ezz paid the Qorvis Communications Company $204,463 over the course of six months in 2008. As stated in the report, Qorvis "facilitated and coordinated media and press appearances on behalf of the foreign principle, as well as provided media monitoring and analysis. The registrant also assisted in preparing and drafting speeches [for the NDP conference]."[35]

In fact, both the Policies Secretariat and the annual conferences had important roles in the grooming of Gamal, which explains why Ezz's main financial contribution was directed to them. As Joshua Stacher writes, "Gamal Mubarak fully consolidated his position as an executive elite by 2002. Subsequent annual NDP conferences left no room for doubt . . . [In the 2004 annual conference] . . . party Secretary General al-Sharif's most substantial contribution was to introduce Gamal Mubarak, who was frequently interpreted and praised throughout his speech by the party faithful . . . The Policies Secretariat strength within the party appeared to be the 2004 conference's key outcome. The president's address stressed that the key objective was to introduce younger elements into the party with the aim of pushing them to take up positions of responsibility."[36]

Ezz's direct financial support to the regime was not limited to the project of hereditary succession, but he also supported the survival of Mubarak's regime. For instance, Ezz funded Mubarak's 2005 presidential campaign. This funding included, among other things, the payment of the staff who worked for three months during the parliamentary campaign in the party's office in Roxy. The program of the 2005 presidential campaign—with all its components and promises—was prepared in Ezz's NGO. Moreover, after Ezz headed the NDP Organization Secretariat in 2005, he appointed more employees to assist him in the daily work of the Secretariat. For instance, the NGO had, for each governorate, one employee representing it to handle the daily work of the Organization Secretariat. In addition, these employees worked on solving the problems of the MPs. One university professor who worked in this NGO for a couple of years explained the power of Ezz through the involvement of his NGO in all the details of the ruling party and parliament. He said, "All important legislation is studied in the NGO before being submitted to the parliament. Also, the NGO prepares answers to NDP parliamentarians whenever there are interpellations submitted from the opposition, so they can defend the minister. Whenever there are important parliamentary sessions, employees in the NGO are in charge of texting messages to NDP parliamentarians to attend and vote . . . This NGO is the kitchen of policies. It is making the policies of the country."[37]

The substantial funding that Ezz was donating to the ruling party and Mubarak's 2005 presidential election suggest how he emerged as an oligarch a la Russia. As mentioned in Chapter 1, the Russian oligarchs made their wealth during Yeltsin's rule by buying state-owned assets at cheap prices during privatization. In return, Russian oligarchs donated substantial funding to Yeltsin during his reelection campaign. Similarly, Ezz, as mentioned earlier, bought the state-owned Al Dekheila factory at a much cheaper price than its true value; in return, he provided substantial funding to the regime through his funding of the ruling party and Mubarak's 2005 presidential campaign. Even though the presidential election was noncompetitive, Ezz's substantial funding suggests his emergence as an oligarch who attempted to influence the policies for his own interest.

It seems that before the rise of the young Gamal and other businessmen like Ezz in the party, the NDP did not need substantial funding. This is because since its establishment in 1978, the NDP has relied on the state for its funding. For instance, the NDP headquarters overlooking the Nile River in downtown Cairo was inherited by the NDP from its predecessor,

the Arab Socialist Union (ASU). It used to be the building of the governorate and was built using public funds.[38] The NDP depended on the state's
largesse. It received funds from the state budget and freely used state media
to advertise.[39] Before the rise of Gamal in the NDP, the party was engaged
in fewer activities and therefore needed a smaller budget. For instance,
party conferences were held every three years and sometimes every five
years. They were not held every year, as specified in 2002 by the new party's
bylaws.[40] There was no need to fund a campaign for Mubarak's presidential election, as there had been in 2005. This is because Mubarak used to
renew his presidential term through a referendum every six years before
the amendment of Article 76 of the constitution in 2005, which allowed for
direct presidential election. In addition, the NDP used to secure a majority in each parliamentary election through the rigging of votes; however,
after the judicial supervision of elections in 2000, the situation changed,
and "the NDP started using the rich people to run for election because
they pave their ways into the election by paying money."[41] For instance,
the 2005 parliamentary election witnessed an increase in vote buying. As
Samer Soliman wrote,

> According to some reports, the price of a vote had climbed to more than 500
> L.E. in such electoral districts as Nasr City, where there was a neck-in-neck
> race between the business tycoons Fawzi Al-Sayyid and Mustafa Al-Sallab.
> Parliamentary seats have become subject to the laws of supply and demand.
> Clearly there was a greater demand, largely due to the judicial supervision of
> the polls ... On the supply side, people sensed the increased demand for their
> votes, and rising unemployment and the economic doldrums into which the
> Egyptian economy had sunk induced many to sell them. Those willing to sell
> naturally held out for the highest bidder. In the electoral districts where the
> competition was the most intense or in which business magnates were most
> determined to obtain a People's Assembly seat with the prospect of a par-
> liamentary immunity that comes with it, the going price of a vote soared.[42]

This suggests how limited democratic reforms made by the regime
through elections had increased the trend of corruption. But corruption
occurred through vote buying not only in elections but also inside parliament. This was evident when Ezz—who emerged as an oligarch a la Russia,
as mentioned earlier—served his own interest by influencing the amendment of Law 3 of 2005 on the Protection of Competition and the Prohibition of Monopolistic Practices in a way that allowed him to enhance his
monopolistic practices, which suggests symptoms of state capture by certain businessmen. The draft of Law 3 of 2005 went through many stages.[43]
First, Minister of Trade Rashid Mohamed Rashid proved that there was a

monopoly in the steel industry and called for toughening the penalty for monopolies by making the penalty proportionate with what monopolists make. As a result, the government proposed a draft law that provided for penalizing monopolists with 10 percent of their sales revenues. Then, when the bill was submitted to the Consultative Assembly, its members asked to raise the fine to 15 percent.[44] When comparing the various stages of drafting the law and its final form, it is clear that all the suggested penalties were more severe than what was legislated in the final form.

In the final draft of the law, the penalty was changed from 15 percent of a monopoly's sales revenues to a maximum fine of three hundred million EGP.[45] It is worth mentioning that if the monopolies were fined at 15 percent, Ahmed Ezz would have to pay 1.7 billion EGP.[46]

The leadership seems to have been aware of how Ezz passed the monopoly law to enhance his monopolistic practices; however, Mubarak did not take any serious action to stop Ezz. As former Speaker of Parliament Fathy Sorour has confessed,

I complained to the President, and told him that [this law] should not pass. So, the President talked to the party's secretary general Safwat El Sherif to resolve the issue. El Sherif came to my office and called in Ezz and told him about the president's objections . . . however, Ezz stuck to his guns and said that he is not going to change the law, and in case I will try to amend it, he will tell the NDP majority to refuse it . . . At this stage, I felt that Ezz is more powerful [than the President] and he represents a dangerous power and disobeys the President.[47]

This infers how the relationship between the regime and Ezz developed from mere co-option to mutual dependency. On the one hand, the regime could not turn against Ezz, since he was the main sponsor for the ruling party, Mubarak's presidential campaign, and the project of hereditary succession of Gamal Mubarak. On the other hand, since Ezz made his fortune through illegal practices, he then needed the regime for protection.

Despite the mutual dependency between Ezz and the regime, when the January 25, 2011, protests started, this relationship became a liability to the regime. In an attempt to offer concessions to the protestors, the regime fired Ezz from the party on January 29, and on the February 3, Ezz was banned from traveling. The extent of the mutual dependency between Ezz and Mubarak's regime meant that the survival of one depended on the other. The flip side of this relationship was that when one collapsed, both collapsed. For instance, when Ezz was fired from the party, this had an impact on the party's ability to mobilize its members during the protests. As a former senior member of the NDP Ali El Din Hillal said, "Ezz was one of the first sacrificial lambs that Mubarak offered up to the crowds because of the population's disdain of him as a leading crony capitalist. Yet, when Ezz left, he took more than four hundred names and contacts of party organizers from across the country. Even had it wished to countermobilize, the party cut its own organizing arm off."[48]

One week after the collapse of Mubarak's regime, Ezz was taken into custody for prosecution, and his financial assets were frozen. Ezz's prosecution reconfirms the mutual dependency that developed between him and Mubarak's regime. Had the Mubarak regime not collapsed, it is less likely that Ezz would have been sent to trial.

Over the last three years (2011–2014), Ezz has been on trial in two cases. The first involves the illegal gain of 6.4 billion EGP between 2003 and 2011 because of his illegal acquisition of Al Dekheila. The second trial was for the illegal sale of steel licenses. In August 2014, Ezz's appeals were accepted, and he was released on bail. He paid one hundred million EGP due to money laundering charges, illicit gains, and the illegal acquisition of Al Dekheila. Ezz is currently under retrial.[49]

Under Mubarak, this form of mutual dependency, in which the regime and Ezz were equally strong and could threaten each other, was considered an exception to the rule rather than the rule. In Ezz's case, the exception occurred because he merged economic and political power. Apart from this exception, different forms of clientelism have emerged between Mubarak's regime and businessmen in which the regime was stronger and could protect or threaten a businessman in his business and political career; in other cases, the increase in the financial power of businessmen allowed them to have a bargaining relationship with the regime despite their illegal business activities, which led to a semiclientelistic relationship. The following case of loan MPs will discuss this point.

The Case of Loan MPs

Before discussing the case of the loan MPs, I start by providing background on businessmen and the banking sector in the 1990s during economic liberalization. One of the economic reforms implemented in the 1990s that enabled businessmen to trade bank money was abolishing the restriction on lending volume to a single customer, strict loan conditions, and credit ceilings to both public and private banks.[50] For instance, during the 1990s, 46 businessmen held around 47 percent of Cairo Bank's loan portfolio. Two of these businessmen had loans worth more than the bank's capital base.[51] Moreover, according to a report on the banking sector during the 1990s, 343 clients received 42 percent of the overall credit facilities allocated to the private sector. Also, out of this group, only 28 clients received 13 percent of the overall credit.[52] One of the corrupt cases in which banks made unguaranteed loans to businessmen was the case of loan MPs, as the following section will discuss.

The case of loan MPs started in 1994 when the head of Al Nile Bank's board of directors, Issa El Ayouty, returned from a six-month business trip to Saudi Arabia. Upon his return, El Ayouty found out that his daughter, Alia El Ayouty, vice president of Al Nile Bank, had married MP businessman Mahmoud Azzam in May 1995 against her father's will. He also discovered that his daughter illegally gave loans from the bank to her husband and other businessmen close to her husband. In order to protect himself against these illegal banking practices, El Ayouty brought accusations against his daughter to the Organization of Administrative Control, the Central Bank, and the prosecutor general.[53] As a result of these accusations, in August 1995, the prosecutor general started investigations with members of the Organization of Administrative Control, which revealed the following: NDP MP businessman Mahmoud Azzam used his close relationship with Alia El Ayouty, vice president of Al Nile Bank, to get loans worth more than 179 million EGP. Knowing that Azzam did not provide any guarantees for these loans and that the Central Bank forbade the banks to deal with him, Alia El Ayouty did not register the loans in his bank accounts.[54]

NDP MP Ibrahim Aglan, board member of Al Dakahlia Bank, used his relationship with Tawfik Abdou Ismail,[55] director of Al Dakahlia Bank and head of the Planning and Budget Committee of the People's Assembly, and gave loans to his brother, businessman Yassin Aglan, which were worth more than two hundred million EGP, without requiring guarantees.[56]

Khaled Mohamed Mahmoud, an NDP MP and son of the former minister of local government, used his relationship with Alia El Ayouty in Al Nile Bank and Tawfik Abdou Ismail in Al Dakahlia Bank to get unguaranteed loans from both banks worth tens of millions of EGP.[57] The investigation further revealed that the group of four NDP MPs mentioned previously formed a network of 18 individuals that included businessmen and bankers who managed to get loans from eight different banks,[58] including Al Nile Bank and Al Dakahlia Bank.[59]

The investigation of the four loan deputies started when parliament, on December 13, 1995, gave them permission to testify in front of the prosecutor general but without removing their parliamentary immunity.[60] One month later, parliament agreed to withdraw their immunity based on a request from the minister of justice.[61] During the trial of the loan deputies, they retained their memberships in parliament. In fact, this was possible due to the institutional impediments in the 1971 constitution, as Article 96 stated, "No membership in the People's Assembly shall be revoked except on the grounds of loss of confidence or status or loss of one of the conditions of membership or the loss of the member's status as worker or farmer upon which he was elected or the violation of his obligations as a member. The membership shall be deemed invalid on the grounds of a decision taken by two-thirds of the Assembly members."

Based on this article, the loan deputies were protected and kept their memberships in parliament during their trial, as one author observed, "What was interesting to observe was that even during the trial, the state continued to protect its corrupt politico-economic entrepreneurs. Ironically, instead of being dismissed from parliament or at least having their membership frozen pending court rulings, these MP businessmen continued 'business as usual': in the mornings they stood in the court behind bars accused of squandering public funds and harming public interests while in the afternoons they were acting in Parliament as public representatives and as the people's legislators."[62]

Then, in 2002, the Supreme Security Court ruled against the accused, and they got prison sentences ranging from 7 to 15 years in prison. The corruption of these businessmen led Judge Ahmed Ashmawi to state in his court ruling that "the case is not a case of members of parliament, because the parliament withdrew their membership when it knew that they are criminals . . . It is not also a case of loans, because what they did was not taking loans from banks but rather they were looting the money of the banks. The court feels sorry for being unable to pass the death penalty against the accused . . . I ask the legislator to amend the law in order to make the death penalty the maximum punishment in this type of case."[63]

But after the court (which is independent in its decisions) sentenced the loan MPs, the regime continued to protect them by finding a way for their release, even though they had been proven guilty. This was evident when Kamal El Shazly suggested in 2004 that parliament amend Article 133 of the Central Bank law.[64] The newly amended article of Law 164 of 2004 was issued to change some articles of Central Bank Law 88 of 2003. According to the old article, when a court case is filed, and before the final court ruling takes place, the accused can make a settlement with the banks in which the accused is required to pay back all the money he or she acquired in return for the banks dropping all charges.[65] The old article suggested that the relationship between the regime and the businessmen was authoritarian clientelistic one based on credible threats of coercion. This meant that either businessmen should pay all the money they looted or they would be jailed. However, the newly amended article[66] is based less on coercion and more on negotiation, as it made it possible for the accused to negotiate a repayment of part of his or her debts in return for dropping all charges, even after the final court ruling had found him or her guilty.[67]

There was a debate among bankers over the amendment of this law. There were those who argued that reconciliation with the businessmen was necessary and not a special favor to support them. For instance, Mahmoud Abdel Aziz, former head of the Federation of the Egyptian Banks, defended the newly amended article by saying that "this amendment was a must and not an option . . . because when a businessman borrowed money from the banks his aim was to make a project; however, when he started the project he may find that the taxes were raised, and the feasibility studies were made on the basis that the dollar, for example, costs three [Egyptian] pounds and now became seven [Egyptian] pounds . . . This is why we reconciled with our clients, and exempted them from hundreds of millions [of Egyptian pounds]."[68]

On the other hand, Ahmed El Baradei, who headed the Cairo Bank from 2000 to 2005, found that many irregularities happened during the 1990s and argued against this law. For instance, he said,

> There is a difference between a crime and the insolvent customer . . . If you did not commit a crime, and you are an insolvent customer, then you should pay back to the bank everything you have, except a minimum amount to leave, like a house and a car if you need it for work . . . None of those who have been sent to court were insolvent customers, but they were presented to court for crimes that should be punished by the law; unfortunately, Law 164 allows you to steal and then reconcile with the banks by paying any amount and keeping part of your loot, and the charges are dropped.[69]

El Baradei's argument seems to be more plausible when comparing the difference between the banking practices of the businessmen in the 1980s and the 1990s and the political-economic environment in the two periods. For instance, according to Hassan Hussein, former head of Misr Bank Al Motahad, "In the 1980s, there were respected businessmen who worked in trade and industry. They would open a letter of credit and when the goods arrived, they would pay the banks. But in the 1990s, businessmen were trading with the banks' money. For example, those who had political connections bought pieces of land for a nominal price. Then they would get loans from the banks based on the value of this piece of land after the bank had highly inflated its price. These people were involved in unproductive activities and made money using state-owned lands."[70]

The increase in the volume of bank loans has been possible because of the implementation of economic liberalization. As mentioned earlier, economic reform in the banking sector has allowed for the abolishment of the restriction on lending volume to a single customer, strict loan conditions, and credit ceilings. Empirical figures suggest that bank loans have aggravated economic conditions. For instance, when Atef Ebeid headed the cabinet in 1999, he found a loss of fifty billion EGP.[71] The fiscal implications of these loans suggest why the regime chose to negotiate with the businessmen over settling their debts. As Hussein explained, "Since Farouk El Okda [who is a close associate of Gamal Mubarak] was appointed governor of the Central Bank in 2004, the most important thing was to amend the Central Bank law and reconcile with the businessmen. El Okda wanted to change the environment. There was a general pressure on the banks to reconcile with the businessmen and not to arrest them . . . they don't pay back the whole amount but negotiate on paying part of it, and they will get out."[72]

We can term this clientelistic relationship that developed between the regime and the businessmen who took unguaranteed loans as semiclientelistic. This new clientelistic relationship allowed businessmen to bargain and negotiate with the regime on paying only part of the money they looted from the banks.[73] In this semiclientelistic relationship that emerged in the context of the economic liberalization, the bargaining induced compliance by the threat of benefit removal. "Benefit" here means paying only part of the money they had looted from the banks.

The case of loan MPs also suggests that the Egyptian state was predatory in the sense of Peter Evans: those who controlled the state (for example, the businessmen and bankers co-opted by the Mubarak regime) were looting at the expense of the interests of the rest of Egyptian society.[74] Stephan Roll observed that in a surveillance regime like Egypt, public banks could not have been giving loans worth millions of dollars without the knowledge of the leadership because the banks' reconciliation with businessmen was based on a political decision by the leadership.[75] As Hussein noted, "Before any reconciliation with the clients, the head of any bank, public or private, should ask the permission of the governor of the Central Bank, who is directly appointed by Mubarak. This makes it all a very political decision."[76]

The following section will examine the case of Ramy Lakah, who, despite his trouble with the banks, was able to develop a different clientelistic relationship with the regime.

The Case of Ramy Lakah: A Cosmetic Opposition Businessman in Parliament

Ramy Lakah is an Egyptian-French, Catholic businessman whose private business includes construction, health care equipment, and aviation. Since the mid-1990s Lakah had been in financial trouble with the banks,[77] which made him enter into an authoritarian clientelistic relationship with the regime in order to seek protection.

In an interview, the former head of Cairo Bank, Ahmed El Baradei, explained Lakah's financial corruption. He said, "Lakah's problem was fraud and not the inability to pay back his debts to the bank. Lakah has been accused of fraud by the Capital Market Authority, the Investigation of Public Funds, and the Organization of Administrative Control. In 1998, Lakah falsely inflated the capital of his companies by increasing the value of its shares. Lakah then sold ten percent of one of his artificially inflated companies to the Cairo Bank for 120 million EGP. Then Lakah got loans from the bank based on the fraudulent papers and the artificially inflated value that he claimed for his companies."[78]

Lakah's financial corruption explains why he was trying to ingratiate himself with the regime, as the case of Al Kosheh suggests. For instance, in August 1998, two Copts were murdered in Al Kosheh, a village in Sohag Governorate. Most of the citizens living in this village are Coptic Christians. During the process of investigation, hundreds of Copts were tortured while in detention. The Egyptian Organization for Human Rights (EOHR) published a report on the Internet about Al Kosheh events. The main objective of the report was to write about police brutality without addressing the position of Copts in Egypt. Nevertheless, the report mentioned that in order to avoid sectarian hatred, the police did not want to accuse Muslims of murdering the Copts and had to attach the crime to a Copt.[79] Through the EOHR report, international newspapers had access to information about this event. For instance, the British newspaper *Sunday Telegraph* wrote a story in October 1998 about the brutality of Egyptian police with the Copts; however, the article exaggerated considerably and had little similarity to the EOHR report. For instance, the article ran a headline stating, "Egyptian Police 'Crucify' and Rape Christians—Thousands of Copts in Egypt Have Been Nailed to the Doors of their Homes, Beaten, Tortured as Authorities Crack Down on Non-Muslims."[80]

At the time this report was published, Lakah was a board member of the EOHR, and he claims that his membership in this organization triggered his first clash with the regime.[81] However, evidence suggests that Lakah was rather supportive of the regime. For instance, in response to the *Sunday Telegraph* coverage of Al Kosheh events, Lakah published several advertisements in foreign newspapers, such as the *New York Times*, the *Herald Tribune*, the *Washington Post*, and the British *Daily Telegraph*, in which he denied the persecution of Copts and demanded no interference in Egyptian national affairs.[82]

Moreover, in March 2000, during Mubarak's visit to Washington, DC, a group of emigrant Copts who were living in the United States organized a demonstration in front of the White House while holding pictures of the Coptic victims of Al Kosheh, thus accusing the Egyptian government of discrimination against Copts.[83] As a result, Lakah funded trips from New York and New Jersey to Washington, DC, for a large number of emigrant Egyptians to support Mubarak during his visit to Washington, DC. As journalist Adel Hamouda observed, "I saw Lakah in Washington, DC; in the middle of the demonstrations in the garden next to the White House . . . There were hundreds in the demonstrations. The participants were Muslims and Copts who don't know discrimination and intolerance. As for the other side, counter demonstration participants were very few."[84] In 2000, Lakah ran in the parliamentary election as an independent candidate. But in 2001, a court verdict withdrew Lakah's membership in parliament because of his dual nationality. Lakah then fled Egypt without paying back his loans to the banks and lived between London and Paris.[85]

Based on Lakah's financial accusations (mentioned previously), the Supreme Security Court then issued a court ruling in January 2003 to sequestrate Lakah's money and properties. Despite the court ruling, the prosecution did not investigate this criminal case.[86] However, this does not mean that Lakah's legal case in the court has been terminated; Lakah's file at the Prosecutor General's Office has not been closed. In other words, "Lakah's file is in the drawer of the prosecutor general; it is neither closed nor opened."[87] This means that in politically sensitive cases, the prosecutor general conducts investigations against the accused and refers him or her to court based on a decision from Mubarak. The judicial authority law enabled the regime to either protect or threaten businessmen like Lakah. As one author writes, "Under the 1972 law on Judicial Authority, the general prosecutor is appointed by presidential decree from among vice-presidents of courts of appeal, counselors of the Court of Cassation, or chief public attorneys . . . no specific qualifications or conditions are required of the new appointee. The appointment of the general prosecutor has remained a political decision made solely by the political authority, which is the president of the republic."[88]

This suggests that in Lakah's case, the regime used threats of coercion—for example, to open his corruption file at any time. This led to the formation of an authoritarian clientelistic relationship between the regime and him. This also explains why Lakah fled the country out of fear of being prosecuted. Then, nine years later, Lakah reconciled with the banks due the amended Central Bank Law 164 of 2004 (discussed earlier), which allows local banks to settle disputes with clients if debts are repaid; charges are then dropped. According to Lakah's bank reconciliation, two-thirds of his debts were forgiven, and he returned to Egypt.[89] In this authoritarian clientelistic relationship, Lakah continued playing the role of an opposition candidate who is supportive to Mubarak after his return to Egypt. For instance, in a newspaper interview in 2010, Lakah was asked if he supported the nomination of Mubarak for another term. He said, "I support President Mubarak; because he represents stability, but I am not supporting the NDP . . . I will only support Mubarak because he is now the most convenient candidate . . . I don't think Ayman Nour or Mohamed El Baradei can fill his position."[90]

Unlike Lakah, other opposition businessmen refused to enter into a clientelistic relationship with the regime since they were critical of Mubarak, his son Gamal, and his inner circle, as the following case of Anwar Esmat El Sadat demonstrates.

The Case of Anwar Esmat el Sadat: A Real Opposition Businessman in Parliament

Anwar Esmat El Sadat is a businessman and a nephew of former President Anwar El Sadat. Upon the death of President Sadat, Mubarak ordered the arrest of Esmat El Sadat (President Sadat's younger brother) and his sons, including Anwar, on charges of making profits through their ties with the late President Sadat. However, the prosecution's investigation later proved that they were innocent.[91] Anwar's older brother explained what happened to them: "Our money was sequestrated [for a number of years], and we were jailed for eight months and thirteen days, during which time the press followed the orders of the authorities and drummed it into people's heads that we were thieves."[92]

El Sadat's private business includes tourism and maritime trade. In 2005, he engaged in politics by running for parliamentary election as an independent candidate in the Al Tala constituency of El Monofeya's governorate. As soon as he was elected to the People's Assembly, El Sadat removed his name from all his private companies and devoted himself to politics. After his election to the People's Assembly, the regime tried to co-opt him, but he said, "After I was elected to the People's Assembly, I was asked by Ahmed Ezz to join the NDP; however, I refused because the voters elected me as an independent parliamentarian . . . Ezz asked me to join the NDP to make sure I am not going to criticize the government or present interpellations."[93]

Then, two years after his election, he was expelled from parliament. According to El Sadat, there are two reasons he was expelled from parliament: first, his request for an investigation by the socialist public prosecutor into Zakariya Azmi, the presidential chief of staff and a member of Mubarak's inner circle, and second, an interpellation he submitted about the monopolization of El Sokhna Port by one of Gamal Mubarak's closest friends.[94] The following section will discuss these two points.

On February 3, 2006, El Salam 98 ferry—which is owned by Mamdouh Ismail, a business tycoon, member of the Consultative Assembly, and close associate of Azmi—sank in the Red Sea after a fire on board. The boat was carrying more than one thousand passengers. The parliamentary fact-finding committee concluded that Ismail was responsible for this disaster.[95] Six weeks after the sinking of the boat, the Consultative Assembly lifted the immunity of Ismail. Its slowness in lifting Ismail's immunity allowed him to flee the country. This was possible, as opposition members of parliament said, because of his friendship with Azmi.[96] After Ismail fled the country, El Sadat requested an investigation of Azmi by the socialist public prosecutor. In his request, El Sadat accused Azmi of helping Ismail monopolize maritime transport in the Red Sea and facilitating his escape from the country after the sinking of El Salam 98 ferry. However, due to the institutional and legal constraints in the People's Assembly bylaw, the steering office of parliament refused to send this request to the socialist public prosecutor. Even though the request for investigation was dropped, this was a tough accusation for Azmi. As the then Speaker of Parliament Fathy Sorour told El Sadat, "It was the first time I had seen Azmi shaking like this in parliament, when you asked for an investigation of him."[97]

Moreover, El Sadat submitted an interpellation in which he accused Gamal Mubarak of awarding one of this closest friends and a classmate at the American University in Cairo, Omar Tantawi, contracts that would enable him to monopolize El Sokhna Port.[98] According to El Sadat, after this interpellation, Sorour told him, "Now I can say that you are about to travel from parliament," hinting that he would be expelled from parliament soon.[99] In fact, it was not long after Sadat presented this interpellation that he was expelled from parliament. The background of his expulsion is related to a check in the amount of half a million dollars that El Sadat issued to guarantee the economic activities of one of his friend's companies. When his friend's company went bankrupt, El Sadat found that his company was also declared bankrupt. The bankruptcy of a parliamentarian means losing his or her integrity to stay in parliament in accordance with Article 96 of the 1971 constitution, which states that "no member in the People's Assembly shall be revoked except on the grounds of loss of confidence or status or loss of one of the conditions of membership . . . The membership shall be deemed invalid on the grounds of a decision taken by two-thirds of the Assembly members."

El Sadat met with Sorour and explained to him that the court rule is flawed and that he is not directly involved in the case. Sorour told him there was no problem as long as he was going to appeal in court. But in the evening of the same day, Sorour called El Sadat and said, "Come to my office tomorrow morning. It's urgent . . . new things have come up." On the following day, El Sadat met Sorour in his office, and Sorour told him, "You should know there are legal and constitutional matters, and there are political matters. Regarding the latter, I have no control over them. I have been asked [by the authority] to expel you from parliament. And God be with you."[100]

Sorour convinced El Sadat to pay half a million dollars to the opponents of his friend's company to get from them a certificate of discharge that would support his case in parliament. The following day, before attending the parliamentary session, El Sadat paid the money, even though he did not have to. Then during the parliamentary session, Sorour asked the members to vote on the dismissal of El Sadat from parliament, since the court had declared his bankruptcy; however, El Sadat sent a petition to Sorour asking to postpone the voting to the evening session until he got an official document saying that the court of appeals would issue its final ruling on the following day. But Sorour insisted on the vote, and El Sadat was expelled from parliament. As El Sadat said, "This was a game."[101]

Even though El Sadat was stripped of his parliamentary membership, the court of appeals ruled in his favor to stop implementation of the ruling that declared his bankruptcy. Then El Sadat raised a case in court and got compensation from parliament, but his membership had already been dropped.[102] The case of El Sadat suggests how businessmen who refused to enter a clientelistic relationship with the regime have been weakened politically, which prevented them from becoming a real opposition.

The following section will examine how the regime used its obedient parliamentary businessmen to act as intermediaries with clients in their constituencies.

The Case of Mohamed Abul-Enein: A Patron-Broker-Client Relationship

As mentioned in Chapter 1, with the introduction of economic liberalization, the state withdrew from the provision of social services. This section discusses how economic liberalization transformed the clientelistic relationship between the regime and parliamentary businessmen from dyadic to triadic, thus including the regime as a patron, businessmen as brokers, and voters as clients. In this triadic relation, the regime plays the role of a patron who subcontracts businessmen to act as brokers in the provision of social services to voters in their constituencies. The services offered by the parliamentary candidates seem to be of significance to the voters. For instance, in the 2005 parliamentary election, candidates who acted as brokers distributed to potential voters CDs, pens, mobile phones, and meat, and in some cases, they offered to pay phone bills. In other cases, parliamentary candidates also traded food for votes. When the 2005 parliamentary campaign occurred during Ramadan, candidates sponsored free meals in poor neighborhoods. In some constituencies, families were given vouchers to claim free chicken. In other constituencies, fast food was delivered to homes.[103]

Illustrative of patron-broker-client relationships is multimillionaire Mohamed Abul-Enein.[104] He started his business during the period 1973–1987 as an importer and distributor of different types of ceramics. Then, in 1988, he established his own factory, Ceramica Cleopatra.[105] In 1995, the regime co-opted Abul-Enein when he was appointed by Mubarak to the People's Assembly.[106] Then, from 2000 to 2010, Abul-Enein was elected to the People's Assembly as an NDP member representing the El Giza constituency in El Giza Governorate, and he also headed the Industry and Energy Committee in parliament. While Abul-Enein's co-option started on the political level, it soon became economic when he was allocated state resources in illegal ways. For instance, in an interpellation submitted to the People's Assembly by Gamal Zahran, head of the independent parliamentary bloc, he uncovered the corruption of the regime in the case of Abul-Enein when he violated Article 95 of the 1971 constitution, which states that "no member of the People's Assembly shall, during his term, purchase or rent any state property or sell or lease to the state or barter with it regarding any part of his property, or conclude a contract with the state in his capacity as entrepreneur, importer or contractor."

According to Zahran's interpellation, during Abul-Enein's first term in parliament (1995–2000) as a member appointed by the president, he bought from the state at nominal prices large pieces of prime land for multiple uses (agriculture, industry, etc.) in strategic locations like Shark el O'wainat in the governorate of El Wadi El Gedid, in Misr Ismailia Road, and in the Gulf of Suez.[107] It is worth mentioning that parliamentarians are supposed to respect the laws and the constitution. For instance, Article 90 in the 1971 constitution states that "before exercising his duties, the member of the People's Assembly shall take the following oath before the Assembly: 'I swear by God Almighty that I shall sincerely safeguard the safety of the nation, the republican regime, attend to the interests of the people and shall respect the Constitution and the law.'"

The leadership seems to have been aware of how Abul-Enein acquired this land. For instance, on different occasions President Mubarak made official visits to Abul-Enein on his agricultural land in Shark el O'wainat (as mentioned earlier, it is one of the lands that he bought in illegal ways).

During these visits, Abul-Enein would brief Mubarak about the agricultural development on his farm.[108] This suggests that President Mubarak not only was aware of the corruption in the selling of lands but also seems to have encouraged it as long as the lands were given to his own co-opted businessmen.

The fact that Abul-Enein made his fortune through illegal practices, which seem to have been encouraged by the leadership, suggests why he accepted the role of a broker to the voters in his constituency by replacing the state in the provision of social services. For instance, Abul-Enein makes an annual profit in his business of 150 million EGP. He spends around 15 million EGP in his constituency yearly in the form of social services to the poor.[109] As one of Mubarak's co-opted businessmen, Abul-Enein supported the regime until the outbreak of the revolution on January 25, 2011. For instance, evidence suggests that on February 2, 2011, Abul-Enein and other businessmen and NDP members were involved in hiring thugs who were holding swords and were mounted on horses and camels to break up the protests on February 2, 2011. This case became known later as the Battle of the Camel.[110]

*Mohamed Abul-Enein in Transformation under
Mohamed Morsi and Abdel Fattah El-Sisi*

After the Twenty-Fifth of January Revolution, Abul-Enein started to get in trouble. He was under trial in the Battle of the Camel,[111] and the government confiscated the land that he got in the Gulf of Suez during Mubarak's rule.[112] Moreover, in one of the speeches of Mohammed Morsi, the Muslim Brothers (MB) candidate, during his presidential campaign as in May 2012 in Suez Governorate, he criticized Abul-Enein and said that his business history is black. Morsi referred to the state-owned lands that he bought with nominal prices because of his close relationship with Mubarak's regime.[113] These unfortunate events that happened to Abul-Enein after the collapse of Mubarak's regime suggest why he chose to disclaim his relationship with the old regime. Despite Morsi's criticism of Abul-Enein during his presidential campaign, Abul-Enein attempted to ingratiate himself with the new regime. For instance, after Morsi won the presidential election in June 2012, Abul-Enein published a paid advertisement in several newspapers congratulating him for winning the election.[114] Moreover, Abul-Enein ordered his media outlets—which he established after the collapse of Mubarak's regime and included the online newspaper *Sada al Balad* (Echo of the Country) and a news channel with the same name—not to criticize the MB. Authors who were against the MB were not allowed to write for his online newspaper, while those sympathetic with them were allowed to publish their articles.[115] Before Morsi continued forty days in office, Abul-Enein, on different occasions, announced his support of him and his *Nahda* (Renaissance) project.[116]

In August 2012, Abul-Enein was among a delegation of eighty businessmen invited to accompany Morsi in his visit to China. Official statements during this trip stated that the regime was willing to reconcile with businessmen affiliated with Mubarak's regime as long as they were not involved in cases of corruption.[117] But it seems Abul-Enein was not one of those businessmen that the new regime was willing to reconcile with. For instance, when Abul-Enein introduced a proposal to one of Morsi's advisors to fund an international economic conference to promote Egypt after the revolution, his proposal was refused by the MB. This is because the MB did not want to present Abul-Enein to society with a new image after the Twenty-Fifth of January Revolution.[118] Abul-Enein seems to have realized that his business interests did not coincide with the interests of the MB, which explains why he later was one of the businessmen who used their media outlets to criticize the MB until Morsi's removal on July 3, 2013, by the Supreme Council of the Armed Forces.[119]

After the election of President Sisi in June 2014, Abul-Enein—as he did with Morsi—started presenting his loyalty to the new president. In different places in El Giza Governorate, Abul-Enein posted banners with slogans supporting Sisi.[120] Abul-Enein seems to continue playing the role of broker to the new regime under Sisi as he did with Mubarak. For instance, as soon as Sisi assumed office, Abul-Enein announced that he was going to pay around 250 million EGP to establish industrial schools that aimed to create a cadre of professionals to strengthen Egyptian industry.[121]

From 2011 to 2014, Abul-Enein shifted his political support from the NDP under Mubarak to the MB under Morsi to finally supporting Sisi. This suggests that he is willing to support any president, regardless of political background, as long as it aligned with his own economic interests.

Businessmen in the 2005 Parliamentary Election

Unlike Abul-Enein, whom Mubarak's regime sought to co-opt, other businessmen competed to play the role of brokers to the regime. This was evident in the 2005 parliamentary election, when in each constituency there were generally three to five businessmen running for the same seat. This competition was among NDP businessmen, independent businessmen who were members in the NDP but were not nominated, and businessmen who were real independents, as well as other candidates. The average amount spent on these campaigns ranged from five to seven million (EGP).[122] For instance, in the 2005 parliamentary election, Shahinaz El Naggar, an NDP member who ran as an independent candidate—since she was not nominated by the party—spent around ten million EGP on her parliamentary campaign in the El Manial constituency of Cairo Governorate. After winning the election, she registered herself in the parliament as an NDP member.[123] El Naggar is a hotelier who comes from a rich family. In her constituency, she provided monthly stipends for five hundred families, ranging from twenty to fifty EGP, in addition to other charitable activities, such as giving gifts to orphans on Orphan's Day and providing material for upholstery to poor women who were getting married. Also, her health center provided services to her constituency at a nominal price (50 piasters per patient). In the same constituency, El Naggar's competitor, Mamdouh Thabet Mekky, was a millionaire businessman working in the leather industry. Mekky was nominated by the NDP as the official party candidate and lost against El Naggar. After his election to parliament in 1990 in the El Manial constituency, he established a social service bearing his name, which provides vocational training and medical services to people in the constituency.[124]

Similar patterns of NDP businessmen who played the role of brokers in their constituencies while running against each other are evident in the 2005 parliamentary election. For instance, in the Kasr El Nil constituency, both NDP members—Hossam Badrawi, a medical services entrepreneur, and Hisham Moustafa Khalil, a wealthy businessman—ran against each other. While the former was nominated as the official party candidate, the latter was not nominated, despite his membership in the party. Khalil was registered in parliament as an NDP member after winning the election. During the parliamentary campaign, Khalil provided services to the constituents. For instance, in poor areas in the Kasr El Nil constituency in Cairo Governorate, such as Boulaq, many constituents did not have tap water, and Khalil paid for water to be delivered to their houses. In addition, he paid to repair streets and paint houses in this area. In the Al-'Aini area in the Kasr El Nil constituency, Khalil also paid for 1,500 meters of sewage pipe to be brought to the residents of this area. His competitor, Badrawi, also provided social services. His two NGOs in the constituency supported four hundred orphans, and he provided free medical care at a local clinic.[125]

The regime has created a divided environment among NDP businessmen running for parliamentary election. The institutional mechanism for this division was the electoral law introduced in 1990 for individual candidacy, which replaced proportional representation. Unlike proportional representation, which prevented intraparty competition, the new electoral law encouraged competition among party members (for example, businessmen). The intraparty competition between NDP businessmen seems to have been advantageous to the survival of the regime, since it encouraged each of these businessmen to invest more in social services to win the support of the voters; at the same time, it prevented their unity and ensured their fragmentation.

Conclusion

In this chapter, I have argued that in the context of economic liberalization, the regime of Hosni Mubarak attempted to stay in power by using different types of co-option of businessmen. These varieties of co-option varied from authoritarian clientelism, semiclientelism, and patron-broker-client relationships. But Ahmed Ezz had an exceptional clientelistic relationship with the regime, which started by mere co-option and developed into mutual dependency. However, such a relationship was an unintended consequence of developing clientelistic relations with businessmen in light of economic liberalization.

These varieties of clientelistic relationships were achieved through the formal institution of parliament, the ruling party, and elections, as well as the informal institutions of corruption and nepotism. The regime rewarded loyal parliamentary businessmen with immunity from prosecution and, therefore, protection for the illegal ways in which they increased their wealth—for example, through obtaining bank loans without collateral. Loyal businessmen in parliament were also rewarded by the regime by being able to buy state-owned companies and state-owned lands at very low prices. Indeed, parliamentary businessmen bought state-owned lands despite this being against the laws of parliament. The market reforms introduced after 1990, in the name of economic liberalization, facilitated these corrupt and illegal practices. Indeed, it is not only that loyal businessmen in parliament were financially rewarded for their loyalty to the regime. Economic liberalization provided new opportunities for economic predation on the part of businessmen, while participation in parliament and the NDP enabled some businessmen to shape decision making in a way that is symptomatic of state capture. Businessmen also helped the regime maintain its legitimacy by providing social services in their constituencies, which compensated for the withdrawal of state spending on welfare services after the introduction of the economic reform program.

In other words, in the context of economic liberalization, a new oligarchy that included businessmen both was a response to economic reforms and was facilitated by economic reforms and structural adjustment. Overall, this chapter has demonstrated that there has not been only one type of regime-businessmen co-option since 1990. The regime's relationships with businessmen have showed variety and flexibility in terms of co-option. The divided environment among them clearly prevented businessmen from being structurally powerful, providing a check on the regime, and playing a democratizing role. In other cases, businessmen supported the survival of the regime without their direct engagement in politics, as the following chapter will discuss.

4

The Social Networks of the Mubarak Family and the Businessmen

Introduction

The primary concern in this chapter is to conceptualise the personal relationships that developed between Mubarak with certain businessmen. This chapter argues that there are businessmen who did not engage in politics, for example, by running for parliamentary elections or joining political parties but who developed personal clientelistic relationships with Mubarak as well as with high-level government officials like businessmen Ahmed Bahgat and Mohamed Nosseir. Other businessmen, such as Naguib Sawiris (hereafter referred to as Naguib to avoid confusion with the rest of his family members) and his family, created network relationships with the Mubarak family. In these traditional clientelistic relations, businessmen varied in their proximity to Mubarak, his family, and high-level government officials, which had implications for the reallocation and abuse of state resources (for example, the selling of state-owned lands and state-owned enterprises at reduced prices, tax evasion, and the borrowing of public bank loans without collateral).

Then, in return for benefiting from economic liberalization through their personal relationships with Mubarak, his family, or high-level government officials, these businessmen provided support for the survival of Mubarak's authoritarian regime. For instance, they provided television and newspaper support to Mubarak, his family, and his regime, as well as philanthropic and charitable activities to compensate for the state's withdrawal from the provision of social services. On the other hand, businessmen who failed to enter into patron-client relationships with the regime have been subject to coercion in their businesses, as in the case of Wagih Siag.

This chapter builds on the work of John Sfakianakis,[1] who argues that Egypt's economic reform provided an opportunity for the emergence of network relations, which helped Mubarak's regime survive and enriched his ruling coalitions, including businessmen and bureaucrats who turned into businessmen. But my findings are distinct from Sfakianakis's, since I argue that there are businessmen, like Hussein Salem, and bureaucrats who turned into businessmen, such as Minister of Housing Ibrahim Soliman, who entered into patron-client relations with Mubarak and his family, and their role was not limited to providing support for the survival of Mubarak's authoritarianism; they also contributed to the enrichment of the Mubarak family. As Amr Adly writes, "The Mubaraks [served] as the nodes of broader networks of state officials and crony businessmen. In this setting, Mubarak and his sons would use their formal and informal leverage to issue public acts that would allocate public assets and market positions to people who are closely allied to them with the final aim of self-enrichment . . . [In] this pattern of self-enrichment . . . the state ceases to pursue public good and serves the private interest of its rulers and their associates."[2]

Businessmen who entered into traditional patron-client relations with Mubarak, the Mubarak family, or high-level government officials are used as examples in this chapter. The aim is to substantiate how the varieties of clientelistic relationships that developed between the regime and businessmen during economic liberalization have helped renew Mubarak's authoritarianism and the self-enrichment of his family.

The Case of Ahmed Bahgat: A Businessman Affiliated with the Regime

Ahmed Bahgat is a self-made businessman who became, in only a few years, one of Egypt's business tycoons. In 1982, Bahgat finished his PhD at Georgia State Institute of Technology in the United States. Subsequently, he succeeded in inventing an electronic guiding device that showed Muslims the correct direction in which to pray. Bahgat received $1 million for his invention.[3] In 1984, when Mubarak was visiting the United States, Bahgat managed to meet with him. During the meeting, Mubarak convinced Bahgat to return to Egypt. Mubarak told Bahgat, "If people like you don't come to Egypt, who is going to develop the country?" After this meeting, Bahgat decided to return to invest in Egypt.[4] The fact that Bahgat sought out a meeting with Mubarak could demonstrate that he wanted to create personal relations with the president, which paid off in terms of his being able to create economically beneficial patron-client relations with the regime. For instance, upon his return from the United States in 1985,

Bahgat established a new company that manufactured televisions. Until 1985, regulations prohibited private companies from producing televisions; however, an exception was made for Bahgat. As one author noted, "Indeed, [Ahmed Bahgat] used his ties with senior officers to obtain a license to manufacture Gold star televisions."[5] During the 1990s, Bahgat's group expanded to include diversified companies that produced products such as household appliances, furniture, electronics, and medical equipment. One of Bahgat Group's biggest projects was Dreamland, a real estate development established in one of Cairo's new suburbs: 6th of October City. This project includes residential communities, recreation, entertainment, shopping and sporting facilities, and it was built on 1,950 feddans (one feddan equivalent to 1.038 acres). Bahgat seemed to have managed to secure this large plot of land by relying on his networks with the regime. In the early 1990s, the then minister of housing and new communities, Ibrahim Soliman[6] (1993–2005), sold 1,950 feddans of land in 6th of October City by direct order to Ahmed Bahgat for much less than its original price.[7]

For instance, Soliman sold Bahgat the 1,950 feddans for a price of fifty Egyptian pounds (EGP) for each meter, and the money was supposed to be paid in installments. But this price did not reflect the real value of the land. Bahgat then paid only five EGP for each meter and did not continue paying the installments. Bahgat then repriced the land through the stock exchange and sold parts of it with a newly inflated price (thirty times more; for example, 1,500 EGP per meter). In addition, he got loans from public banks and used the land that he obtained by illegal means as collateral. These loans exceeded two billion EGP.[8] This example shows how the 1990s experienced a significant upward shift in the types of corruption that the regime was engaging in. Unlike in the 1980s, when the regime allowed only Bahgat's company to produce televisions, in the 1990s the regime started allocating state resources (for example, state-owned lands) to private individuals. As Timothy Mitchell explains,

> The state also subsidizes urban property developers, selling public land cheaply and putting up the required expressways and bridges in rapid time . . . If one's first reaction is amazement at the scale and speed of these developments, one soon begins to wonder about the contradictions. The IMF and Ministry of the Economy make no mention of the frenzied explosion of the capital city, and the state's role in subsidizing this speculative neoliberalism goes unexamined. A bigger problem is that structural adjustment was intended to generate an export boom, not a building boom. Egypt was to prosper by selling fruits and vegetables to Europe and the Gulf, not by paving over its fields to build ring roads. But real estate has now replaced agriculture as Egypt's third-largest non-oil investment sector, after manufacturing and

tourism. Indeed, it may be the largest non-oil sector, since most tourism investment goes into building tourist villages and vacation homes, another form of real estate.[9]

Bahgat continued expanding his private business, and in 2001, he founded the private channel, Dream TV. A background for the landscape of private media is needed before discussing the case of Dream TV. Although there are private channels in Egypt, they are not independent. This is because the ownership structure of private channels allows the government to automatically be awarded partial ownership. For instance, in the case of Dream TV, the government owns 10 percent of the station. Also, private channels that operate in the government's media production free zone, located in 6th of October City, are offered tax exemptions and land. This helps them cut the expenditures of the normal costs of operation, but such a privilege does not seem to be for free. This is because to operate in this zone, any channel requires a license from a state body (the General Authority for Free Zones), which has the right to cancel licenses for channels that criticize the government and its policies.[10]

Bahgat did not seem to care about the content of the channel; he established the channel only to market his product. For instance, at the time Bahgat established Dream TV, he owned a number of factories, and he would spend around forty million EGP a year on advertising. So instead of paying this money for advertisements, he got the idea of establishing his own television station where he could advertise his products.[11] However, one year after its establishment, Dream TV became embroiled in controversy in 2002 when it broadcast a lecture held at the American University in Cairo by the Egyptian intellectual Mohamed Hassanein Heikal, in which he raised the issue of hereditary succession in Egypt. This issue, concerning the possible "inheritance" by Gamal Mubarak of his father's presidency, was considered a "red line" in public debate. In addition, talk shows such as *Ra'is al-Tahrir* (Editor in Chief), presented by Hamdy Qandil, and *'Ala Al-Qahwa* (At the Coffee Shop), presented by Ibrahim Eissa, criticized the shortcomings of the Egyptian government. In 2003, Qandil and Eissa were both suspended for criticizing the Egyptian government.[12]

However, Ibrahim Eissa blamed his dismissal from Dream TV on Bahgat's dependency on the regime: "When I signed for Dream, I had my conditions: to be allowed to express myself freely and present what people are feeling . . . Things were going perfectly, but after great success and marvelous reactions, their eyes were opened and the scissors of the editors had to start . . . But when the prime minister himself insists on cancelling my program in order to support Ahmed Bahgat in this financial troubles, this is really a question mark."[13]

Eissa's words suggest that Bahgat had violated the patron-client relationship with the regime by allowing criticism of the government to be expressed on his television channel, leading the regime to enforce this patron-client relationship by using the banks to threaten Bahgat's business. For instance, Bahgat denied that he had defaulted on any loans, saying in 2002 that his total assets (1.7 billion EGP) were more than the total sum he had borrowed from the banks over a number of years (1.6 billion EGP).[14] Yet, in May 2004, the government prevented Bahgat from traveling abroad until he settled the billions of pounds he owed to the National Bank of Egypt and the New Housing Communities Authority.[15] As Dream TV's Chief Executive Officer claimed, "Even if Bahgat was not in a financially vulnerable position that necessitated the government support of his business, it remains within the government's capacity to *put him in one.*"[16]

The regime's enforcement of its clientelistic relations with Bahgat could explain why Bahgat continued supporting the regime. For instance, in the 2005 Egyptian presidential election, which was the country's first presidential election, there was a limit on the time allocated by state television to each presidential candidate. To counter this limit, the Mubarak campaign made a deal with Dream TV. According to the deal, Dream TV would have exclusive rights to broadcast Mubarak's campaigns, but this did not have any effect on the channel's coverage of the other candidates. At the same time, Dream TV benefitted from this deal, since the demand for advertisements during the broadcast of Mubarak's campaign was three times the average for that time slot.[17]

Since Dream TV is owned by one of the co-opted businessmen by the regime, it is therefore not surprising that it continued its support for the regime during the mass protests against Mubarak in 2011. A few days after the outbreak of the Twenty-Fifth of January Revolution, Mona El Shazly—the host of *El Ashara Masa'* (The 10 p.m.), one of the most popular talk shows on Dream TV—was supportive of Mubarak following his second speech, in which he said that he was not going to run for president again and would stay only until the end of his term in September 2011.[18] After airing this speech on her talk show, El Shazly cried and sympathized with Mubarak. A few days later, El Shazly revealed on the air that she had been instructed how to cover the demonstrations. She said, "They told us to say 'dozens' of demonstrators."[19]

The fact that Bahgat was one of the clients co-opted by the regime and that his interests coincided with the survival of the regime is best illustrated by the problems he faced after the fall of Mubarak. The banks confiscated the assets and properties of Bahgat in Dreamland in amounts equivalent to his debts, worth 3.2 billion EGP.[20] This suggests that Mubarak's regime used Bahgat's debts to threaten him to be obedient to the regime and to support it. If Bahgat had not obeyed, the regime could have put Bahgat's business in financial trouble at any time. We could term this type of relationship between the regime and Bahgat, which is based on credible threats of coercion, "authoritarian clientelism."

An example similar to Bahgat's Dream TV and freedom of expression is the case of Ibrahim El Moallam and *Al-Sherouk* newspaper. El Moallam is a businessman who did not engage in politics. He owns Al-Sherouk Publishing House and also the daily independent newspaper *Al-Sherouk*, which was established in 2009. But before discussing his case, it is important to provide background on the regulations for publishing newspapers. There are three types of newspapers: government-owned newspapers, political parties' newspapers, and private newspapers. First, the editors in chief of the government-owned newspapers, *Al-Ahram*, *Al-Akhbar*, and *Al-Gomhuriya*, were appointed by the president of the republic, which made them supportive of the government. Second, established political parties have the right to publish newspapers, but Article 14, Law 40 of 1977 empowers the Political Parties Committee (PPC) to stop a party's newspapers and activities if the committee deems it necessary to the national interest (1971 constitution).[21] The third type of newspaper is private and requires a license from the High Press Council, which is constituted by a decree from the president of the republic; the speaker of the Consultative Assembly serves as the chair. The council decides within forty days on an application. In case of refusal, the council provides reasons to the applicant, who may appeal to the court; however, the law does not clarify the reasons for refusal. In fact, it is not easy to obtain a license to publish a newspaper because security forces have to approve it. For instance, while the license should be approved within forty days by the High Press Council, applications were usually delayed, which meant that license applications were refused.[22] The structure of ownership of newspapers is another difficult condition to establish for private newspapers. This is because newspaper companies must exist in the form of cooperatives, and no single person can own more than 10 percent of a newspaper company's overall capital. However, according to one author, "It is unclear whether these rules are enforced in practice; at least some major print media titles appear to be owned, or at least controlled, by individual businessmen."[23] This means that the regime has the right to prevent a businessman from having complete ownership of a newspaper if it applies this condition. But at the same time, they may ignore this condition and give a newspaper license to a businessman who has entered a patron-client relationship with the regime. For instance, Ibrahim El Moallam seems to have been allowed to have the majority of shares in *Al-Sherouk* because he developed a patron-client relationship with Suzanne Mubarak, the wife of President Mubarak.

This relationship started when Suzanne Mubarak was visiting the Heliopolis Club and El Moallam asked permission from her guards to greet her. Then the relationship started to develop when he met her in the Alexandria Library and told her, in front of the people there, "Mrs. Mubarak, I am your servant before I am the servant of Egypt." A few weeks later, El Moallam was invited by Mrs. Mubarak to attend an event at Masr El Gadida Library. As soon as she arrived, El Moallam greeted her and kissed her hands.[24] Through this patron-client relationship, El Moallam started to print books for Suzanne Mubarak for the yearly Reading for All Festival. This is an initiative launched in 1991 by Mrs. Mubarak that attempted to provide books to the underprivileged classes, and El Moallam made millions from printing books for this yearly festival.[25]

However, it seems that El Moallam violated this patron-client relationship with the Mubarak family when, in the summer of 2010, the novelist Alaa El Aswany wrote a series of weekly articles in *Al-Sherouk* in which he criticized the project of hereditary succession and Mubarak's authoritarian regime. As a result, the regime used threats of coercion when security forces went to El Moallam's carton factory and closed it with red wax, claiming the factory did not have a fire extinguisher. El Moallam understood that the real reason was El Aswany's articles. For two weeks, El Aswany did not write his weekly articles.[26] But after El Aswany resumed writing and wrote an article criticizing the failure of Mubarak in ruling the country, El Moallam's factory was closed again. El Aswany was told that there was a lot of pressure put on El Moallam by State Security because of his articles, which were critical of the regime and also Mubarak. El Aswany decided to stop writing for *Al-Sherouk* newspaper, since he did not want to cause more problems for El Moallam in his work.[27] This suggests that the regime formed an authoritarian clientelistic relationship with El Moallam by threatening him in his private business.

While proponents of neoliberalism argue that private ownership of media presents a challenge to the state monopoly of media and can become an avenue for criticizing ruling regimes,[28] the cases of Dream TV and *Al-Sherouk* newspaper contradict the existing literature on neoliberalism. As mentioned earlier, increasing private ownership of media did not challenge the editorial content of the state-owned media; it complemented it. This also seems to conform to Eberhard Kienle's argument about how the regime controlled the information market that emerged as a result of economic liberalization, which increased authoritarianism.[29]

The following case will examine businessman Mohamed Nosseir, who, like Bahgat and El Moallam, developed an authoritarian clientelistic relationship with the regime.

The Case of Mohamed Nosseir

In 1974, Mohamed Nosseir established the Alkan Group, which, by 2002, was made up of 11 companies and engaged in activities including construction, petrol, pharmaceuticals, aviation, travel, and cotton yarn manufacturing, in addition to financial services.[30] In the early 1990s, Nosseir was invited by his childhood friend, Mamdouh El Beltagui, the then Cairo provincial secretary of the National Democratic Party (NDP), to join the party; Nosseir attended few party meetings and decided not to continue. Also, in the late 1990s, Nosseir was offered the position of minister of trade, but he refused.[31] Nosseir is a businessman who chose not to engage in politics, but rather relied on his good relationship with the government. When asked if he was a member of Egypt's "charmed circle," he said, "No, no . . . To the charmed circle I say: good luck. But I believe that the further away one is from power and the lower one's profile, the better. I have a good relationship with the government. I respect it, but I do not like close involvement."[32]

In fact, Nosseir's good relations with government officials allowed him to benefit from the privatization process. As Sfakianakis explains,

> Certainly, the biggest privatization that Egypt experienced in the early stages of the privatization process was the sale of Coca Cola in 1993. It was a deal that involved most prominently, among other members of the political elite, the quintessential elite businessman of the 1990s, Mohamed Nosseir. He benefited from his relations with Atef Sidqi [the then prime minister] as well as Atef Ebeid [the then minister of public-sector enterprises] to purchase with little competition the Coca Cola factory, which he resold two years later, at a price more than triple its cost. After all, Nosseir and the rest of the crony business elite were only doing what the structure of the economy had allowed them to do: provide politically helpful services to the regime.[33]

However, Nosseir's case demonstrates how good relations with the regime did not always guarantee increased wealth. While Nosseir's networks enabled him to make profits from the privatization process, in other instances, his relations could not protect his business, as in the case of the Citadel project. The idea of the Citadel project started in 1997 when Nosseir was invited, with a group of businessmen, to meet with Mubarak and the cabinet of ministers. The aim of the meeting was to discuss the implications of Israel's integration in the economy of the region after the 1993 Oslo agreement—for example, Israel's investment in the region, the possibility that it would control the economy of the region, and the potential for Egypt to lead the region economically. Mubarak raised the question of whether Egypt was ready to attract investors. Nosseir answered by saying that Egypt should have financial centers like Canary Wharf in London and La Defense in Paris. Mubarak looked at Nosseir and asked, "Can you establish such a center?" Nosseir answered, "I will do it, president."[34] Nosseir's answer suggests that not only was his relationship with Mubarak was based on subordination and obedience to the regime, but it also entailed asking private businessmen to finance and provide projects for the public good. Reports suggest that this type of relationship between businessmen and the regime was not uncommon. Apparently, Mubarak reminded successful businessmen "that personal wealth entailed social obligations . . . [He] secured a commitment from entrepreneurs to fund the construction of a considerable number of public schools. When he found out that the commitment was not translated into reality he unambiguously threatened the hesitating donors that social mobility could work both ways, downward as well as upward."[35] The regime's authoritarian clientelistic relationship with Nosseir means that he was one of those businessmen whose businesses could be threatened if they did not provide support to the regime in the form of public projects. This may explain the flow of resources from Nosseir to the regime in the form of charitable activities. For instance, one of his charitable projects was the renovation of Om Dinar Village in the Imbaba district in cooperation with the government. This included changing the water and sewage systems and renovating the schools, the health unit, and the youth center.[36]

The obligatory nature of contributions in this authoritarian clientelistic relationship suggests how predatory the state was, as Margaret Levi defined it, which means it would do anything to take money from society.[37] But here the regime chose to develop this predatory relationship with businessmen, who have benefited from economic liberalization and, in return, had to provide support to the regime.

In 1998, Nosseir got the required approval and started preparing for his two-billion-EGP project on land, which he bought in 1976 in the Muqqatam district adjacent to the Cairo Citadel. (The Citadel is a twelfth-century walled fortress located next to Mohamed Ali Mosque and is considered one of the landmarks of Cairo.) Nosseir labeled his project "the Citadel," and it included a financial center, housing, entertainment, a shopping mall, the Egyptian stock exchange, offices, cinemas, an underground garage, and a five-star hotel.[38] But in 2006, the Governor of Egypt froze construction at the site after the Supreme Council of Antiquities (SCA) at the Ministry of Culture and a number of archaeologists complained that the construction was illegal and could threaten both the Citadel and Mohamed Ali Mosque.[39] By 2006, Nosseir had spent three hundred million EGP on the design and early stages of construction.[40] Then, after a long battle between the SCA and Nosseir, the SCA involved the United Nations Educational, Scientific, and Cultural Organization, which recommended lowering the height of the complex, and Nosseir scaled it back.[41] It appears that the authoritarian clientelistic relationship between the regime and Nosseir obliged him to build this project without carrying out the necessary preliminary research into the site. He paid a price for his blind obedience, since his project was delayed for a number of years. However, as will be discussed later in the chapter (in the section on the monopoly of telecommunications), Nosseir also obtained personal financial gain from his relationship with the regime.

The following section examines the case of billionaire Naguib Sawiris. Unlike Bahgat and Nosseir, who developed an authoritarian clientelistic relationship with the regime, Naguib's relationship with the regime was based on mutual dependency, as the following section will discuss.

The Case of Billionaire Naguib Sawiris

Diane Singerman focuses on how the context of political repression of lower-income Egyptian families, the *sha'bi* (popular sector), creates informal networks that help them in making a living, finding employment, and gaining access to education and subsidized services. But these networks involved different corruption measures, such as bribing teachers and officials in charge of exam results and using violence and fraud to obtain subsidized goods.[42] Singerman's argument could be contrasted with the role of the families at the elite level, such as the Sawiris family, who rely on their networks to gain access to state resources through different corrupt means, as the following section will discuss.

The patriarch of the Sawiris family is Onsi Sawiris, whose father was a lawyer and landowner. Onsi is the father of Naguib, Samih, and Nassif. In 1950, Onsi established his first construction company. In a few years, it became one of the largest contractor companies in the country. But in the 1960s, his company was nationalized, and for five years, he worked for his own company and received a monthly salary from the government. In 1966, Onsi was allowed to travel to Libya, where he stayed for 12 years. However, after Sadat's signing of the Camp David Accords, Libya considered Egypt to be an unfriendly country, leading Onsi and many other Egyptians to leave Libya. Onsi returned to Egypt in the late 1970s and established his own company, Orascom Construction Industry (OCI). By the early 1990s, OCI became the largest private-sector contractor, and it diversified its activities. Each of its diverse sectors became an independent identity. For instance, in 1998, Naguib, the eldest brother, bought the first government-owned mobile operator in Egypt (Mobinil) and established

Orascom Telecom (OT), which monopolized the telecom industry (as will be discussed later in the section on the monopoly in the telecommunications sector). The second part of OCI to become independent, by the late 1990s, was Orascom Hotels and Development (OHD), which was headed by the middle brother, Samih. By the mid-1990s, Nassif, the youngest brother, headed OCI, which became a multinational construction company.[43] In 1998, the Sawiris family established the Renaissance Company, which managed several movie theatres. Also, Nassif was a member of the Business Secretariat in the NDP. In 1995, Naguib Sawiris's mother, Yousria Loza, was one of the ten people appointed by Mubarak in the People's Assembly. The Sawiris family's relationship with the regime was not only through parliament and the ruling party. For instance, on different occasions, Suzanne Mubarak inaugurated the development market organized by the Sawiris Foundation for Social Development. During these events, Mrs. Mubarak would meet with Onsi Sawiris and his wife Youria Loza, who would brief her about the activities funded by the Sawiris Foundation.[44] On another occasion, Suzanne Mubarak inaugurated the nursing institute funded by the Sawiris Foundation in El Gouna, Hurghada. Onsi Sawiris, Samih Sawiris, Naguib Sawiris, and Yousria Loza attended this event and met with Mrs. Mubarak.[45]

The Sawiris family used its networks with the Mubarak family to shape laws to benefit the family's private businesses. For instance, in 1997, an investment incentive law was passed to offer fiscal exemptions to very large companies in the cinema industry, of which there were only two: a public-sector company and the other Sawiris company, Renaissance.[46] This legislation suggests symptoms of state capture by the Sawiris family. As Kienle explains,

> Of course, nothing would have prevented the Sawiris brothers from informing the regime of their wish that their company, Renaissance, be granted special treatment. They were clearly in a position to transmit such a request, probably to the President himself. They owned and managed companies that for instance in the field of public works and defense installations, provided services no other company in Egypt was able to provide. With important interests in the United States, they could simply have withdrawn from Egypt, had they been treated with insufficient respect. Curtailing their business activities in Egypt or destroying their companies would have worked against the interests of the regime itself; arresting them for whatever reason would have prompted the collapse of their business run according to the recipes of "hands-on-management," which made the owners indispensable.[47]

The size of the Sawiris family business and its importance for the Egyptian economy meant that the state was practically obliged to tolerate the family's illegal business practices. For instance, in order for Naguib's OT to be able to get Mobile contracts in countries like Jordan and Algeria, it had to increase its capital. In 1999, OT used false bank certificates to raise its capital by four hundred million EGP. As a result of this increase, the company had the right to issue stock market shares. The capital market authority confirmed that these certificates were false and refused them. However, it did not inform the prosecutor general and only asked the Sawiris family to raise the OT capital by the equivalent (four hundred million EGP). Moreover, the capital market authority failed to instruct the Sawiris family to abide by the law immediately, which meant that the Sawiris family had ample time to profit from the falsified certificates. OT immediately issued forty million stock market shares, and each was sold for 55 EGP. This made a profit of 2.2 billion EGP. This simply means that the Sawiris family used a small portion of the profit made through selling these falsified certificates to raise its capital.[48]

The state's tolerance of the Sawiris family's illegal business practices seemed to have helped in the expansion of the Sawiris's business. For instance, Naguib's OT became one of the largest conglomerates in Africa, the Middle East, and Asia. By 2007, OT had expanded its operations in countries like Algeria, Tunisia, Pakistan, Bangladesh, and Iraq. In 2008, Naguib was ranked sixtieth on Forbes's list of the world's wealthiest people.[49]

While the Mubarak regime enabled the Sawiris family to abuse state resources and engage in illegal practices for personal enrichment, in return, the Sawiris family provided political support to Mubarak and his regime. This was evident in the media outlets that Naguib founded (the private newspaper *Al-Masry Al-Youm* and the private television channel, ONTV). The independent newspaper *Al-Masry Al-Youm* was founded by Naguib and other businessmen in 2004, and he owned 33 percent of its shares. Although its news coverage is considered to be neutral and balanced and to discuss both positive and negative news about the government,[50] when it came to the president, his wife Suzanne, and his son Gamal, it avoided direct criticism.[51] Magdi El Galad, editor in chief of *Al-Masry Al-Youm*, was asked in a 2010 television interview on the Modern Horya channel about his opinion on publishing news in *Al-Masry Al-Youm* that supported Gamal Mubarak's run for president after his father. He answered that he would not publish such news, which infers that the newspaper was trying to present itself as neutral, but he added that, on a personal level, he supports Gamal. For instance, El Galad said, "My personal opinion is I may vote for Gamal for president because we are from the same generation ... He may do good things for the country ... I am with the new blood ... On a personal level, I love and respect Gamal. He did good things in the economy."[52]

When the editor in chief of *Al-Masry Al-Youm* praised the young Mubarak during a television interview, he indicated sympathy for the project of hereditary succession. In 2007, Naguib launched a private television satellite channel called ONTV, which supported the regime, since it had "a vague political agenda, to counter what he considers the negative impact of 'religious extremism.'"[53] Moreover, in October 2010, the popular ONTV talk show *Baladna Belmasry* ("our country" in Egyptian dialect) hosted by the outspoken media figure and editor of *Al-Destour* newspaper, Ibrahim Eissa—was suspended, and Eissa was dismissed from the channel. Sources suggest the reason behind Eissa's dismissal was the channel's opposition to his criticism of prominent figures in the regime.[54] The timing of Eissa's dismissal was the run-up to the 2010 parliamentary elections, when there was a clampdown on criticisms of and opposition to the regime in anticipation of the transfer of power to the young Mubarak.[55]

Despite Naguib's support for the regime through his private media, he was the main financier of the Democratic Front Party (DFP), which was an opposition party established in 2007. In the following chapter, I examine what happened to businessmen who founded or joined political opposition parties. Yet Naguib was not subjected to the same treatment as these other opposition businessmen. In an interview with the then president of the DFP, Osama El Ghazaly Harb, he explained,

Naguib's fortune is billions, so donating to the party around one million EGP a year is nothing for him, unlike other businessmen who prefer to donate money to the ruling party for political support and to accumulate wealth and get protection from the regime. Naguib is considered an exception. Most of his investments are abroad. He is considered relatively independent because no one is completely independent of the regime. The stability of the Sawiris family business empire is good for the sake of the country. For example, if Orascom falls, this can affect the stock exchange and the Egyptian economy . . . Naguib is strong.[56]

Harb's words reconfirm that the size and importance of the Sawiris family businesses protected Naguib from any negative consequences of his funding of an opposition party. The regime needed the Sawiris family's investment and was not in a position to turn against them. At the same time, while Naguib was the main financier of the DFP, this opposition party did not represent a challenge to the regime. (It was, as I discuss in the next chapter, a "loyal opposition party.") Nevertheless, allegedly, when Naguib wanted to become a member of the party, security told him not to join it, and he agreed not to.[57] In other words, the relationship between the regime and Naguib seems to be based on mutual bargaining rather than on credible threats of coercion (as in the previously mentioned cases of Bahgat, El Moallam, and Nosseir).

Naguib stated his support for Mubarak on many occasions. For instance, in an interview with Charlie Rose in 2008, Naguib said, "I support Mubarak because he is a wise man and did a lot of things for Egypt."[58] Naguib continued his support for Mubarak during the 18 days of the revolution; for instance, after the outbreak of the revolution, he called the private television channel El Mehwar and cried out of sympathy and love for Mubarak. In a television appearance with BBC Arabic, he claimed that Tahrir Square does not represent the Egyptians, insisted that Mubarak should stay, and said that this was also the opinion of many Egyptians. He also repeated this opinion in a phone call to his channel, ONTV, by saying that he was against the removal of Mubarak.[59]

The size and importance of the Sawiris family fortune protected it from the threats of coercion that the Mubarak regime made to other businessmen in its networks. Unlike other clientelistic networks between the regime and businessmen, the Sawiris family participated in a more symmetrical clientelistic network with the regime. The regime needed the Sawiris's investments because if their businesses were in trouble, as mentioned earlier, this could affect the Egyptian economy. This may explain why the state tolerated the Sawiris family's illegal business practices. At the same time, the Sawiris family depended on the survival of Mubarak's regime for their wealth, which explains why they provided political support for the regime, while their wealth also protected them from abuse by the regime. This suggests the development of a clientelistic relationship between the regime and the Sawiris family based on mutual dependency.

Naguib Sawiris in the Post-Mubarak Period

Ahmed Ezz (discussed in the previous chapter) and Naguib Sawiris developed a relationship of mutual dependency with the regime. But the fact that Naguib did not engage in politics made him maintain public neutrality toward Mubarak and allowed him to transform himself from an ally of Mubarak into a supporter of the Twenty-Fifth of January Revolution. For instance, after the collapse of Mubarak's regime, Naguib claimed on a television interview that the regime had persecuted him because he had an independent opinion and defended the truth.[60] Moreover, a few months after the Twenty-Fifth of January Revolution, Naguib established the Free Egyptian Party (FEP). Naguib did not hold any position in the party, but he was its main financier. Naguib continued disclaiming his relationship with Mubarak's regime, which is illustrated by his words during a media conference of the FEP when it was being established. He said, "There are no conditions for joining the Free Egyptian party. The only ones who are not allowed to join it are the remnants [*feloul*] of the old regime—the NDP members of parliament and the local councils—who have spoiled political life."[61]

In June 2012, the MB candidate Mohamed Morsi (2012–13) was elected president. Naguib seemed to have been concerned about the prospects of his family business under the rule of the MB. This is because in Morsi's speech on October 6, 2012, "he singled ... [the Sawiris family] out, and said [they] owe taxes."[62] A few months after Morsi's speech, the finance minister initiated a criminal case against Onsi Sawiris and his youngest son, Nassif, for alleged tax evasion. According to the accusation, the OCI owed the state 14 billion EGP in taxes on profits it had gained from selling its cement sector in 2007 to the French company Lafarge. As a result, in March 2013 the prosecutor general put the names of the father, Onsi, and his son, Nassif, on the arrival watch list. This means that they were to be detained as soon as they arrived in Egypt.[63] However, a few months later, the tax authority reconciled with the Sawiris family when the family agreed to pay around $1 billion in installments over five years with an immediate payment of $357 million. As a result, Onsi Sawiris and his youngest son returned to Egypt and the travel ban on them was lifted.[64]

Since Morsi's rule was against Naguib's business interests, it is not surprising, therefore, that he would fund—as he admitted—the Tamarod (Rebel) movement to remove him. The movement was founded by a handful of young activists who collected, by June 30, 2013 (one year after Morsi was sworn into office in 2012), more than 22 million signatures for a petition demanding that Morsi step down. Collecting millions of signatures from citizens all over the country should have been a difficult task, since the young activists needed financial and administrative support. But this task seems to have been possible because Naguib allowed the Tamarod movement to use facilities in the offices and branches of his FEP all over the country.[65] On June 30, 2013, millions of Egyptians went to the streets demanding that Morsi leave, which allowed the military to interfere on July 3, 2013, and remove Morsi.

After examining the cases of both Naguib and Nosseir, the following section will examine how economic liberalization under Mubarak has strengthened authoritarianism by allowing both of them to monopolize the telecommunications sector.

The Case of Monopoly in the Telecommunication
Sector: Naguib Sawiris and Mohamed Nosseir

The first Global System for Mobiles (GSM) network was launched in 1996 by Telecom Egypt (TE), which is owned by the government and controlled the telecommunications sector. In 1998, TE was transformed into a corporation and a joint-stock company, and the government owns 80 percent of its shares.[66] In the same year, the National Telecommunication Regulatory Authority (NTRA) was established as a semi-independent body "whose role is to oversee all telecommunications activities such as the allocation of frequencies, granting licenses, monitoring the quality of services and prices and preventing monopolies."[67] In May 1998, the TE offered to sell its first GSM. Both Naguib and Nosseir submitted a bid. Nosseir's bid was higher than Naguib's, but it was the latter who won the first mobile line (Mobinil). Six months later, Nosseir got a license for the second mobile line and chaired Vodafone Egypt (formally branded "Click").[68] By giving Naguib the first mobile license instead of Nosseir, the government helped enhance his profits. This is because Mobinil, as the first mobile operator, inherited the state-owned mobile company with around eighty thousand subscribers; however, Vodafone had to start from scratch to attract customers, and it spent 1.1 billion EGP to build its infrastructure.[69]

Why did Naguib get the first mobile line instead of Nosseir? One author explained this by saying that this could not have been possible without "Sawiris enjoy[ing] good relations with the Mubarak regime, since such licenses were usually awarded to individuals with friendly ties to the ruling party."[70] While Nosseir also had good relations with the regime—as illustrated previously by his purchase of Coca-Cola—the size and importance of the Sawiris family businesses in comparison to Nosseir suggests that the Sawiris family had greater structural power based on the size of its business. For instance, before TE sold its first GSM to the private sector, Mervat El Telawi, in her capacity as a Minister of Social Insurance (1997–99), bought one quarter of TE's shares with money from social insurance. El Telawi aimed to double the money derived from insurance because this was one of the companies that could make high profits. However, then Prime Minister Kamal El Ganzouri forced her to sell these shares because he wanted to sell TE shares to only one investor.[71] The investor to whom El Ganzouri wanted to give the first GSM was Naguib.

Several years later, Nosseir seemed to have still been angry with El Ganzouri for not awarding him the first license. This may explain why he blamed El Ganzouri for economic conditions in the early 2000s. He said, "The crisis is because of mistakes made by the government. Not Prime

Minister Atef Ebeid's . . . Former Prime Minister Kamal El-Ganzouri, in his final months, crippled the economy."[72]

Both Naguib and Nosseir used their networks with government officials to enhance their monopolistic practices. For example, both mobile companies (Mobinil and Vodafone) were granted market exclusivity until the end of 2002. Then, at the end of the two mobile operators' four-year exclusivity period, TE applied for and bought a third mobile license from the NTRA; however, after buying the license, TE returned it to the NTRA and relinquished the project. In an interpellation submitted to parliament by Abu El Ezz El Hariry, he argued that TE could have made a guaranteed profit from the third mobile network and questioned the reasons for postponing it.[73] On the one hand, government officials argued that a third network was not economically feasible.[74] This opinion was also shared by Mohamed Nosseir, who said, "The market at present cannot and should not sustain a third competitor . . . The revenues of the two existing networks are falling . . . Not on a large scale, but they are going down. The rate of new customers coming to the networks has also dropped dramatically. And so a third entrant will only take clients away from the two existing networks."[75]

Naguib also was against a third mobile network entering the market, citing the bad economic conditions during this time. For instance, he said, "There's definitely a place for a third company. But the current economic situation is bound to affect the new entrant at a time when people are saving money because their incomes are being reduced. Tourists are staying away and people are losing their jobs. I think it will be difficult to attract new clients."[76]

On the other hand, other sources suggest that the reason for the postponement of the third mobile network was that the two mobile companies wanted to enhance their monopolistic practices. For instance, evidence suggests that both Naguib and Nosseir bribed Mohamed Nazif, the then minister of telecommunications, and Akil Beshir, the TE chairman, to postpone the third mobile network's entrance into the market.[77] Moreover, empirical figures support the argument that the market was not saturated. For instance, from 2002 to 2005, the number of customers for the two mobile operators (Mobinil and Vodafone) increased from 4 million to 14 million.[78] Empirical figures also suggest that both Naguib and Nosseir made a lot of profit by monopolizing the market. For instance, Mobinil profits increased from 425 million EGP in 2002 to 915 million EGP in 2003. And Vodafone profits increased from 345 million EGP to 830 million EGP in 2003.[79]

But after the postponement of the third mobile line, both Mobinil and Vodafone had to pay 1.45 billion EGP to NTRA. Mobinil agreed to pay its share of 780 million EGP in installments over five years. As for Vodafone

Egypt, it paid its share by selling 25 percent of its shares to TE.[80] How did Nosseir manage to implement this Vodafone transaction in a way that allowed him to make profits at the expense of TE? In fact, Nosseir had strong relations with TE Chairman Akil Beshir, who had been his business partner, with a 15 percent share, since 1975 in one of his private companies.[81] Beshir justified this decision by saying that "forming a partnership with Vodafone was a better option" than launching a third mobile network.[82] Yet empirical figures suggest that this transaction was in favor of Nosseir rather than TE. For instance, when in 2002 TE bought 25 percent of the shares, it bought 60 million shares with 619 million EGP. This means the price of the share is 10.4 EGP. Then, in 2006, TE bought another 24 percent of Vodafone Egypt's shares at a price of one hundred EGP for one share. But this was an overrated price, since its price in the market at this time did not exceed thirty EGP; this raises questions about who benefited from this transaction. Suffice it to say that Nosseir, who owned 5 percent of shares in Vodafone Egypt (which is equivalent to 12 million shares), bought them with sixty million EGP. In this transaction, Nosseir sold these shares for 1.2 billion EGP. By analyzing the annual profits that Nosseir was making from his ownership of Vodafone shares, we find out that it did not exceed thirty million EGP.[83] While Nosseir made huge profits from this transaction, TE got loans from the banks worth 5.4 billion EGP to buy 24 percent of Vodafone's shares.[84]

Supporters of neoliberal economics argue that deregulation leads to efficiency and greater competition. For instance, in the United States, as a result of the deregulation of telecommunications from 1984–87, the profitability of mobile companies rose in 1984 relative to 1981; however, it then fell by 1987 due to competition. From 1981 to 1987, the productivity of these firms increased. Also, competitive pressures from new entrants to the telecommunication industry encouraged incumbent companies to reduce their prices from 1984 to 1987.[85]

However, in Egypt, deregulation of telecommunications did not lead to competition between the two mobile companies Mobinil and Vodafone; it led to a duopoly in the market, which enabled both Sawiris and Nosseir, through their network relations with the regime, to make large profits at the expense of the state.

The following section examines the case of businessmen Hussein Salem and Wagih Siag. While the former developed a particular patron-client relation with Mubarak, the latter failed to enter into a patron-client relation with the regime.

The Case of the Taba Land: Hussein Salem versus Wagih Siag

Wagih Siag is an Egyptian businessman who holds Italian citizenship. Siag never engaged in politics. He comes from a well-known family in the hotelier business. In 1989, Siag bought a piece of land in Sinai Governorate from the Egyptian government for 1.5 EGP per square meter. The total amount paid was 975,000 EGP for 650 thousand square meters. This land is six kilometers from the town of Taba[86] on Egypt's border with Israel. After Siag bought this land, the Egyptian government started building infrastructure—a water desalination plant, an electricity plant, an airport, and so on. All these projects have raised the value of the land. Siag's project included a hotel called Siag Resort and a gambling casino. The land had many advantages: it was only 1.5 kilometers from the sea, and Siag had a license to build eight meters above sea level. From 1990 to 1994, Siag started basic construction of the project, and in 1994, he entered into an agreement with the Israeli company, Lumir. However, in 1995, the then minister of tourism, Mamdouh El Beltagui, canceled the contract for sale of the land to Siag. Siag met with El Beltagui, who asked him if he had an Israeli partner. Siag told him no but that he had just signed a contract with an Israeli agent for a time share. El Beltagui asked Siag to cancel the contract with the Israeli agent, which he did. However, El Beltagui decided to continue with cancelling the sale contract, claiming that Siag would not be able to finish the project in the agreed-upon time. This was despite the fact that Siag was proceeding with the project per the agreed-upon schedule. Siag met again with El Beltagui, who told him, "I have taken orders from higher authorities to take the land. I have to implement the order despite my will. This order is bigger than me."[87]

Then, in 2002, the president issued Decree 205 to expropriate the property, allocate it to public benefit, and use it as instructed by then Prime Minister Atef Ebeid. Ebeid issued Resolution 315 of 2003, declaring that a natural gas pipeline would be constructed on Siag's land.[88]

The gas was to be exported to Israel through the East Mediterranean Gas (EMG) Company, which is a gas company established in 2000; businessman Hussein Salem had the majority of the shares. (EMG will be discussed later in this section.) This means that Siag's land was not really expropriated for public benefit but was reallocated by the regime to another businessman. Then, when Siag discovered Salem's name in this project, he understood the reason for taking his land from him. Siag said, "This is corruption to the extent that the president and his entourage [networks] are above the law."[89] According to political scientist Hassan Nafei, "El Beltagui did not take the land from Siag because he had an Israeli partner. Egypt has official relations with Israel and deals with tens of Israeli companies. In addition,

Siag had already canceled his contract with the Israeli company. The most likely reason for taking the land was to give it to Salem."[90]

So Siag filed a suit against the minister's resolution in the administrative court. Even though Siag won the case, the court decision was never implemented. Siag won another court ruling, which canceled the president's and prime minister's decrees. Despite Siag having won all the cases, no steps were taken by the government to give him back his land.[91] This suggests that Siag was not part of any patron-client relationship with the regime that would help him protect his business, as he implied in the following words: "Egypt is owned by some people in the regime. But I am an outsider . . . I found that out later on when the court rulings were never implemented. At the beginning, I thought that when a minister or a prime minister is removed, things will change. For instance, when Ahmed El Maghrabi, who is my friend, became the minister of tourism in 2004, I thought the court ruling would be implemented; however, nothing has changed."[92]

Although Siag was not protected by the regime, he was protected by his Italian nationality. When Siag realized that there are people in Egypt who are above the law, he used his Italian citizenship and filed a lawsuit before the International Arbitration Centre of the World Bank[93] in 2005. Siag asked for compensation based on the price of the land at this time and also the price of the real estate he had built.[94]

But what is the importance of Hussein Salem to the regime? And why did the regime favor Salem rather than Siag in the case of the Taba land? A brief background about Salem is important to understanding his relationship with the Mubarak regime and even the president himself. Salem is an Egyptian-Spanish businessman. (He was born in Egypt and acquired Spanish citizenship as an adult.) He is an ex-intelligence officer who, in the late 1970s, was appointed as the Egyptian commercial counselor in Washington, DC. In 1980, Salem resigned from his government job and started his first company, the Egyptian American Transportation Company (ETSCO), and two of his partners were former CIA officers.[95] In his book *The Veil*, journalist Bob Woodward claims that Mubarak, who was at this time Sadat's vice president, was the one who helped Salem establish ETSCO in order to transport US weapons to Egypt and that, in return, Mubarak received commissions.[96]

The relationship between Salem and Mubarak continued and evolved until Mubarak became president. For instance, one of Salem's friends, Ambassador Amin Yousri, revealed a story that showed how close Salem was to Mubarak: "In the mid-1990s, I met with Salem at the Semiramis Intercontinental Hotel in Down Town Cairo. While we were drinking coffee, an American Jewish businessman approached Salem and asked if he could facilitate a meeting with Mubarak. In the next morning, I saw picture of this businessman standing next to Mubarak in the newspaper."[97]

It seems that Mubarak and his family formed a particular patron-client relationship with Salem so that he could enhance their self-enrichment. For instance, a statement from the prosecutor general said that Salem built the Mubarak family four villas, which were estimated at forty million EGP. The Mubarak family paid only 14 million EGP in return for helping Salem buy large plots of land in Sharm El Sheikh.[98]

For instance, from 1988 until 2010, Salem acquired 2.5 million square meters of land in Sharm El Sheikh, where he constructed and ran two water desalination plants, a huge golf course, a massive conference hall, and the luxurious hotel chain Maritime Jolie Ville. This chain consists of three five-star hotels in Sharm El Sheikh: Jolie Ville Resort and Casino, Jolie Ville Golf and Resort, and Jolie Ville Royal Peninsula Hotel. Salem bought the land where he constructed these projects for much less than its real price. For instance, he bought the land at the per-meter price of two to five EGP, while the real price ranged from five thousand to fifty thousand EGP.[99] This suggests how the reallocation of state resources to Salem was possible through his clientelistic relationship with Mubarak and his family. As Mamdouh El Zoheiry, former governor of South Sinai Governorate (1993–97), admitted during the prosecution investigation in May 2011, "The land has been given to Salem without any auction . . . Salem could not have gotten these large plots of land in one city [Sharm El Sheikh] without his strong friendship with Mubarak."[100]

It is worth mentioning that unlike the previously mentioned Bahgat and Nosseir—who were involved in an authoritarian clientelistic relationship with the regime and had to provide services (for example, in the form of media support to the regime or charitable activities)—Salem did not have to play this role. It seems that his role was to provide services only to the Mubarak family. For instance, his only charitable activity in Sharm El Sheikh was the building of a mosque in 2008, which is located a few minutes from the Mubarak family villas but far away from the citizens of the city.[101] This suggests that the mosque was built specifically for Mubarak to pray in rather than for the citizens. Salem's lack of social provision in Sharm El Sheikh is an example of how the regime marginalized the Bedouin from national development. As one of the Bedouin put it, "Hussein Salem and his friends who invested in Sharm El Sheikh have not provided us with any service that we can remember; however, they increased our suffering and made us feel marginalized . . . We never worked in their hotels . . . My modest tourist project was a cafeteria in a tent that was shut down by the regime because it did not have a license."[102]

Also, young workers who came from other governorates to work in Sharm El Sheikh were complaining that they paid high rents for small apartments (around 1,500 EGP per month) and that they paid a lot of money for water. Unfortunately, Salem did not provide them with any services like affordable accommodations or cheap water. For instance, through his water desalination plants, he was selling one cubic meter of water for 16 EGP.[103]

The regime continued to reallocate state resources to Salem. This was evident in two business projects that dealt with Israel. It should be noted that there is much hostility in Egyptian society toward the Camp David Accords, signed in 1979, and normalization with Israel. For instance, in the early 1990s, professional syndicates were against normalization with Israel and threatened its members with an investigation if they traveled to Israel. Also, the Union of Egyptian Authors dismissed one of its members because he visited Israel and wrote a book about it.[104] Any business relationship between Egypt and Israel is perceived by Egyptian society as normalization. Despite the hostility of Egyptian society toward normalization, the Egyptian regime engaged in business relationships with Israel. For instance, the idea for one of the projects with Israel that was assigned to Salem started after the 1993 Oslo agreement with the Palestine Liberation Organization, when Israeli Prime Minister Yitzhak Rabin, Israeli Foreign Minister Shimon Peres, and Mubarak agreed to establish a joint-venture oil refinery project. Three years later, the Middle East Refinery Project (MIDOR) was established with 80 percent private capital divided equally between Egypt and Israel and a 20 percent share for the Egyptian Petroleum Company. Salem's Israeli partner in MIDOR was Yossi Maiman (whose name will appear again in Salem's gas company, EMG), owner of the Israeli company Merhav.[105] However, MIDOR was not a successful project and faced several problems. For instance, it did not have former experience in the oil industry, and banks were reluctant to finance its activities. Also, MIDOR was the outcome of a political decision, which did not take into consideration that the market was already saturated.[106] Salem's Israeli partner, Maiman, sold his share to the National Bank of Egypt. Sources suggest that "Salem secured a commission for himself for managing to get the bank into the deal!"[107] Despite the failure of MIDOR, Mubarak assigned to Salem another business project with Israel. The new project aimed to export gas to Israel through EMG (which, as mentioned earlier, was established in 2000 on land expropriated from Siag). EMG was formed by a partnership between businessman Hussein Salem, who owned 65 percent; the Egyptian National Gas Company, which owned 10 percent; and Israeli businessman Yossi Maiman, who owned 25 percent.[108] In an interview, Salem admitted that it was Mubarak who asked him to export gas to Israel. For instance, he said, "Mubarak told me that the gas deal with Israel will be a strategic point in the relations between Egypt and Israel."[109] But some sources suggest that the gas deal benefitted Israel, the Mubarak family, and Salem at the expense of Egypt. Egypt sold the gas to Israel at a very low price, which led to the loss of $714 million.[110] Moreover, a Kuwaiti newspaper, *Al-Jarida Al-Kwaitia*, published documents that accused both of Mubarak's sons (Alaa and Gamal) of making commissions worth hundreds of millions of dollars in return for their support for exporting gas to Israel.[111] In 2008, Salem sold his shares in EMG, reporting, "My $95 million investment increased to half a billion dollars by the time I sold my share in the [EMG]."[112] This suggests that Egypt was a "predatory state," as conceptualized by Peter Evans.[113] Those controlling the state (for example, the Mubarak family and their associate Hussein Salem) were looting for their own interests at the expense of the interests of the rest of Egyptian society.

The case of the Taba land illustrates the flow of resources from private businessmen (for example, the expropriation of Siag land) to the Mubarak family and their associate (for example, Salem). Despite the regime's coercion in expropriating the land from Siag, in the end, he got compensation by seeking support from an external agency: the Arbitration Center in the World Bank. In 2009, Siag won his case against the Egyptian government, and the International Arbitration Center ordered the Egyptian government to pay him $132 million. As a result, Siag sought, through the International Arbitration Center, to confiscate the money of both Misr Bank and the National Bank branches in Paris and London.[114]

Siag seems to have realized that since there is no rule of law, he could only do business in Egypt by entering into a patron-client relationship with the regime. This became possible after he won his case in the International Arbitration Center. The regime stopped using coercion (for example, when it expropriated his Taba land by force) with Siag and agreed, for the first time, to negotiate with him. We can term this clientelistic relationship that emerged between Siag and the regime, which is based on bargaining, "semiclientelism." The regime's negotiation with Siag allowed him to resume his investments in Egypt, provided that he waive all lawsuits and claims relating to his disputes with the government in front of Egyptian courts and other bodies of litigation abroad.[115] This means that the bargaining relationship induced compliance by the threat of the removal of benefits (for example, returning to invest in Egypt) and not the threat of coercion. In return, Siag agreed to get paid only $74 million.[116]

At the end of January 2011, a few days after the outbreak of the uprising, Salem flew to Dubai on a private jet with a bag containing $500 million in cash. He then escaped to Spain, where he was arrested in June 2011 by Interpol. Salem was accused, as mentioned earlier, of corruption charges and of exporting gas to Israel for less than the market price. Salem escaped extradition because of his Spanish citizenship. Then, in June 2012, Salem was sentenced in absentia to 15 years in prison for squandering public funds in the gas deal with Israel. Salem appealed against the conviction. In the second trial, in September 2014, Salem was sentenced in absentia to 10 years in prison.

This case suggests that not only was the new political economy of authoritarianism aiming at the survival of the authoritarian regime; it was also aiming at the enrichment of the Mubarak family. This became possible when the Mubarak family developed a particular patron-client relationship with Salem. Then, in return for Salem helping in the enrichment of the Mubarak family, the regime helped and protected him in accumulating wealth in illegal ways.

The Case of the Mubarak Family and Its Associates: Different Levels of the Chain of Beneficiaries

This section shows that the self-enrichment of the Mubarak family occurred not only by creating particular patron-client relationships with businessmen but also by creating clientelistic relationships with high-level government officials. Former Minister of Housing Ibrahim Soliman is a case in point. Soliman was born in Bab El Sha'aria, which is a poor suburb in Cairo. Soliman's father started his career as a carpenter and later owned a small workshop to manufacture furniture in Bab El Sha'aria. After finishing his bachelor's degree in engineering, Soliman traveled on a government scholarship to Canada to get his PhD. Soliman earned his PhD and returned to Egypt to lecture in Ain Shams University. In the early 1980s, Soliman opened a small engineering consultancy office; however, after his appointment to the cabinet in 1993, he closed it. In 2005, Soliman was elected to parliament as the NDP candidate representing the El Gamaliya constituency.[117]

Suzanne Mubarak, at one time, would send Soliman to France to buy her expensive antiques. Also, Soliman was in charge of decorating the presidential palaces.[118] This suggests the particular patron-client relationship that developed between the Mubarak family and Soliman. Based on this relationship, the Mubarak family would use Soliman to help in their own self-enrichment. For instance, in 2006, Soliman allocated large plots of land for a company called Palm Hills in 6th of October City. Fifty-five percent of the company is owned by Mansour[119] and El Maghrabi[120] (both are maternal cousins), who are from the circle of business tycoons associated with the Mubarak family. Palm Hills is the second-largest real estate company in Egypt. Soliman allocated the land by direct order, which is in violation of the auction law.[121] According to the amended tender law (Law 89 of 1998), which replaced the former tender law (Law 9 of 1983), the state is obliged to sell the land to investors by bidding rather than by direct order.[122]

After the Twenty-Fifth of January Revolution, documents revealed that Alaa Mubarak was a shareholder in Palm Hills, with 3.6 percent of its capital. Alaa sold some of his share in Palm Hills to El Mansour and El Maghrabi on March 10, 2008, for 247.7 million EGP, making a profit of 218 million EGP.[123]

One year later, Alaa made another profit from Palm Hills. For instance, during the General Assembly meeting of Palm Hills on March 31, 2009, Alaa's name appeared with the names of other shareholders. During the meeting, a decision was made to raise the value of the shares of Alaa from 33 million EGP to 49 million EGP. This profit was made because of the allocation of an additional 11 million square meters to Palm Hills through direct order. Evidence suggests that the beneficiaries were not only members of the Mubarak family but also their close associates. Other names were mentioned during the Palm Hills assembly meeting, including Omar Tantawi (Gamal Mubarak's closest friend and classmate at the American University in Cairo) and Mamdouh El Gammal (Gamal Mubarak's father-in-law).[124]

At the top of the chain of beneficiaries for self-enrichment were the Mubarak family and its associates (friends and in-laws). Then, at a lower level of the chain of beneficiaries, there were high-level government officials like Soliman, who in return for helping in the enrichment of the Mubarak family, were allowed to accumulate wealth through their own clientelistic relations. For instance, an interpellation submitted to parliament by opposition parliamentarian El Badri Farghali stated that EnviroCivic Consultancies (which is a small engineering consultancy office), owned by Ibrahim Soliman's brother-in-law Diaa El Mouniri, had monopolized the implementation of the Ministry of Housing's construction projects since the appointment of Soliman to the cabinet in 1993. During the period from 1993 to 2000, the cost of the projects implemented by EnviroCivic was eight billion EGP. Around 98 percent of these projects were awarded to EnviroCivic through the Ministry of Housing.[125] This suggests how, within a few years, Soliman became a very rich businessman. For instance, in the early 2000s, Soliman bought a big villa in Heliopolis built on four thousand square meters. He also bought a villa looking out on the sea along the north coast of Marina Compound in the western part of Alexandria Governorate. The total cost of both villas was around forty million EGP.[126]

In March 2012, Soliman was sentenced to eight years in prison and was fined 2.18 billion EGP for squandering public funds and selling state land for less than its market value. After spending 24 months in prison, the court accepted his appeal. He was released without bail and is currently under retrial.

Soliman's case suggests how the new political economy of authoritarianism that started in the early 1990s allowed businessmen to accumulate wealth by entering into patron-client relationships with high-level government officials. It also suggests how high-level government officials like Soliman took advantage of economic liberalization and turned into businessmen.

Conclusion

Proponents of economic liberalization argue that market reforms like privatization and deregulation improve economic efficiency by reducing the role of the state and increasing the degree of private-sector competition.[127] However, in Egypt, the process of economic liberalization has led to corruption and cronyism. Examples of cronyistic practices, such as those mentioned in this chapter, were evident in the nontransparent sale of state-owned assets (for example, the sale of state-owned lands in 6th of October City to Bahgat, the sale of the state-owned Coca-Cola factory to Nosseir, the sale of the state-owned first mobile line to Naguib, and sale of state-owned lands in Sharm El Sheikh and natural resources to Salem). This suggests how state-owned assets have been transferred below their value and without competition to a few selected businessmen who benefited from economic liberalization at the expense of the rest of the citizens.

The regime's clientelistic relationships with businessmen have not been static. This is because economic liberalization has reproduced clientelism in various forms (for example, authoritarian clientelism, semiclientelism, and mutual dependency), which helped maintain Mubarak's authoritarianism. The regime developed authoritarian clientelistic relationships with both Bahgat and Nosseir based on credible threats of coercion. In such relationships, the regime allowed Bahgat and Nosseir to benefit from economic liberalization; in return, we find a flow of resources from them to the regime in different forms, such as media support and social services.

Economic liberalization has allowed Naguib to form an exceptional clientelistic relationship with the regime. Naguib and his family business have invested in different sectors of the economy (for example, telecommunications, real estate, tourism, media, and the cinema industry), which led to the development of a mutually dependent relationship with the regime.

Based on this relationship, it was in the interest of the Sawiris family to support the Mubarak family and his regime through his media outlets and philanthropic activities.

In the case of Siag, after he won his case against the government, he entered into a semiclientelistic relationship with the regime. This relationship was based on bargaining and the threat of the removal of benefits rather than the threat of coercion.

The clientelistic relationships between the regime and businessmen have not only aimed at the survival of Mubarak regime; in some cases, Mubarak and his family developed particular patron-client relations with certain businessmen or high-level government officials with the aim of self-enrichment, as in the cases of Salem and Soliman.

Unlike businessmen examined in this chapter who chose not to engage in politics and who relied on their personal relationships with the regime, the Mubarak family, or government officials, other businessmen engaged in politics by joining the opposition. The following chapter will examine how the regime dealt with opposition businessmen.

5

Businessmen in the Opposition

Introduction

This chapter aims to answer the question of how the Egyptian authoritarian regime dealt with businessmen in opposition parties and opposition movements who refuse to be co-opted. To answer this question, this chapter builds on the work of Ellen Lust-Okar,[1] which finds that Egypt's authoritarian regime maintained its survival by creating a divided political environment between the legal and illegal opposition. However, my findings are distinct from Lust-Okar's, since I argue that in Egypt, the regime renewed its authoritarianism by creating a divided political environment among parties and movements in the opposition on other levels. On one level, the regime co-opted some businessmen in legalized opposition parties and used them to create a divided political environment inside those opposition parties that refused to be co-opted by the regime's clientelistic chain. On another level, the regime created a divided political environment among parties and movements in the illegal opposition.

This chapter begins by discussing the significance of businessmen in opposition political parties in the context of regulations for establishing political parties under Mubarak. It also introduces Holger Albrecht's[2] typology of political opposition in order to understand the attitude of the Mubarak regime to different opposition figures. It then goes on to discuss several cases—like those of Moussa Mostafa Moussa in the Ghad Party, El Sayyid El Badawi in the Wafd Party, Medhat El Haddad in the Muslim Brothers (MB) Organization, and Hani Enan in the Kefaya (Enough) movement—that illustrate how the regime dealt with different opposition businessmen in order to suppress the political opposition as a whole.

Businessmen in Egypt's Political Opposition

In Egypt, the funding of political parties seems to be restricted by regulations stated in the constitution. For instance, according to Article 11 of Law 40 of 1977,[3] parties are not allowed to accept funds from abroad or from a company or institution (even if it is Egyptian). The resources of the party are composed of the subscriptions and donations of its members and the profit it makes from noncommercial activities (for example, issuing newspapers); however, under authoritarianism, political parties find it difficult to create a wide base of members who can subscribe to political parties. This means that the subscription of party members cannot cover the routine expenses of political parties, which include spending on election campaigns, party conferences, and other expenses for establishing offices all over the country, their administrative staffs, and so on. That is why having a significant number of wealthy members is important to provide funding for political parties. For instance, regarding South Korea under the Park Chung-hee regime (1961–79), Alexander Kim remarked that "no party could be effective unless it had many wealthy members, or unless it could secure secret illegal donations—something the ruling party could do, but which an opposition party would find immensely difficult."[4]

As mentioned in Chapters 3 and 4, most businessmen preferred to join the ruling party or remained independent and relied on their network ties with the regime. Despite the limited number of businessmen in the opposition, the regime attempted to co-opt them; otherwise, they could use their structural and financial power against the regime. For instance, in each of Egypt's opposition parties or movements, the regime co-opted the most prominent businessmen, as in the case of the businessmen Moussa Moustafa Moussa in the Ghad Party, El Sayyid El Badawi in the Wafd Party, and Hani Enan in the Kefaya movement.

Albrecht[5] has distinguished between different types of opposition under authoritarianism:

1. Regime-loyal opposition, which works within the confines of the authoritarian regime and includes legalized political parties.
2. Tolerated opposition, which emerges in society independently from the state and which the state keeps under control by using a mix of co-option and coercion.
3. Antisystem opposition, which includes Islamic movements and groups that advocate human rights and democracy. These groups reject the discreet forms of co-option by the regime. The regime

forbids these groups from participating in the formal political process and may also legally prosecute them.

4. Radical opposition, which challenges the authoritarian regime to the extent that it is perceived as dangerous. In such cases, the regime would use high levels of repression, which would lead to its exclusion from the formal political process.

The significance of Albrecht's typology is that it promotes understanding of how the regime was dealing with the opposition, especially during the different stages of its transformation.

Opposition Businessman: Moussa Moustafa Moussa and the Ghad Party

The Ghad Party was established as an opposition party in 2004. It included members from different professional backgrounds in addition to businessmen. The aim of those who joined the party seems to have been to achieve democracy. As wealthy businessman and senior member of the Ghad Party Omar Said Al-Ahl said, "One of the main objectives of the Ghad Party—before its establishment officially and after it was founded—was to amend the constitution . . . The 1971 constitution gives the president enormous power . . . He is everything . . . We wanted to limit the power of the president . . . and also limit his tenure."[6]

However, this stated aim is contradicted by the actions of some of the Ghad Party's members. Multimillionaire and businessman Moussa Mostafa Moussa is a case in point. In 1981, the Moussa family started the SCIB Company, which made paints, construction chemicals, and waterproofing products. By 1997, their SCIB Company expanded and partnered with the Sawiris family. In 2004, Moussa started engaging in politics. He was one of the founders of the Ghad Party and became deputy chairman of the party. Moussa's brother Ali was one of Gamal Mubarak's closest friends and was a member of the Policies Secretariat of the ruling party. But before discussing the involvement of Moussa in politics and how his role in the Ghad Party was an obstacle to democracy, the following section will give a brief background on the circumstances under which the Ghad Party was established and about its leader Ayman Nour.

Nour graduated from the Faculty of Law at Mansoura University and later earned a PhD from Russia. He worked as a lawyer and had a law office in downtown Cairo. He was also a journalist who wrote a daily column in the Wafd newspaper. In 1995, Nour was elected to parliament as a Wafdist member in Cairo Governorate in the Bab El Sha'aria constituency. As a political activist from a loyal opposition party, which was legal and worked within the confines of the authoritarian regime, Nour promised the then minister of parliamentary affairs, Kamal El Shazly, that he would not cross the red line and criticize Mubarak. Moreover, Nour "developed excellent relations with high-ranking government ministers, and provided State Security with information on the Wafd party activities to curry favor with the regime"[7]

However, after his reelection to the 2000 parliament, Nour ran for the position of deputy speaker in parliament and got 161 votes out of 454. This was considered a high number of votes for an opposition member of parliament, which also suggests that he must have gotten most of the votes from National Democratic Party (NDP) members, since they represented 88 percent of the seats in the 2000 parliament.[8] According to Nour, after this event, he "started to be targeted by the regime."[9]

But how did the regime target Nour? Inside each opposition party, the regime had co-opted political activists and businessmen. For instance, in the Wafd Party, Noaman Goma'a had been co-opted by the regime, since he became a vice president of the party. Goma'a is a very wealthy lawyer who represented several multinational companies. Part of his wealth could be attributed to his connection with the regime. For instance, in the early 1990s, when Goma'a was vice president of the Wafd, he used his friendship and connections with then Minister of Agriculture Youssef Wally and bought large plots of agricultural land in Giza Governorate at much less than the market value.[10] Since Goma'a was co-opted by the regime, it is not surprising that he would be used to get rid of Nour, as the following section will discuss.

In March 2001, a few months after Nour ran for the position of deputy speaker in parliament, Noaman Goma'a, the then president of the Wafd Party, fired Nour. The background of his expulsion from the party is related to his support of Farid Hassanein, a Wafdist parliamentarian who was charged by Goma'a of inciting rebellious actions in the party. Goma'a expelled both Hassanein and Nour, even though Nour was only one of many of Wafdists present during this incident. According to Hassanein, "Goma'a is just using the incident to get even with Nour, because he doesn't like him and is jealous of him . . . In the beginning I had thought that Nour was paying for my supposed mistakes, but I soon discovered that it was the other way round."[11] Since Goma'a was co-opted by the regime, firing Nour from the party does not seem to be a decision that he made by himself. As Nour said, "Goma'a was told by the authorities that I am dangerous and can challenge his leadership, and he should get rid of me."[12]

After his dismissal from the Wafd a few months later, in October 2001, Nour joined the Egyptian Socialist Arab Party (hereafter referred to as the

Misr Party). Nour was appointed by Gamal Rabie, the president of the Misr Party, as the first deputy of the party and also the editor in chief of the party's newspaper. The Misr Party was an inactive party. For instance, since May 2000, it had not published its newspaper; also, in the 2000 parliamentary elections, it did not nominate candidates. On October 25, 2001, the Misr Party informed the Higher Parties Council (HPC) of new changes in its leadership. On the same day, at night, another Misr Party member—Wahid El Oksory, who is a retired military officer—held a party meeting in his house that included five hundred discontented party members. During the meeting, Rabie was dismissed from the party and El Oksory was elected party president.[13]

At the same time, the regime continued to prevent Nour from participating in the formal political process (for example, it prevented him from joining legalized political parties like the Misr Party). So, as with the Wafd Party, when the regime used its co-opted party member, Goma'a, to get rid of Nour, in the case of the Misr Party, the regime used its co-opted party member, El Oksory, to create a division in the party, hence preventing Nour from being a member of the party. Nour commented on El Oksory's claims of gathering the party's discontented members: "I've seen his house. It fits ten people—thirteen maximum . . . it was a tactic by the government to create infighting so they had a reason to close the party due to a leadership struggle"[14]

In fact, a few days later, the HPC froze the Misr Party's activities because of the dispute among its leadership.[15] Similar patterns, in which the regime used its agents to create division inside opposition parties, are evident in the case of the Ghad Party, as the following section will discuss.

Before examining the division inside the Ghad Party, I will start by giving a background on how it was established. After the Misr Party was frozen, Nour started drafting a program to establish a new party to be called the Mostakbal Party. While working on the program of the Mostakbal Party, Nour received several phone calls from the authorities asking him to call Gamal Mubarak and invite him to join the new party; however, Nour refused.[16] This suggests that Nour refused to be co-opted, which signaled to the regime that he had been transformed into an "antisystem" opposition member.

Then one day, Nour read in *Rose Al-Youssef* magazine that the young Mubarak would establish a party called the Mostakbal Party, so Nour decided to change the name of his new party to Ghad (which is closer in meaning to the Mostakbal).[17] Nour belonged to the "antisystem" opposition and refused to be co-opted by the regime (by inviting the young Mubarak to join his party), so it is not surprising that the establishment of Nour's Ghad Party would face several obstacles by the regime, as the following section will discuss.

The establishment of political parties is subject to Law 40 of 1977, which required the creation of political parties to be in accordance with the will of the regime. According to the law, a special committee was to be established, named the Political Parties Committee (PPC). This committee is in charge of receiving all applications for the creation of new parties. Fifty of the founders of an organization wishing to be recognized as a party are required to issue powers of attorney to its deputy founder. According to Article 8 of Law 40 of 1977, the head of the Consultative Assembly serves as president of the PPC, and the following are the members of the committee: the minister of justice, the minister of interior affairs, the minister of the People's Assembly, and three ex-judges or their deputies, who should not be affiliated to any party and are chosen by the president.

This means that the PPC is a tool of the government and is used to manipulate the creation of political parties according to the will of the regime. In the words of one author, "The committee owes its loyalty to the executive and thus the formation of the parties is effectively at the discretion of the government."[18] It is worth mentioning that between 1977 and 2000, the PPC only licensed the application of the Socialist Labor Party. The other opposition parties that were created during this period were approved by administrative court rulings that overturned the decisions of the PPC.[19]

Similar patterns of controlling opposition political parties are evident in other authoritarian countries. For instance, in Jordan, the main concern of King Hussein bin Talal in legalizing political parties was to make sure that "such parties agreed in advance to support the constitution and the monarchy."[20] Similarly, in Morocco, when King Hassan reestablished the multiparty system in 1977, "potential parties were forced to demonstrate their allegiance to the king and his policies if they were to be allowed to compete."[21]

According to Wael Nawara, one of the founders of the Ghad Party and a businessman who owns a small advertising company, "Since Nour has refused to be co-opted by the regime, then the PPC rejected three times to give his Ghad Party a license."[22] In the third attempt to establish the Ghad Party, its founders submitted to the PPC five thousand powers of attorney, while the law required only fifty. The party founders issued the powers of attorney to its two deputy founders, Nour and Moussa, in the public notary office.[23] Even though the party had submitted many more than the required number of powers of attorney, the PPC claimed that the Ghad Party's platform did not differ significantly from those of already established parties.[24] As Eberhard Kienle argues regarding the PPC's licensing the creation of new parties, "most of the programmatic conditions were so vague and general that it was easy to reject almost any demand for the creation of a new party by pointing to one section or another of its manifesto."[25]

But after the PPC refused to create the party for the third time, the Ghad Party challenged the PPC decision in the administrative court. In order to avoid losing the case, PPC chairman Safwat El Sherif offered Nour a new deal: stop the judicial process, and in return, the Ghad Party would be awarded its party license. Nour accepted the deal.[26]

After being granted PPC approval on October 28, 2004, the Ghad Party was supposed to abide by the red line and avoid criticizing Mubarak. However, after the establishment of the Ghad Party, it emerged as a "radical" opposition that refused to be co-opted—to the extent that it was perceived by the regime as dangerous, which was illustrated by two events. First, after the Ghad Party was officially established on January 19, 2005, its seven members of parliament presented a project for a new constitution. It should be noted that until this time, amendment of the constitution was considered taboo. Mubarak had repeatedly said that there was no need to amend the constitution. For instance, in an interview in the early 1990s with prominent journalist Makram Muhammad Ahmed, Mubarak said, "The various groups that wish to change the Constitution seek different and conflicting goals. In all frankness . . . I am not in favor of such a change at present, since tampering with the Constitution is dangerous . . . and will pit different classes and different interest groups against each other. I do not wish to engage in polemics over the Constitution . . . this is not the time for it; we are in a process of development."[27]

One decade later, Mubarak's regime seemed to have insisted on the same opinion regarding the amendment of the constitution. For instance, when in 2004 Safwat El-Sherif was asked during a party meeting about the possibility of amending the constitution, he said, "The amendment of the constitution is possible, but it is not a priority at this time in order to preserve the unity of the society."[28]

Second, the party appointed Ibrahim Eissa[29] as the editor in chief of its newspaper.[30] Eissa was considered an opponent of Mubarak and of hereditary succession. Appointing Eissa as an editor in chief meant that the party's newspaper would be criticizing Mubarak and the hereditary succession of his son Gamal. The fact that the Ghad Party emerged as a "radical" opposition party may explain why on January 27, 2005, the party's leader, Ayman Nour, was arrested and stripped of his parliamentary immunity. Nour was arrested ninety days after the establishment of the party and nine days after his party presented a proposal for a new constitution. Nour was accused of forging signatures for the powers of attorney that were submitted to the PPC.[31]

Even if Nour had forged these signatures himself, or if someone else had, Nour was the one to be arrested as soon as the case was triggered, even though the powers of attorney were issued to both of the party's deputy founders, Nour and Moussa. In fact, two days before the arrest of Nour, Moussa had traveled abroad. Moussa's sudden travel at this time seemed to have been tailored by the regime. For instance, according to a retired judge and senior member in the Ghad Party, "I do not doubt that Moussa was told by the authorities to travel abroad at this time. This is the way of the authorities. They would tell you travel without telling you the reasons for it."[32]

It is also less likely that Moussa would have been arrested in the same way as Nour. Moussa has good relations with the regime, and his brother Ali is one of Gamal Mubarak's closest friends.[33] Upon his return from abroad, Moussa was taken from the airport by a police car to State Security, where he was interrogated for nine hours, after which he was acquitted.[34] But Moussa should not have been acquitted. Since both Nour and Moussa were deputy founders of the party, they both should have been tried. Moreover, Nour should not have been the only one to be blamed for the forged signatures for powers of attorney. Before the submission of the powers of attorney to the PPC, they were kept in Moussa's office, not Ayman's. As a businessman, his office had facilities to keep the documents, photocopy them, and so on. However, during the investigation, Moussa was told by State Security to say that he had nothing to do with the powers of attorney.[35] To save himself from any trouble, Moussa followed the instructions of State Security. For instance, after his meeting with State Security, Moussa went to meet Hisham Kassem (a senior member of the Ghad Party) in his office to evaluate what happened to Nour. Moussa's conversation with Kassem reflects the fact that he had been threatened by State Security to the extent that he started turning against Nour rather than supporting him. As Kassem said, "Moussa told me that we have to play it down; otherwise, they will destroy us. We should not organize press conferences or say that what happened to Ayman is political oppression. He asked me to adopt his point of view and that this would be for the sake of both the party and Ayman."[36]

In light of the discussion at the beginning of this chapter on the co-option of opposition businessmen, the regime co-opted Moussa, who was the party's vice president and one of its wealthiest businessmen, especially after it perceived how Nour's Ghad Party had been transformed into a "radical" opposition party. Moussa's co-option by the regime is illustrated by his attempt to change the party's policies. This co-option was part of a regime strategy to exclude Nour, who was considered by the regime to be dangerous and therefore part of the "radical" opposition, and to maintain the Ghad Party as part of the "regime-loyal" opposition. Before the arrest of Nour, the regime had scheduled a national dialogue between the NDP and the opposition parties, and the Ghad Party was one of the parties invited. The first session of the dialogue took place after the arrest of Nour, and the then secretary general of the Ghad, Mona Makram Ebeid, replaced Nour in the session and presented the party's proposal for a new constitution.[37] The new constitution presented by Ebeid on behalf of the party was titled "Tomorrow's Constitution: Their Words Are for History and Our Words Are for the Future," which included 209 articles that aimed to introduce a liberal platform.[38] After the arrest of Nour, Moussa was ordered by the regime to replace Ebeid in the following session of the national dialogue. During this session, the then secretary general of the NDP, Safwat El Sherif, asked Moussa whether the Ghad Party still insisted on an immediate constitutional amendment. Moussa responded by saying no—that they would postpone the constitutional amendments and that it would be up to President Mubarak to decide when to amend the constitution.[39] According to Ebeid, "During a party meeting, Moussa recounted to us that after he had told the National Dialogue that there would not be a request for constitutional amendments, Kamal El Shazly pointed to him with the thumb upwards."[40] Ebeid interpreted this as a sign of approval from the regime.[41] This confirms that the regime considered Moussa to be a member of the "loyal" opposition that worked within the system it created.

Another sign of Moussa's co-option by the regime was his immediate removal of Ibrahim Eissa as editor in chief of the Ghad Party's newspaper following his return from abroad and Eissa's replacement with a journalist with strong ties with State Security.[42] Approximately two months later, Nour was released; however, charges against him were not dropped. A few months later, Nour ran in the first presidential elections, which took place in September 2005. He came in second after Mubarak. During the presidential elections, Moussa did not make any financial contributions to the Ghad Party's campaign, while his associate in the party, Ragab Hillal Hemeida, put banners in the streets to support Mubarak. Simultaneously, in an indirect way, the regime sent Nour a message saying that if he gave Moussa his position in the party, there could be concessions regarding his court case. This meant that Moussa would direct the party as the authorities wanted. However, after the presidential election, Nour fired both Moussa and Hemeida.[43] As a result, in May 2006, Nour lost his court appeal and was sentenced to five years in prison "for what most people believe are trumped up fraud charges"[44]

The sentence of Nour, however, was not a sufficient solution to deal with a "radical" opposition party. Since the party had already been legalized by the regime, creating a divided environment inside the party was one way to destroy it. To create this division, the regime used its co-opted businessman inside the party, Moussa. For instance, Moussa and Hemeida, following State Security instructions, formed another wing of the Ghad Party and held a General Assembly for the party. Those who attended the

General Assembly were not members of the party but workers from Moussa's factories and other non–Ghad Party members. These members elected Moussa as president of the party and showed their loyalty to the regime.[45] Moreover, in October 2005, Moussa issued a newspaper called the *Ghad*. In its first edition, it called for Gamal Mubarak to be the next president of Egypt.[46] From 2005 to 2007, Moussa filed several court cases against Nour over the Ghad Party. Then in 2007, the PPC, headed by the then NDP secretary general and head of the Consultative Assembly, Safwat El-Sherif, approved Moussa's wing of the party as the legal party.[47]

The division in the Ghad Party resulted in two wings of the party—one legal, approved by the regime, and headed by Moussa and the other illegal, unlicensed, and headed by Nour. The fact that Moussa's wing was a tool created by the regime to destroy the originally legalized Ghad Party is reflected in the way Moussa viewed his party's role in the opposition. For instance, he said, "we respect [Mubarak]. He is the President of Egyptians. We are not against him. Going in elections does not mean that you disrespect someone."[48]

Moreover, in return for Moussa's role in creating division inside the Ghad Party, he was rewarded in his political career with a seat in the Consultative Assembly in the 2010 elections in the Giza constituency. In his daily column in *Al-Destour* newspaper, Ayman Nour writes, "Moussa has been looking for years for a constituency in which to run for election, but the Giza district was not one of his choices; however, it was the choice of the security machinery."[49] The elections were apparently rigged in favor of Moussa, as political activist Mohamed Abou El Ghar said, "The casting of the ballot showed that Moussa had more than 100,000 votes, despite the fact that those who voted in the elections were only a few thousand."[50] Similarly, in an interview with the Washington-based think tank, the Carnegie Endowment, Nawara (2010) said, "Opposition candidates and National Democratic Party candidates enter the electoral race with a predetermined outcome. This was shown in the [June 2010] ... [Consultative Assembly] elections. In the Giza district, the National Democratic Party candidate was defeated by the government-supported Ghad Party candidate. The reports indicated that 7,000 voters participated while the Ghad Party candidate—who was not even from the district—received 119,000 votes. This is a miracle; how can a candidate who is not from the National Democratic Party receive 119,000 votes when there are only 7,000 voters?"[51] The jailing of Nour was a signal from the regime to political activists and businessmen that whoever attempted to become a member of the "radical" opposition would end up in jail. In addition, the division in the party weakened Nour's wing, since it became unlicensed by the regime. As a result, in addition to many of the ordinary members who left Nour's wing, all big businessmen also left it. For instance, big businessmen who were already members of the party realized that direct confrontation with the regime would not lead to the democracy they aimed for; in addition, there was the risk of being harmed in their businesses. As one senior member in the Ghad Party said, "There were a number of businessmen who joined the Ghad Party, like Omar Said Al Ahl and others; however, after the arrest and trial of Nour, the goal they wanted to achieve [democracy] was not accomplished, so they left the party . . . And after the split between Ayman and Moussa, no businessmen joined the party."[52]

Other businessmen who were aspiring to join the Ghad Party changed their opinions and decided to join opposition parties that were officially licensed by the regime. For instance, Mohamed Mansour Hassan, a multimillionaire, businessman, and son of Mansour Hassan (a prominent politician and former minister under Sadat), attended party meetings in December 2004 before the arrest of Nour and was considering becoming a member of the party. One month later, Nour was arrested, and Hassan continued attending the meetings during the 45 days of Nour's arrest. After his temporary release, Nour met with Hassan and asked him to officially join the party, but Hassan refused and told Ayman, "This is not a true party. During the period of your arrest, I attended the party meetings regularly and noticed that there were elements planted in the party [by State Security], like Moussa, that aimed to stop it from working . . . Moussa and his associates in the party should be dismissed."[53]

However, from his perspective as a politician, Nour thought that it was too early to make this decision. A few months later, Nour dismissed Moussa, and the regime created a division in the party that resulted in two wings. Then Nour called Hassan, asking him to join his wing; however, Hassan refused again. Later on, Hassan decided to join the Democratic Front Party (DFP), which is an opposition party established in 2007 that is not "radical" in its opposition to the regime. Hassan's case shows how the regime's co-option of a businessman like Moussa in the Ghad Party reduced the credibility of the party as belonging to the opposition, which made Hassan reluctant to join the Ghad Party. Even after Nour dismissed Moussa from the party, the division the regime created within the Ghad Party resulted in Nour's wing becoming unlicensed by the regime. Instead of joining an unlicensed party, some opposition activists preferred to join a nonradical but licensed opposition party rather than a "radical" party not approved by the regime. For instance, Hassan admitted that the DFP is not as "radical" as the Ghad Party. He said,

We were not confronted by the authorities . . . You should know that until now, we have not yet succeeded, and success is what leads you into danger . . .

Our party has few members, and we are not popular in a way that threatens the regime. They are monitoring us very closely to see what we have achieved. If they find that we are popular enough and have followers, then, this would be their indicator. We are not like the Ghad Party that had a charismatic leader like Ayman Nour. Also, the Ghad started very strong during its establishment. For example, they were texting messages to inform people about their new party, and unlike our party, Nour was surrounded by a large number of youth.[54]

As a result, Nour's wing of the Ghad Party was left with a handful of small businessmen who decided to remain and continue in challenging the regime. However, their presence in the party did not represent any challenge to the regime because they were not financially strong. As for Moussa's wing, it also did not represent any threat, since it remained subordinate to the regime.

In other cases, the regime co-opted businessmen from loyal opposition parties in order to tame a radical newspaper. The following section on El Sayyid El Badawi and *Al-Destour* newspaper will discuss this point.

Pharmaceutical Tycoon El Sayyid El Badawi, President of the Wafd Party: The Case of *Al-Destour* Newspaper

El Sayyid El Badawi is a pharmaceutical tycoon. In 1996, El Badawi established Sigma Pharmaceutical Industries. He was elected to the Wafd Party's Higher Committee in 1989. In 2000, El Badawi became the Wafd Party's secretary general, and in 2010, he was elected president of the party. In 2008, he founded the satellite television channel Al Hayat.[55] Then, in August 2010, after he was elected president of the Wafd Party, El Badawi and Reda Edward (another businessman in the Wafd Party's highest committee) bought *Al-Destour* newspaper. *Al-Destour* is an independent newspaper and was considered the most critical of the regime. The total amount paid in 2010 for *Al-Destour* was 16 million Egyptian pounds (EGP), and El Badawi had the largest percentage of shares.[56] Three weeks after buying *Al-Destour*, El Badawi fired its editor in chief, Ibrahim Eissa, who had previously been editor in chief of the *Ghad* newspaper before Moussa took over the party. Eissa had been known as a critic of the Mubarak regime. *Al-Destour* was launched in 1995 but was banned by the authorities in 1998 because it published a statement by al-Jama'a al-Islamiyya (the Islamic Group) that contained a death threat to three Coptic businessmen, including Naguib Sawiris.[57] In 2001, the Supreme Administrative Court ruled in favor of publishing *Al-Destour*, but it was not until 2004 that the regime allowed it to reopen. The clashes between the regime and Eissa did not end after the reopening of *Al-Destour*, and in

2008, Eissa was sentenced to prison for six months for publishing an article that questioned Mubarak's health.[58]

The buying of *Al-Destour* two months before the parliamentary elections of 2010 and one year before the scheduled 2011 presidential elections, especially among rumors of potential hereditary succession, suggests that El Badawi was co-opted by the regime to suppress any opposition. After being fired by El Badawi, Eissa commented that the regime wanted "absolute silence on the part of the press as parliamentary and presidential elections approach."[59]

Evidence suggests that El Badawi had entered into a clientelistic relation with the regime. This may explain why a very rich businessman and an opposition politician paid millions to buy an antiregime newspaper, fire its editor in chief, and destroy his reputation in such a way. El Badawi's pharmaceutical business seems to have expanded because of his connections with the regime. In 2005, Mubarak visited El Badawi's pharmaceutical company, Sigma. At this time, El Badawi's pharmaceutical factory was a small one, and it was not common for Mubarak to inaugurate small factories. Two years later, El Badawi's factory became one of the largest and most important pharmaceutical factories in Egypt.[60] Moreover, to operate his satellite television channel, Al Hayat, he needed government licenses, and "it was believed that the Mubarak regime handed out such licenses only to loyal individuals that it trusts."[61] El Badawi's relations with the government have also helped him violate laws[62] and keep its security services at bay.[63] For instance, the Ministry of Health issued Decree 350 of 2009 to prohibit the sale of Tramadol—a pharmaceutical painkiller—and classified it as an addictive drug.[64] Despite the ministry's decree, El Badawi's pharmaceutical company continued selling Tramadol, claiming that it was not addictive and could be sold with a prescription, thereby enhancing its profit.[65]

This clientelistic relationship, while benefitting El Badawi greatly on an economic level, operated to limit his political independence. El Badawi knew that the regime could easily remove him from his position as the party's president by creating a division inside the party—like what happened with his predecessors, Noaman Goma'a and Mahmoud Abaza.[66] This suggests that El Badawi's business career (for example, his pharmaceutical company and satellite channel) and political career (for example, his leadership of the party) were very dependent on the regime. In cases of disobedience, the regime was able to use credible threats of harming him economically and politically. This type of clientelism is authoritarian in nature.

To protect himself, El Badawi played the role of an obedient, "loyal" opponent to the regime. For instance, this was evident in the first three weeks after El Badawi bought *Al-Destour* and before he fired Eissa. As Eissa related, "One day Reda Edward called me and said, 'stand beside El Badawi for the sake of the Wafd, and stop the daily column of Ayman Nour.'"[67] But Eissa refused. In fact, Al-Destour was the only newspaper that allowed Ayman Nour to write a daily column, "Shebak Nour" (Nour's Window), when he was imprisoned. That a jailed person could manage to send his daily column clandestinely to a newspaper and be published is considered an unprecedented event. After Nour was released from prison, he continued writing his daily column in *Al-Destour*.[68] In another incident, El Badawi called Eissa regarding an article that Mohamed El Baradei had written on the anniversary of the 1973 (October) War. In the article, El Baradei wrote that in the 37 years since the 1973 war, Egypt "had not progressed politically or economically."[69]

El Badawi told Eissa that the article threatened their interests: "It will cause us many problems."[70] But Eissa insisted on publishing the article. So to prevent Eissa from publishing the article, El Badawi decided to fire him from *Al-Destour*. Edward told Eissa, "We were about to be destroyed today because of El Baradei's article . . . Mubarak himself was going to destroy us and threaten our interests."[71] After the firing of Eissa, El Badawi was much criticized in the media and also by his party members To calm the situation, he sold his *Al-Destour* shares to his partner, Reda Edward. El Badawi later apologized to the Wafd Higher Committee by saying that the "Al-Destour incident was the worst decision he'd ever made."[72]

El Badawi is not an exceptional case of a businessman in a "loyal" opposition party like the Wafd Party who was co-opted by the regime. For instance, business tycoon Salah Diab owns Pico Company, which includes diversified activities such as petroleum services, agriculture, and real estate development and is one of the businessmen who benefited during the Mubarak regime. Diab is also a member in the Wafd's High Committee. After the Twenty-Fifth of January Revolution, investigations revealed that in the mid-1990s, Diab bought 750 feddans (one feddan equivalent to 1.038 acres) on Cairo-Alexandria Desert Road from the government for the purpose of reclaiming the land for agriculture. However, Diab did not use the land for agricultural purposes and instead built resorts on it and made big profits. Moreover, Diab bought the land at much less than the market value, for three hundred EGP per feddan, while the value of a feddan at this time was eight thousand EGP.[73]

Diab became supportive of Mubarak's regime despite his membership in the Wafd Party. In 2004, Diab and other businessmen established the daily independent newspaper *Al-Masry Al-Youm*,[74] in which he owned the highest number of shares. As mentioned in the previous chapter, *Al-Masry Al-Youm* never criticized the president and his family. Moreover, on different occasions, Diab confirmed his loyalty to Mubarak's regime. One year before the scheduled 2011 presidential election, Diab was asked in a newspaper interview if he would vote for Mubarak. He said, "Of course I will vote for Mubarak . . . No one can doubt his patriotism . . . I might differ with him on his ways, but I don't differ with him on his goals . . . He is improving many things in the country."[75]

Unlike El Badawi, who entered into an authoritarian clientelistic relationship with the regime, other businessmen refused to enter the regime's clientelistic chain—for example, members of the MB, who as a result were detained, tortured, and prosecuted by the regime. The following section will discuss how the regime dealt with MB businessmen.

Muslim Brothers Businessmen and the Case of the Al Azhar Militia

Unlike opposition parties that are legalized by the PPC and lack the ability to mobilize the masses, the MB under Mubarak was a banned organization, but it was legalized after the Twenty-Fifth of January Revolution. It had operated semiclandestinely and had a large number of supporters throughout Egypt. Popularity of the MB is usually considered to be a result of its extensive social network, which provides services to the poor.[76] So why would the Egyptian regime allow the MB to function despite its illegality and popularity? To answer this question, we should understand the different types of relationships between the MB and the Mubarak regime.

In the 1980s, the MB was an opposition organization "tolerated" by the regime. In order to keep it under control, the regime had used both coercion and co-option with the MB. Regarding the former, the regime created a division between the MB and the other legal opposition parties by refusing to grant the MB official admission to the system.[77] Simultaneously, the MB was allowed to run in the 1984 and 1987 parliamentary elections on the party list of the legal opposition parties (the Wafd and the Labor Parties respectively).[78] Hesham Al-Awadi explains the reasons for Mubarak allowing the MB to engage in politics in the 1980s: "Mubarak had no option but to reconcile himself with political and social forces until his regime stabilized. He also tolerated the Muslim Brothers, alongside leftists and the Wafd Party, in order to create a broader national front against the threat posed by the extremist *al-jihad* and *al-Jama'a al-Islamiyya* groupings. By accommodating the [MB] in the political process in 1984 and 1987, Mubarak aimed to buy the support of the moderates and to signal that the new regime was not antagonistic to the Islamist movement in general, but only towards its violent wing."[79]

At the same time, during the 1980s, the MB was a weak opposition organization that could not attempt to challenge the regime. This may explain why it accepted the role of a "tolerated" opposition organization.

As the then MB supreme leader Omar El Tulmasani implied, "When we were released from the 1981 detention, we were in a state of near recession. We set to looking for a lawful means to carry out our activities without troubling security or challenging the laws. Allah saw fit to find us a lawful way in the views of officials. The parliamentary session had just ended and thinking began on the new parliamentary elections. It was the opportunity of a lifetime, and had the [MB] let it slip from their hands they would surely be counted among the ranks of neglectful."[80]

On the societal[81] level, the regime allowed the MB to engage in professional syndicates, university student unions, and charitable organizations, provided they did not merge their social services with politics.[82] As a "tolerated" opposition organization, it seems that there was an unspoken contract between the MB and the regime. The MB was allowed to operate as long as it respected the regime's rule (for example, their social activities were apolitical). As one MB member of the Engineering Syndicate said, "In the initial years of our presence in the syndicate we did nothing but services, services, services. We did not speak politics, because we realized that if we did so from the outset, people would not listen. We needed to provide services first. As a result, people began to gather round us. It was only then that we could talk to them about our political views. We would expect them to support us, since by then they knew us better."[83]

However, the regime's tolerance toward the MB changed after it started violating the rules of the game. This was evident when the MB merged the social services offered to the victims of the 1992 earthquake with politics. As Al-Awadi writes,

> It is possible that the regime was worried by media comments on the failure of the state in contrast to the success of [the MB]. However, what certainly aggravated the regime was the way [the MB] turned the crisis into a political campaign. The movement exploited the earthquake-damaged areas and promoted its political concerns by displaying banners that carried the slogan "Islam is the solution." These banners were placed on tents and in relief headquarters belonging to the movement or the syndicates that it controlled. This was the same slogan that the MB had used in 1987 to run its political campaign for parliamentary elections, and despite the different context, the repetition of the slogan confirmed the regime's scepticism.[84]

When the MB used the slogan "Islam is the solution" in the early 1990s, the regime started to consider the MB a "radical," rather than a "tolerated," opposition. This is because not only was the MB refusing co-option; it also started to challenge the regime. At the same time, the regime continued to create a division between the MB and the illegal opposition.

For instance, in 1993, after the renewal of Mubarak's term in a referendum, he held a national dialogue with the legal opposition parties and did not invite the MB. As Lust-Okar writes, "Explicitly excluding the Muslim Brotherhood and other illegal opposition forces, Mubarak underscored the red line between acceptable and unacceptable opposition. The Dialogue had a rocky start as the opposition members and the government argued over the composition of its membership and, more importantly, over the agenda, but the majority of moderate, legal opponents eventually chose to play the game, shoring up the regime."[85]

Once the MB became a "radical" opposition organization, the government moved to suppress it. Throughout the 1990s, the regime cracked down on members of the MB and tried them in military courts, accusing them of attempts to revive an illegal organization. The 1966 law of the military judiciary states that "during the state of emergency, the President of the Republic has the right to refer to the military judiciary any crime which is punishable under the Penal Code or under any other law."[86]

For instance, around 1,033 civilians were tried in military courts during the period from 1992 to 2000, which resulted in 92 death sentences and 644 prison sentences.[87] It is worth noting that verdicts in military courts are subject to ratification only by the president, and they are unappealable.[88] The first trials of MB members by military courts during Mubarak's regime were concomitant with the 1995 parliamentary elections, when 84 MB members were arrested and 54 of them were tried by military courts and got prison sentences ranging from three to five years. The second trial occurred in 1996 and is known as the case of the Wasat Party. This case was triggered after a number of young MB members applied for legal party status under the name of the Wasat, which was refused by the PPC. As a result, 13 MB members were arrested, and 8 were tried by military courts and got prison sentences ranging from three to five years. The third trial of MB members by a military court was in 1999. It was known as the case of the professional syndicates because of all the 20 individuals arrested were members of syndicates and 15 of them were sentenced from three to five years. The fourth trial of MB members by a military court was in 2001 and included a number of university professors. Twenty-two MB members were arrested and 15 were tried by military courts and got prison sentences ranging from three to five years.[89] The regime has also cracked down on the MB on other occasions (in 2004 and 2007) that will be discussed in detail later in this section.

Even though the regime started prosecuting the MB after it became a "radical" opposition organization, it continued to violate the rules of the game. For instance, the MB ran in the 2000 parliamentary election, which was the first election to be held under judicial supervision, as independent candidates. The MB candidates got 17 seats in parliament—compared to only 1 seat in the 1995 parliament—and thus represented the largest opposition bloc.[90] This suggests how the MB started to become a concern for the regime. For instance, Sherif Wally, the then NDP Giza youth secretary and a member of the Consultative Assembly, implied that the MB was on the verge of becoming a challenge to the regime when he said, "It was not all clean elections. Sometimes we had to stop the Muslim Brothers from emerging . . . Especially a lot in the third stage [of voting], because in the first stage not a lot of people [i.e., MB-inclined voters] entered [the process]. In the second stage they entered and they found themselves successful. So in the third stage they didn't believe it, so they began [turning out in greater numbers]. They were moving like hell!"[91]

In return for the MB winning 17 seats in parliament, the regime continued to crack down on them. The best illustration of the regime's crackdown on the MB is the case of MB businessman Medhat El Haddad. After graduating from the Faculty of Engineering at Alexandria University, El Haddad established a number of companies, which included construction, real estate investment, import/export, and conference organization. El Haddad was also politically active. He ran in parliamentary elections several times (the Consultative Assembly in 1995 and the People's Assembly in 1995 and 2005) and lost them all. According to El Haddad, each time he ran for election, the result was forged in favor of the ruling party candidate. After each election, El Haddad raised a case in the court about the forging of election results. In 2000, he got compensation from the court for the forging of the 1995 Consultative Assembly[92] elections, and in 2001, he got compensation from the court for the forging of the 1995 People's Assembly[93] elections. On different occasions during the 1990s, El Haddad was arrested by State Security and sentenced by the court because he belonged to an illegal organization. But his arrest in May 2004 seemed to have been a message from the regime that it would start using more violence with the MB. For instance, El Haddad was arrested at his house at midnight and taken to Mazara't Tora Prison. He was detained in Mazara't Tora with 57 other MB members, who came from different professional backgrounds; they included businessmen, university professors, engineers, pharmacists, and accountants. The State Security police closed 21 companies, pharmacies, and commercial stores that the MB owned in six different governorates. Then, on June 5, 2004, El Haddad and around 11 other MB detainees were kidnapped by State Security police from Mazara't Tora. They were put in a microbus, blindfolded, handcuffed, and taken to a secret prison in Madinat Nasr, located around ten meters under the State Security building. After the prisoners arrived, State Security started using different types of torture on El Haddad and the other MB detainees. For instance, El Haddad was slapped severely by the State Security police several times on his face. The State Security police took out of his trousers, and every few hours someone would stop by and threaten to kill him.[94] Another of the MB detainees, businessman Mohamed Osama, was stripped of all his clothes by the State Security police and was given electric shocks in sensitive parts of his body. Then, after six days of torture, they all returned to Mazara't Tora Prison and were detained for six months.[95]

Another example of how the MB continued to violate the rules of the game was when, in March 2005, they organized a demonstration that included ten thousand demonstrators who were asking for a quicker pace of reform.[96] The MB slogans demanded more freedom and an end to emergency law. This means that the MB crossed the red line, since they were not allowed to challenge domestic issues in demonstrations. They were only allowed to hold big demonstrations on foreign policy issues (for example, Palestine and Iraq).[97] One author explained that this new strategy of the MB was "a response to [their] thorough exclusion from the national dialogue [held few weeks earlier] . . . and the emergence of Kefaya."[98] Even though the government harassed hundreds of MBs, they continued to hold big demonstrations. For instance, in a single day on May 4, 2005—on the occasion of Mubarak's birthday—the MB organized 41 surprise rallies in which seventy thousand people from 18 governorates participated.[99] The MB held this demonstration independently, without cooperating with the other political forces; also, they held the demonstration without informing State Security in order to get the required approval.[100] As a result of this demonstration, a few days later, several hundred members of the MB were arrested, including one of its senior leaders, Essam El Arian.[101]

A few months later, the MB started preparing for the 2005 parliamentary elections. Before the elections, the Guidance Bureau asked the MB offices in the governorate to prepare a list of potential candidates who would run for election, and the list exceeded more than two hundred candidates. At this stage, the regime seemed to have been trying different tactics to suppress the MB, since outright coercion and persecution was not working. Instead, the regime tried co-option, which was evident when State Security held meetings with Khairat El Shatter (the second deputy of the MB supreme guide and a millionaire businessman) and asked him to contest only 120 seats out of the 444.[102] The fact that El Shatter agreed to meet with State Security suggests that being a "radical" opposition organization did not prevent the MB from bargaining with the regime when it was in the MB's interest.

But the regime's "voter intimidation and ballot stuffing failed to stop the Brothers' affiliates from winning a historic eighty-eight seats,"[103] which suggests that the MB continued to refuse to be co-opted. The 88 seats won by the MB in the 2005 parliamentary election seem to have been much more than what the regime expected in its political bargain with El Shatter. For instance, one author commented on the significance of the MB's success in the 2005 election. He writes, "The Muslim Brothers' success at the ballot box did not merely reflect the growing popularity of the Islamist group. It also marked a fundamental change in the Brothers' strategy, of working toward active political participation rather than merely seeking to survive."[104]

After the MB won 88 seats in the election, it held a press conference in which Mahdi Akif, the then MB supreme guide, said that he would instruct the newly elected MB members to push for democratic reforms, mainly to reduce the powers of the president and put a limit on the president's tenure.[105]

The one responsible for this transformation was El Shatter, which made him a particular target for punishment by the regime.[106] The regime punished El Shatter and other MB members one year after the 2005 parliamentary elections in what became known as "the case of the Al Azhar militia." The background to this case was that in December 2006, a dozen young MB students attending Al Azhar University held a military-style parade demonstration. During the demonstration, the MB students wore black uniforms and masks and marched from the student center to the university's main gate. Six of the masked students stood in the middle of a square formed by the other MB students; they performed martial exercises reminiscent of demonstrations held by Hamas and Hezbollah.[107] After this parade, progovernment newspapers like *Al-Watani Al-Youm*, the mouth piece of the NDP, and the semiofficial daily newspaper *Al-Ahram* started a negative campaign against the MB. For instance, the headline of an article in *Al-Ahram Daily* stated that "the group ordered its militias to travel abroad for military training in preparation for taking over the regime."[108] The regime seized the opportunity by exploiting fear of the rise of Islamists to power and their potential use of violence, and it started its largest crackdown on the MB from December 2006 to January 2007. During this period, State Security forces arrested 40 members of the MB, including businessmen and university professors. Out of the 40 arrested, 25 were sentenced by the military court and got prison sentences ranging from three to seven years. The accusations included money laundering and financing an illegal political organization.[109] The arrest of MB businessmen aimed at breaking their financial power, and the most prominent of the arrested MB businessmen was Khairat El Shatter, whose assets were frozen. Companies owned by the accused businessmen were closed, and their products were confiscated. These companies included publishing houses, import/export firms, and pharmaceutical and construction companies; the total amount of frozen assets was valued by tens of millions of dollars.[110]

Closing the companies of the MB businessmen could affect their performance in parliamentary elections because MB members are required to donate around 8 percent of their income to the MB.[111] For instance, a university professor who is a member of the Guidance Bureau of the MB and was also sentenced in the case of the Al Azhar militia revealed that "The funding of the MB is from the donations of the members. Everyone pays whatever he can afford. Donations may not be in money; it could be in gifts like providing banners for the parliamentary candidates . . . Supporting the candidates is not a crime. I myself, when I was a candidate for election, some MB members supported me by providing banners, organizing conferences, etc. This is the crime that El Shatter was accused of. But this is not a crime; it is just a political accusation."[112]

Around half of the 25 MB members sentenced in the case of the Al Azhar militia were businessmen, and among them was Medhat El Haddad. Even though he had been arrested and tortured in 2004, he had not stopped participating in politics and was arrested again in 2007 in the case of the Al Azhar militia. When I asked El Haddad why he insisted on engaging in politics by joining the MB and donating money to them, which could have put his life and his private business at risk, he revealed the following:

> I engage in politics because I want the Islamic Shari'a to be the law of the country. Joining the MB is religion [a religious duty], my engagement in politics and business is religion [a religious duty].[113] I work in business and politics to take reward [thawab]. I donate money to the MB because this is the highest of charity [sadaka], it is holy war [jihad] for the sake of God, and it has a double reward. I can die for the holy war [jihad] and become a martyr. What's going on now with the MB is like what happened to the Prophet and his companions. The state securities are like the infidels [koufar], because they confiscate the properties of the MB. It is similar to what the infidels [koufar] did with the companions of the Prophet. We want a civil rule that applies the Islamic Shari'a. If the NDP applies Shari'a, I will join it.[114]

When I asked El Haddad why he thought the regime was excluding and torturing the MB, his answer implied that they were perceived as dangerous to the regime: "The regime wants to protect itself against the MB because [the MB] are popular, and [the regime] fear[s] that we may put [the regime] and its members on trial because of the mistakes they committed against the society, like torturing the people, and the MB in prison, the trial in military court, the emergency law, forging elections, etc."[115]

From El Haddad's answers, we can substantiate the reasons for MB businessmen to engage in politics. It seems that MB businessmen opposed Mubarak's authoritarianism not because they wanted to achieve democracy but because they were willing to sacrifice their lives and private businesses in order to implement Shari'a. This means that their opposition to the regime had to do with their ideological stance rather than their belief in democracy.

Despite the MB's views about mixing religion and politics, it was a "tolerated" opposition organization as long as it was subordinate to the regime and abided by the rules of the game during the 1980s. However, in the early 1990s, the MB was transformed from a "tolerated" opposition organization, on which the regime had used both coercion and co-option, to a "radical" opposition organization that challenged it. As a result of this transformation, the regime started cracking down on the MB. Then, after the MB won 88 seats in the 2005 parliament, the regime made its largest crackdown on the organization. This manifested itself in the case of the Al Azhar militia in 2006–2007, which aimed at breaking the MB's financial power. Then, in the 2010 parliamentary election, the regime reached the opposite end of the spectrum of co-option with regard to the MB, which was extreme exclusion from the political realm. This means that the regime had widened its exclusion of the MB to the extent that it was prevented from gaining any seats in parliament.[116] This new type of MB exclusion had been possible through new strategies employed by the NDP during the 2010 election. For instance, the NDP introduced *el da'ara el maftouha* (the open constituency), in which two or three candidates were nominated by the NDP in the same constituency. The division of votes between the NDP candidates and the MB candidate in a constituency prevented any candidate, especially the MB candidate, from winning in the election's first round (for example, from getting 50 percent plus one of the votes). Then, in the second round, the votes were combined and given to only one of the NDP candidates against the MB candidate.[117]

Unlike MB businessmen, who shifted from "tolerated" to "radical" opposition members, other opposition businessmen began as "radical," then transformed into "loyal" opposition members, like Hani Enan, sponsor of the Kefaya movement. Even though Enan became "loyal" to the regime, the Kefaya movement remained a "radical" opposition organization. The following section will discuss how the regime weakened Kefaya by creating a divided political environment between it and other illegal opposition organizations like the MB.

The Case of Hani Enan: Sponsor of the Kefaya Movement

Hani Enan is a multimillionaire and businessman who imports medical equipment and provides turnkey hospitals. For the last two decades, Enan has been the main importer of medical equipment to Egypt's military forces. On the political level, Enan belongs to the "1970 generation," which was involved in the student movement in Egyptian universities during the 1970s. In 2004, Enan resumed his political activity when he and other political activists founded the Egyptian movement for change, Kefaya.[118] The meaning of the Arabic word *kefaya*, which is "enough," expressed the main demand of the movement: for Mubarak to relinquish power. While the main core of the Kefaya movement consisted of the 1970s generation of activists, like Enan, its membership was also open to all activists in their individual, rather than institutional, capacities. For instance, the movement included political activists from the left like those in the Karama Party (Nasserite), liberals like those in the Ghad Party, and Islamists from the Wasat party, the Labor party, and the MB. What is common among all these parties is that they were not part of the legal opposition, since they were not licensed by the regime, except for the Ghad Party, which became illegal only after the division in the party, as mentioned earlier.

As the only businessman in Kefaya, Enan was its main sponsor. From 2005 to 2008, he spent around three hundred thousand EGP on the movement. The amount he paid covered expenses for organizing receptions, demonstrations, renting an office for the movement, paying salaries for administrative staff, and so on. As a result of his financial contribution to Kefaya, Enan has been slightly harmed in his private business. For instance, after Enan's involvement with Kefaya, his license to submit tenders to the military forces was banned by State Security. To solve this problem, Enan relied on distributers to submit the tenders instead of him. It is worth noting that State Security knew that the distributer was working for Enan.[119] This suggests that the regime started sending warning signs to Enan that if he were to continue funding Kefaya, then his business would be put in more trouble. Enan seemed to have gotten the message and distanced himself from Kefaya and its main aims. For instance, in a newspaper interview with Enan in 2009, he said, "I withdrew from Kefaya because the movement had already played its role in mobilizing the street . . . I am proud of this . . . I see that Kefaya's role has ended . . . and the continuation of some of its leaders in the movement is considered a failure . . . Some of them wished to unite the opposition and to walk in a demonstration of a million protestors that would overthrow the regime . . . But this did not and will not happen in Egypt."[120]

In another newspaper interview, Enan declared his support for Gamal Mubarak to be the future president of Egypt.[121] When I interviewed Enan in 2010, he repeated his new stance—that Kefaya was not intended to be a danger to the regime. He said, "Unlike the MB, who are dangerous to the regime, I am not. I can't mobilize the street, but I can mobilize public opinion. I don't wish to be a danger to the regime; however, I only wish to shake the regime. I push the people, and then they move a bit."[122] The withdrawal of Enan from the movement not only affected the financial ability of the movement but also was a warning sign to other businessmen not to fund or join the movement. Despite the transformation of Enan from a "radical" to a "loyal" opposition member, the goals of the movement remained a threat to the regime. So to weaken the movement, the regime created a divided political environment between Kefaya and the MB (which was the largest opposition group). For instance, on July 20, 2005, both Kefaya and the MB, for the first time, organized a joint demonstration. The MB supporters numbered around five thousand, and Kefaya had only several hundred. The MB shouted slogans like "with our blood and soul, we redeem you, Islam." On the other hand, Kefaya members' slogans directly attacked the regime. They said, "Down with Mubarak" and "Enough with Mubarak." In the middle of the protests, MB members left because they said that they didn't want to insult the president, even though during previous protests—especially in a large one organized by the MB two months before, on Mubarak's birthday (as mentioned earlier)—they criticized him directly.[123] But what were the strategies used by the regime to create this division among parties and movements in the illegal opposition? The regime used different punishments for Kefaya and the MB, which helped prevent their unity. For instance, when MB leaders were asked "why they participate only 'half-heartedly' (if at all) in opposition demonstrations . . . Brotherhood leaders retort that while Kefaya demonstrators get roughed up, their supporters are hauled in for indefinite periods."[124] In other instances, the regime divided the two groups by bargaining with one of them against the other. For example, in December 2006, the Kefaya movement started preparing meetings to celebrate its second anniversary. One of the ideas proposed in these meetings was to hold a big demonstration in front of *Dar El Kada' El Ali*, Cairo's High Court in downtown. One of the members of the MB Guidance Bureau participated in these meetings and agreed that the MB would participate in the demonstration. However, the MB later excused itself and said that it could not participate for internal reasons related to the MB. Then one day after they decided to withdraw from the demonstration, MB senior member Essam El Arian, who was detained in 2005, was released. Sources suggest that a deal was made between the regime and the MB, and in return for not participating in the Kefaya demonstration, El Arian was released.[125]

Due to the divided political environment created by the regime, Kefaya became a weak movement, which could not represent a challenge to the regime. For instance, *Al-Ahram* newspaper carried an interview given by Mubarak to the Kuwait-based *Al-Syassa* newspaper, asking him what he thought when people told him about the Kefaya movement. He said, "This is not bothering me ... I know who is behind them whether it is Kefaya's or other demonstrations"[126] The leadership was assured that he could break the financial power of any opposition businessmen if they crossed the red line and funded an opposition movement. In addition, the regime was successful in weakening any movement through its divide-and-rule tactics.

Conclusion

Albrecht's typology of the opposition enabled an examination of how the regime dealt with different types of opposition, especially during their transformation (from loyal to tolerated to antisystem to radical).[127] If the opposition transforms into antisystem or radical opposition, the regime uses its divide-and-rule tactics to create a divided political environment to weaken the opposition. For instance, Lust-Okar argued that authoritarian regimes created division between the legal and illegal opposition.[128] This was evident when the Mubarak regime labelled the MB as an illegal organization while granting official status to loyal opposition parties. However, this chapter discovered other levels of division created by the regime to weaken the opposition: one level was inside legalized parties, as in the case of the Ghad Party, which resulted in one party being legal and another party being illegal, and another level was among parties and movements in the illegal opposition, as in the case of the MB and Kefaya movement.

But the different levels of division created by the regime among parties and movements in the opposition did not prevent the outbreak of the revolution and the fall of Mubarak's regime, as the concluding chapter will discuss.

Conclusion

Introduction

This book has attempted to address the reasons for the survival of authoritarianism in Egypt during the three decades under Mubarak's rule. To address this issue, I have focused on the case of businessmen in Egypt. Contrary to the scholars who argue that businessmen are agents of democratization,[1] this book has found that in the case of Egypt under Mubarak, they were not. Instead, my research found that under Mubarak, there were businessmen who played a role in supporting authoritarianism for their own economic interests; however, there were also businessmen who opposed authoritarianism and sacrificed their businesses because of their ideological views rather than their belief in democracy.

Empirical Findings

The research question this book set out to answer is, to what degree did businessmen contribute to the survival of authoritarianism during the three decades of Mubarak's rule (1981–2011)? My research has shown that some businessmen played an important role in the survival of authoritarianism. This was contingent on the creation of a new political economy of authoritarianism under the Mubarak regime. First, contrary to Amr Adly's[2] arguments, this work demonstrates that businessmen were able to capture the state and influence policies for their own benefit. Relevant examples are the cases of Ahmed Ezz in Chapter 3 and Naguib Sawiris (hereafter referred to as Naguib to avoid confusion with the rest of his family members) in Chapter 4. Ezz used his power in parliament and amended the monopoly law in a way that enhanced his profit. Naguib used his social network relationship with the Mubarak family to tailor the 1997 investment incentive law, which offered him fiscal exemptions. It was in the interests of both Ezz and Naguib to support Mubarak's authoritarianism, since their interests coincided with the survival of the regime. However, it was also in the interest of the regime to allow these businessmen to become rich. Ezz provided substantial funding to the ruling party and Mubarak's 2005 presidential campaign. Naguib used his media outlets (*Al-Masry Al-Youm* newspaper in which he is a shareholder and his private television channel, ONTV) to provide political support to Mubarak and his regime.

This work built on the argument of John Sfakianakis[3] on how network relations between the regime and its coalitions (businessmen and bureaucrats) provided support to the regime in return for their self-enrichment. However, this book further argues that the regime also allowed bureaucrats to accumulate wealth not only to provide support for the regime but also in return for their help in the enrichment of the Mubarak family. The case of Ibrahim Soliman, the minister of housing in Chapter 4, demonstrates how the private office of his brother-in-law monopolized the projects of the Ministry of Housing after his appointment to the cabinet in the early 1990s. Empirical findings in this work demonstrate that Soliman was encouraged by the regime to accumulate wealth illegally in return for helping in the enrichment of the Mubarak family. This was also a role that businessman Hussein Salem played with the Mubarak family. Empirical findings in Chapter 4 demonstrate how Salem helped enrich the Mubarak family through the East Mediterranean Gas Company, which exported gas to Israel.

Third, empirical findings demonstrate that not all businessmen were supporting authoritarianism for their economic interests. The case of the Al Azhar militia in Chapter 5 demonstrates that the Muslim Brothers (MB) businessmen opposed authoritarianism and sacrificed their own businesses in order to implement Shari'a. This empirical finding is contrary to the argument of Eva Bellin who wrote that businessmen support authoritarianism for their own economic interests.[4]

Empirical findings demonstrate that Egypt has constituted two different types of predatory state.[5] Peter Evans's conception of a predatory state is demonstrated in the case of loan MPs when businessmen and bankers co-opted by the Mubarak regime looted the banks at the expense of the interests of the rest of Egyptian society, as discussed in Chapter 3.[6] Evans's conception of a predatory state is also demonstrated in the case of Hussein Salem, as discussed in Chapter 4. In this case, Mubarak's sons (Alaa and Gamal) made commissions worth hundreds of millions of dollars in return for their support for exporting gas to Israel at a very low price through the East Mediterranean Gas Company, the majority of whose shares were held by businessman Hussein Salem. This gas deal benefitted the Mubarak family and Salem.

Margaret Levi's conception of a predatory state is demonstrated by the extraction of money by force from businessmen when they were asked to finance and provide projects for the public good, as discussed in Chapters 1 and 4. This was also demonstrated in Chapter 1 when the state imposed an unconstitutional tax on public- and private-sector employees working abroad.[7] The two different types of predatory state defined by Evans and Levi, as discussed in this book, demonstrate that the state was harsh toward society and businessmen; however, businessmen co-opted by the regime were allowed to accumulate wealth in illegal ways in return for their donations. The rest of society (excluding businessmen who entered into clientelistic relationships with the regime) got looted and got nothing in return. At the same time, those who controlled the state apparatus, like the Mubarak family, and their associates, like Salem, plundered and fulfilled their interests at the expense of Egyptian society's interests. This, then, explains the failure of Mubarak's political economy of authoritarianism, which was based on predation.

Theoretical Contribution

This work demonstrates that the political economy of authoritarianism in Egypt has relied on co-opting businessmen. As discussed in Chapter 2, under Nasser, the political economy of authoritarianism relied on co-opting businessmen for the purpose of implementing the national development plan. Sadat co-opted the *Infitah* (open-door policy) bourgeoisie, who were linked to foreign capitalism, for the purpose of allying with the West. As discussed in Chapters 2–5, Mubarak co-opted businessmen for the sake of regime survival and the enrichment of his family.

This work examines the different institutional mechanisms of the Mubarak regime's co-option of businessmen. It went beyond the conception of co-option as dyadic and static. This work demonstrates that in light of economic liberalization, the political economy of authoritarianism intersected with different types of clientelistic relationships. Co-option became flexible and took a variety of forms (for example, authoritarian clientelism, semiclientelism, patron-broker-client relationships, and mutual dependency). The varied means of co-opting businessmen demonstrate how the regime prevented them from playing a democratizing role in politics.

Ramy Lakah in Chapter 3; Ahmed Bahgat, Ibrahim El Moallam, and Mohamed Nosseir in Chapter 4; and El Sayyid El Badawi in Chapter 5 entered into authoritarian clientelistic relationships with the regime. These clientelistic relationships were based on their subordination to the regime and were reinforced by credible threats of coercion. The regime used Lakah's file of financial corruption at the Prosecutor General's Office to threaten him. Even after Lakah returned to Egypt and reconciled with the regime by settling his debts with the banks, he was still under a credible threat of having the file documenting his corruption opened at any time, which made him continue in his support of Mubarak and in his subordination to the regime. In the case of Bahgat, the regime used his debts to public banks to threaten his business in case he became disobedient. This ensured that both he and his private channel, Dream TV, were subordinate to the regime. In the case of El Moallam, when his *Al-Sherouk* newspaper criticized the project of hereditary succession and Mubarak's authoritarian regime in one of its articles, the regime used credible threats of coercion by closing his carton factory, claiming as its reason that the factory did not have a fire extinguisher. Nosseir's authoritarian clientelistic relation with the regime was demonstrated by his subordination to Mubarak when he was ordered to establish a financial center, which he called "the Citadel project." This subordination was reinforced by credible threats of coercion when he became one of those businessmen who had to provide support to the regime in the form of charitable activities. El Sayyid El Badawi's economic and political careers were dependent on the regime for survival. This dependency forced him into an authoritarian clientelistic relationship with the regime based on credible threats of losing both his business and his political career if he were disobedient. Therefore, he obeyed the regime when he was ordered to buy the radical newspaper *Al-Destour* in order to tame it. Other businessmen entered into semiclientelistic relationships with the regime—for example, the loan MPs in Chapter 3 and Wagih Siag in Chapter 4. In the case of the loan MPs, as a result of economic liberalization, the credit ceilings of banks were abolished, which allowed businessmen to loot banks' money. This increased the structural and financial power of businessmen and allowed them to enter into semiclientelistic relationships with the regime based on bargaining and less subordination. Similarly, the increase in the financial power of Siag after winning his case against the Egyptian government allowed him to enter into a bargaining relationship with the regime. The loan MPs' bargain with the regime allowed them to pay back only part of the money they had looted from the banks. Siag's bargaining with the regime allowed him to return to Egypt to resume his private business. In both cases, the bargaining relationships induced compliance by the threat of the removal of benefits (for example, the benefit of paying back only part of the money businessmen had looted from the banks in the case of loan MPs and the benefit of returning to invest in Egypt in the case of Siag) and not by threat of coercion.

This work has demonstrated that economic liberalization transformed the relationship between the regime and parliamentary businessmen into a triadic relationship, as mentioned in Chapter 3. This triadic relation involved the regime (as a patron), the parliamentary businessmen (as brokers), and the voters (as clients). In this triadic relationship, parliamentary businessmen played the role of brokers and replaced the state in providing social services to their constituencies.

The varied ways of co-opting businessmen demonstrate how the regime renewed its authoritarianism after the introduction of economic liberalization. One group of businessmen entered into authoritarian clientelistic relationships with the regime based on subordination. These relationships were reinforced by credible threats of coercion. Another group of businessmen entered into semiclientelistic relationships with the regime based on bargaining. The clientelistic relationships based on bargaining induced compliance by the threat of the removal of benefits rather than threats of coercion. A third group of businessmen entered into patron-broker-client relationships with the regime and replaced the state in the provision of social services. In exceptional cases, businessmen Ahmed Ezz and Naguib Sawiris formed a relationship of mutual dependency with the regime. Businessmen who refused to be co-opted by the regime—as in the cases of Ibrahim Kamel and Anwar Esmat El Sadat, discussed in Chapter 3—were punished by the regime and were prevented from engaging in politics.

This means that the regime's co-option of businessmen should not be understood in terms of only one type of co-option. In other words, the regime could not maintain its survival by using only threats of coercion with all businessmen, by bargaining with all businessmen, or by using all businessmen as brokers to replace the state's role in providing services. Instead, the regime maintained its survival and renewed its authoritarianism after the introduction of economic liberalization by using a variety of clientelistic relationships with businessmen.

But how did the Egyptian authoritarian regime deal with the opposition that refused to be co-opted into its clientelistic chain? Mubarak's regime weakened the opposition by creating a divided political environment among political parties in the legal and illegal opposition.[8] But this work further demonstrates that the regime created a divided environment among the opposition on different levels. On one level, the regime co-opted particular businessmen in legalized opposition parties, such as in the case of businessman Moussa Moustafa Moussa in Chapter 5. Moussa was used by the regime to create a divided environment inside the Ghad Party when it turned to radical opposition. This division resulted into two wings: one legal, headed by Moussa, and the other illegal and not approved by the regime, headed by Ayman Nour. The regime's division of the Ghad Party weakened it. Rich businessmen, like Omar Said Al Ahl, Mansour Hassan, and others, left the Ghad Party because this division prevented them from accomplishing the democracy that they were aiming for. On another level, the regime created a divided political environment among the illegal parties and movements, as with the MB and the Kefaya movement discussed in Chapter 5.

The Failure of Mubarak's New Political Economy of Authoritarianism

Mubarak's new political economy of authoritarianism relied on co-opting regime supporters and the loyal opposition. This co-option helped the regime maintain its survival for almost three decades. Mubarak's authoritarian regime seemed to be durable until January 25, 2011, when protestors went to the streets with political and economic grievances. This proved the failure of Mubarak's new political economy of authoritarianism. For instance, in exceptional cases, the regime's co-option of businessmen resulted in unintended consequences. As discussed in Chapter 3, in light of economic liberalization, the regime's relationship with Ezz was transformed from mere co-option to mutual dependency. This work demonstrates that the survival of both the regime and Ezz required mutual dependence. Ezz controlled a lot of organizational data in the party, not only in his capacity as an organization secretary, but also because of his substantial financial funding through his nongovernmental organization (NGO), which was involved in all the details of the party. Three days after the outbreak of the revolution on January 25, Ezz was dismissed from the party. After Ezz's dismissal, he took with him names and contact information for hundreds of party organizers from all over the country. This meant that the organizing arm of the party had been cut off, which made the party unable to mobilize its members to counterbalance the protestors in Tahrir Square.

The regime's control over the private media (its newspapers and channels) by co-opting their owners, as in the cases of Bahgat and El Badawi, did not prevent the protestors from going to Tahrir Square. The call for participation in the demonstration on January 25 was announced a couple of weeks earlier through the social media platform Facebook. The regime had underestimated the role of youth groups and activists using social media and only focused on co-opting the businessmen who owned the private media. For instance, the regime's authoritarian clientelistic relationship with Bahgat ensured that he was subordinate to the regime. Dream TV was supportive of Mubarak in the first few days after the outbreak of the revolution; however, the regime's co-option of Bahgat turned out to be unimportant when the number of protestors in the streets was increasing. At this stage, the Dream TV talk show announcer could not continue to hide the truth from the public and revealed the real number of protestors in the streets.

Naguib, as discussed in Chapter 4, developed an exceptional relationship of mutual dependency with the regime. This meant that the survival of Mubarak's regime was also in his business interest. During the 18 days of the revolution, Naguib continued his support of Mubarak by appearing on different talk shows either on his private channel, ONTV, or on other private channels. During his appearances on these talk shows, he cried out of his love for Mubarak and said that Mubarak should stay in power until the end of his presidential term. Naguib and the other businessmen who controlled the private media could not play a role in preventing the protestors from going to Tahrir Square, and the number of protestors continued to increase until the removal of Mubarak on February 11, 2011.

The patron-broker-client relationships that the regime developed with parliamentary businessmen helped provide social services to the voters in their constituencies; however, the outbreak of the revolution demonstrated that the demands of the citizens had not been met by the state or even its brokers (like the businessmen). This was evident in the slogan of the revolutionaries in Tahrir Square, which asked for "bread, freedom, social justice, and dignity." This means that their demands were not only political but also economic.

The regime weakened parties and movements in the opposition by creating different levels of division among them. However, the different levels of division among the political parties in the legal and the illegal opposition, inside the illegal opposition, and among the political parties and movements in the illegal opposition undermined the possibility that it could form a coalition either for or against the regime. As mentioned earlier, the Twenty-Fifth of January Revolution proved that the real opposition to the regime came from youth groups and social media activists.

Egypt in the Post-Mubarak Period

Under the Supreme Council of the Armed Forces from 2011 to 2012

After the ouster of Mubarak on February 11, 2011, the Supreme Council of the Armed Forces (SCAF)—the country's interim military rulers—dissolved the parliament and suspended the constitution, promising to transfer power to civilian rulers through free presidential elections. The first issue addressed by the SCAF was whether Egypt should amend the 1971 constitution before or after the parliamentary and presidential elections. The SCAF decided to start with elections and with making minor amendments to the 1971 constitution. A committee appointed by the SCAF amended nine articles of the 1971 constitution. On March 19, 2011, the amendments passed in a national referendum with 77 percent support. However, ten days later, the SCAF expanded its power by issuing a "provisional constitutional declaration," which was a document consisting of 62 articles that served as an interim constitution. Out of the 62 articles, only 9 were approved in the March 2011 referendum. The interim constitution gave the SCAF full presidential authority until the election of a president.

One of the amended articles in the interim constitution facilitated the procedures of registering political parties. Registering a party could be accomplished by providing written notification to a judicial committee. The party would be considered legal if the judicial committee did not respond to the notification after thirty days. As a result of this quick process, dozens of political parties were established, and they included Islamist, leftist, liberal, and revolutionary youth parties.[9]

There were businessmen who seized the opportunity of this new political environment and increased their political influence by establishing and funding political parties. For example, Naguib Sawiris initiated the establishment of the liberal, secular Free Egyptian Party (FEP).[10] The Liberal Justice Party received around one million EGP from the wealthy businessman Hisham El Khizandar.[11] Businessmen Ramy Lakah and Anwar Esmat El Sadat established and funded the Reform and Development Party (RDP). The MB established their Freedom and Justice Party (FJP). The party is funded by businessmen affiliated with the MB, including businessman Khairat El Shatter, who was released prematurely in March 2011 by the SCAF.[12]

In a period of six months, the FEP recruited 150 thousand members, and 150 of them stood as candidates in the December 2011–January 2012 People's Assembly elections. This was possible through an expensive party campaign. Evidence suggests that Naguib contributed to 20 percent of the FEP budget up until the parliamentary elections.[13] The result of the performance of political parties funded by the businessmen in the December 2011/January 2012 People's Assembly elections was weak. For instance, the FEP won 3 percent of the seats, the RDP won 1.8 percent of the seats, and the Justice Party won 0.2 percent of the seats. On the other hand, the Islamists won the majority of votes, reaching 73 percent. They were represented in the FJP, which got 47.2 percent, and the more conservative and Islamist Salafi Nour Party, which got 24.3 percent. However, on June 15, 2012, the SCAF dissolved the People's Assembly after the Supreme Constitutional Court ruled that the electoral law was unconstitutional. The court ruled that party members should not have been allowed to contest the one-third of seats designated for independents. Two days later, the SCAF issued an interim constitutional declaration that gave back all legislative powers to itself until a new People's Assembly was elected.

There were businessmen who also funded the campaigns of non-Islamist presidential candidates. For instance, in the second round of the presidential election in June 2012, the competition was between Ahmed Shafik, the last prime minister under Hosni Mubarak, and Mohamed Morsi, the MB candidate. Evidence suggests that the businessmen affiliated with Mubarak's regime provided substantial funding to Shafik's campaign.[14] By the end of June 2012, the MB candidate, Mohamed Morsi, won the presidential election with a small margin over his rival.

Under Muslim Brothers President Mohamed Morsi from 2012 to 2013

Upon assuming power, in July 2012, Morsi issued a presidential decree for reinstating the dissolved People's Assembly, which provoked mass protests by the revolutionary forces. A few days later, Morsi accepted a ruling of the Supreme Constitutional Court suspending Morsi's decision to reinstate the People's Assembly. Then, in August 2012, Morsi started asserting his authority in politics by issuing a constitutional decree that gave him wide-ranging powers. Moreover, Morsi asked for the retirement of field Marshal Hussein Tantawi, the minister of defense who served under Mubarak for two decades, and replaced him with a younger general, Abdel Fattah El-Sisi.

On November 22, Morsi had another clash with the Judiciary when he issued a constitutional decree that put his decisions above judicial review. It is suggested that Morsi feared the Judiciary—which is filled with Mubarak appointments—would dissolve the constituent assembly in charge of drafting the constitution. Morsi took this decision without consulting his ministers, and many of his advisors resigned. The decree was criticized by the revolutionary forces as an attack on the independence of the Judiciary. In response to Morsi's constitutional declaration, members of several political parties and youth political movements—many of whom had voted for Morsi against Shafik—formed the National Salvation Front (NSF).[15] Demonstrations erupted in around 17 governorates, protesting against Morsi's constitutional declaration. Instead of calming the protestors, Morsi announced on December 1 a presidential decree that called for a referendum on a highly contentious draft of the new constitution. By end of December, the constitution passed with 64 percent of votes.

As discussed previously, in the first six months of his rule, Morsi antagonized the Judiciary and several political parties and movements, including those who had voted for him in the presidential election. In addition, there were also the *feloul* (remnants) of the old regime who were already against him. Against this background, a handful of young activists founded, in April 2013, the Tamarod (Rebel) movement to remove Morsi.

The movement collected signatures from Egyptians to demonstrate a vote of no confidence against Morsi. By end of June 2013, the Tamarod movement claimed to have 22 million signatures.

As mentioned earlier, this research demonstrates that under Mubarak, there were businessmen who played a role in supporting his authoritarianism for their own economic interests, like in the cases of businessmen in the ruling party, businessmen from the loyal opposition parties, and businessmen who had network relations with the regime. When Morsi concentrated all powers into his hands, businessmen could have supported his authoritarianism—as they supported Mubarak for a number of years—if his rule coincided with their economic interests. Businessmen's support of Morsi could have been possible through their large media outlets, which shaped the public opinion. For example, there are businessmen who invested in the media under Mubarak—including Naguib, the owner of ONTV and a shareholder in *Al-Masry Al-Youm* newspaper, and Ahmed Bahgat, the owner of Dream TV. Other businessmen established their media outlets after the Twenty-Fifth of January Revolution, including Mohamed Abul-Enein's *Sada al Balad* (Echo of the Country), an online newspaper and a news channel with the same name, and Mohamed El Amin, owner of the private channels Al-Nahar and CBC and the newspaper *Al-Watan*.

Instead of co-opting these media moguls, Morsi provoked them. For instance, after three months of his rule, Morsi mentioned the Sawiris family in his 6th of October speech (as mentioned in Chapter 4), saying they owe taxes to the country. A few months later, the finance minister initiated a criminal case against the Sawiris family for alleged tax evasion. This meant that the Sawiris family's business interests did not coincide with those of Morsi's MB regime. It is not surprising, therefore, that Naguib would provide support to the Tamarod movement, as he admitted in an interview, "The Free Egyptians party, the party that I founded, used all its branches across Egypt to (gather) signatures for Tamarod . . . Also the TV station that I own and the newspaper, Al-Masry Al-Youm, were supporting the Tamarod movement with their media . . . It is fair to say I encouraged all the affiliations I have to support the movement"[16]

In other cases, Morsi started his attack on the *feloul*, businessmen who were remnants of Mubarak's regime, before his election as president. As mentioned in Chapter 3, in one of Morsi's speeches during his presidential campaign, he criticized Abul-Enein. Despite Morsi's criticism, Abul-Enein attempted to ingratiate himself with the new regime. For instance, as soon as Morsi won the presidential election, Abul-Enein published paid advertisements in several newspapers to congratulate him. Moreover, Abul-Enein ordered *Sada al Balad* not to criticize the MB. However, Morsi's MB regime seemed unwilling to reconcile with Abul-Enein. This was evident when the MB refused Abul-Enein's proposal to fund an economic conference about Egypt after the revolution. The MB did not want to present Abul-Enein to society with a new image after the collapse of Mubarak's regime.

The failure of Morsi to co-opt the businessmen who had investments in media explains why they led an opposition media campaign against him when they found that their business interests did not coincide with his rule. For instance, since early 2013, the private media spread rumors that Morsi would lease the pyramids and sell the Suez Canal to Qatar. Moreover, talk shows on these private television channels used to invite only anti-Islamist guests to discuss political events without providing balance by inviting the MB to give their perspectives.[17] On the other hand, the MB has also invested in private media by establishing the *Freedom and Justice* (named after their party) daily newspaper. Businessmen affiliated with the MB also established the television channel Misr 25. However, the MB's engagement in the private media failed to compete with the other private media owned by businessmen.[18] This was evident in the ability of the private television channels owned by businessmen to mobilize citizens against the regime. For instance, on the June 23, 2013—a few days before people went to the streets to demonstrate against Morsi on June 30, 2013 (the first anniversary of Morsi's rule)—four ministers decided to resign. They announced their resignation live on the talk shows of private television channels. This also encouraged other government officials and governors to resign. The talk shows discussed that the regime was losing legitimacy as a result of the resignations of a number government officials.[19] In his speech on June 26, 2013, Morsi referred to some of the businessmen who used their private channels against him. For instance, when referring to El Amin, Morsi said, "He's a tax evader—let him pay . . . He unleashes his channel against us."[20] Morsi also referred to Bahgat, saying that he used his channel to attack him to cover up his debts to the banks.[21]

By June 30, it seemed that the private media channels had been one of the reasons that had contributed in convincing the citizens to lose confidence in the regime, and millions went to the street demanding Morsi's removal. On July 3, 2013, the SCAF arrested Morsi and the top MB leaders and suspended the constitution. The head of the Supreme Constitutional Court, Adly Mansour, was appointed as interim president. The minister of defense, General Abdel Fattah El-Sisi, announced on television that the military had no intention of becoming involved in politics but had to remove Morsi because he failed to meet the expectations of citizens.

Under Interim President Adly Mansour from 2013 to 2014

After the ouster of Morsi on June 30, 2013, his supporters held two sit-ins: one in El Nahda Square in Giza and a larger one in Rabaa Al Adawiya Square in Nasr City. Morsi's supporters promised to remain in the two sit-ins until he was reinstated. Three weeks later, during a speech to recent military graduates, Sisi asked Egyptians to hold mass demonstrations to give him permission to confront violence and terrorism. He said, "I'm asking you to show the world . . . If violence is sought, or terrorism is sought, the military and the police are authorized to confront this."[22] Sisi's words suggest that he was asking for authorization to break up the two sit-ins.

By August 14, 2013, the police interfered to disperse both sit-ins, leaving a disagreement over the number of deaths and injuries. While Human Rights Watch reported one thousand people dead, the Egyptian government reported the deaths of only 627.[23] MB supporters retaliated by burning fifty churches; Christians owned schools and businesses across the country.[24]

After the police breakup of the sit-ins, protests by supporters of the ousted President Morsi became frequent. In November 2013, the interim president, Adly Mansour, enacted a new protest law that required the protestors to ask for permission before protesting in the streets.[25] This law has been criticized by the revolutionary youth and human right groups, since it limited the right to protest that was acquired after the Twenty-Fifth of January Revolution.

Under President Abdel Fattah El-Sisi from 2014 to the Present

In March 2014, Sisi resigned from the military and announced that he was running for presidential election. In support of Sisi's decision to run for election, Arab Gulf countries promised to provide aid to help Egypt deal with its economic problems.[26] In May 2014, Saudi Arabia, Kuwait, and the United Arab Emirates pledged $20 billion in financial assistance to Egypt.[27] During his presidential campaign, Sisi stated that he planned to fund national projects through grants from Gulf countries.[28] In June 2014, Sisi won the presidential election with a landslide victory against his only rival, the leftist politician Hamdeen Sabahi. Those who voted for Sisi included the *feloul* of the Mubarak regime, citizens who wanted stability and security at the expense of democracy, and large segments of the Copts.

During his first month in office, Sisi announced an increase in the prices of fuel and electricity in order to reduce energy subsidies by forty billion EGP.[29] It is suggested that the decision to reduce subsidies was a way to regain the confidence of foreign donors and international institutions.[30] But Sisi was not looking only for outside financial assistance; he sought it also at the local level. For instance, during Sisi's presidential campaign, he asked businessmen to donate one hundred billion EGP to finance the national development projects.[31] After his election, Sisi invited fifty businessmen to a meeting in which he managed to collect more than five billion EGP for his newly established public fund, Long Live Egypt. A number of the businessmen who attended the meeting and donated money were affiliated with Mubarak's regime. For example, some of those who made donations were members of the dissolved NDP, like Mohamed Farid Khamis. Others were members of the dissolved NDP but also had investments in media, like Hassan Rateb, owner of the TV channel El Mehwar, and Soliman Amer, owner of the TV channel El Tahrir. Others had investments in the media and had network relations with the Mubarak regime, like Naguib Sawiris, Salah Diab and Mohamed El Amin.[32] This suggests that Sisi's relationships with some businessmen guarantee him funding for his national development projects and also the political support of these businessmen's private media outlets.

But would the donations that Sisi is seeking from the Gulf countries, the international institutions, and the businessmen help meet the demands of the revolutionaries? On January 25, 2011, the revolutionaries went to the streets demanding "bread, freedom, social justice, and dignity." Bread symbolized the basic daily commodities that were becoming difficult for the poor to afford because of high inflation. Sisi's economic liberalization, which reduced energy subsidies, has affected the energy-intensive industries, like cement, fertilizer, iron, and steel, owned by the private sector.[33] But at the same time, the increase in the price of fuel and electricity has consequently increased the cost of food and public transportation. This burden has fallen on the 30 percent of the population who are living below the poverty line.[34]

The passing of the protest law in November 2013 suggests that in terms of freedom, the revolutionaries have not yet met their demands. The collapse of Mubarak's and Morsi's regimes would not have been possible without the protests through which the citizens expressed their grievances. In an attempt to maintain the right to protest, which was obtained after the Twenty-Fifth of January Revolution, prominent young revolutionaries— including Ahmed Maher and Mohamed Adel of the April 6 movement; Ahmed Douma, a human rights activist; and Alaa Abdel Fattah, a well-known blogger—demonstrated against this law. The police quickly arrested them, and they were charged with protesting without seeking permission and were sentenced and fined.[35] On another occasion, on the fourth anniversary of the revolution, a number of activists marched peacefully to

Tahrir Square carrying flowers to commemorate the demonstrators killed during the revolution. One of the peaceful protestors, Shaimaa El Sabbagh, was shot by the police and died.[36] Despite the police denial of firing shots at the protestors, evidence suggests that she was killed by the police.[37]

Social justice could be achieved through a progressive tax system that funds public educational, health, and transportation systems. Upon assuming office, Sisi issued a law amending the tax code to apply a 10 percent tax on stock market proceeds as well as a 5 percent tax on incomes that exceed one million EGP per year.[38] But Sisi's economic policies are less likely to work unless the country is stabilized in terms of security. Since Sisi was elected in June 2014, there has been an escalation of terrorist atrocities committed by different Islamist groups on the Egyptian army and civilian targets all over Egypt.

After four and a half years of the Egyptian revolution, it has not yet achieved its main goals. It is perhaps better at this stage to say that the revolution is still unfinished. It may take a number of years until the revolutionaries fulfill their dreams. At the same time, we should not ignore the small achievements that we have reached until now. Mubarak has been ousted and is under trial with his two sons, Alaa and Gamal. Egyptians have broken the barrier of fear and have now tasted the fruit of freedom. This suggests that they will not accept being ruled again by an authoritarian regime that does not accomplish their political and economic demands.

Notes

Introduction

1. Maye Kassem. 1999. In the Guise of Democracy: Governance in Contemporary Egypt (London: Ithaca Press); Eberhard Kienle. 2001. A Grand Delusion: Democracy and Economic Reform in Egypt (London: I. B. Tauris); Eva Bellin. 2002. Stalled Democracy: Capital, Labor, and the Paradox of State-Sponsored Development (Ithaca, NY: Cornell University Press); Jason Brownlee. 2007. Authoritarianism in an Age of Democratization (Cambridge: Cambridge University Press); Lisa Blaydes. 2011. Elections and Distributive Politics in Mubarak's Egypt (Cambridge: Cambridge University Press); Ellen Lust-Okar. 2004. "Divided They Rule: The Management and Manipulation of Political Opposition," Journal of Democracy 36(2): 139–56.
2. Barrington Moore. 1966. Social Origins of Dictatorship and Democracy (Boston: Beacon); Charles Moraz. 1968. The Triumph of the Middle Class (New York: Anchor); Eric Hobsbawm. 1969. Industry and Empire (Harmondsworth: Penguin).
3. Bellin. 2002.
4. Nazih Ayubi. 1995. Over-Stating the Arab State: Politics and Society in the Middle East (London: I. B. Tauris).
5. Samuel Huntington. 1991. The Third Wave: Democratization in the Late Twentieth Century (Norman: University of Oklahoma Press), p. 67.
6. Ray Bush. 2012. "Marginality or Abjection? The Political Economy of Poverty Production in Egypt," in Marginality and Exclusion in Egypt, ed. Ray Bush and Habib Ayeb (Cairo: American University in Cairo Press), p. 66.
7. Bellin. 2002.
8. Amr Adly. 2009. "Politically-Embedded Cronyism: The Case of Egypt," Business and Politics 11(4): 1–28.
9. Bellin. 2002.
10. Adly. 2009.
11. The only Policies Secretariat meeting that Gamal Mubarak missed since the establishment of the Secretariat in 2002 was in March 2010 when he was accompanying his father in Germany for treatment. Only half of the members of the Secretariat attended this meeting, which suggests how members, including businessmen, were attending these meetings to meet with Gamal and create a personal relationship with him for their own personal benefit

rather than for the benefit of the party. For more information, see *Al-Masry Al-Youm*, March 10, 2010.

12. Ellen Lust-Okar. 2004.
13. Robert Yin. 1984. Case Study Research: Design and Methods (Beverly Hills, CA: Sage), p. 23.

Chapter 1

1. Jane Kinninmont. 2012. "Bread, Dignity and Social Justice: The Political Economy of Egypt's Transition." Chatham House. Briefing Paper. At http://www.chathamhouse.org/sites/default/files/public/Research/Middle%20East/bp0412_kinninmont.pdf, accessed March 20, 2014.
2. Emad Shahin. 2013. "The Egyptian Revolution: The Power of Mass Mobilization and the Spirit of Tahrir Square," in Revolution, Revolt, and Reform in North Africa: The Arab Spring and Beyond, ed. Ricardo Rene Laremont (London: Routledge), p. 56.
3. Ibid.
4. Kinninmont. 2012.
5. Shahin. 2013. p. 56.
6. Mona El-Ghobashy. 2012b. "The Praxis of the Egyptian Revolution," in The Journey to Tahrir: Revolution, Protest and Social Change in Egypt, ed. Jeannie Sowers and Chris Toensing (London: Verso), pp. 23–24.
7. Shahin. 2013. p. 58.
8. Abdel-Fattah Mady. 2013. "Popular Discontent, Revolution, and Democratization in Egypt in a Globalizing World," Indiana Journal of Global Legal Studies 20(1), pp. 314–15.
9. Shahin. 2013. p. 54.
10. Hossam el-Hamalawy. 2011. "Jan 25: The Workers, Middle Class, Military Junta and the Permanent Revolution." Arabawy blog, February 12. At http://www.arabawy.org/2011/02/12/permanent-revolution, accessed January 10, 2012.
11. Peter Evans. 1989. "Predatory, Developmental, and Other Apparatuses: A Comparative Political Economy Perspective on the Third World State," Sociological Forum 4(4): 562.
12. Eberhard Kienle. 2001. A Grand Delusion: Democracy and Economic Reform in Egypt (London: I. B. Tauris).
13. Amr Adly. 2009. "Politically-Embedded Cronyism: The Case of Egypt," Business and Politics 11(4): 1–28.
14. Eva Bellin. 2002. Stalled Democracy: Capital, Labor, and the Paradox of State-Sponsored Development (Ithaca, NY: Cornell University Press).
15. Maye Kassem. 1999. In the Guise of Democracy: Governance in Contemporary Egypt (London: Ithaca Press).
16. Jason Brownlee. 2007. Authoritarianism in an Age of Democratization (Cambridge: Cambridge University Press).

17. Lisa Blaydes. 2011. Elections and Distributive Politics in Mubarak's Egypt (Cambridge: Cambridge University Press).
18. John Sfakianakis. 2004. "The Whales of the Nile: Networks, Businessmen, and Bureaucrats during the Era of Privatization in Egypt," in Networks of Privilege in the Middle East: The Politics of Economic Reform Revisited, ed. Steven Heydemann (New York: Palgrave Macmillan), pp. 77–100.
19. Nazih Ayubi. 1995. Over-Stating the Arab State: Politics and Society in the Middle East (London: I. B. Tauris).
20. Ray Bush. 2007. "Politics, Power and Poverty: Twenty Years of Agriculture Reform and Market Liberalization in Egypt," Third World Quarterly 28(8): 1601.
21. Nadia Farah. 2009. Egypt's Political Economy: Power Relations in Development (Cairo: American University in Cairo Press), p. 35.
22. Ibid.
23. Ray Bush. 2007. p. 1603.
24. Nadia Farah. 2009. p. 36.
25. Ray Bush. 2009. "The Land and the People," in Egypt the Moment of Change, ed. Rabab El-Mahdi and Philip Marfleet (London: Zed Books), p. 55.
26. Farah. 2009. p. 52.
27. Evans. 1989.
28. Samer Soliman. 2011. The Autumn of Dictatorship: Fiscal Crises and Political Change in Egypt under Mubarak (Stanford, CA: Stanford University Press), p. 38.
29. Cited in Moheb Zaki. 1999. Egyptian Business Elites: Their Visions and Investment Behavior (Cairo: Konrad Adenauer Stiftung and the Arab Center for Development and Future Research), p. 96.
30. Cited in Yahya Sadwoski. 1991. Businessmen and Bureaucrats in the Development of Egyptian Agriculture (Washington, DC: Brookings Institution), p. 253.
31. Hans Lofgren. 1993. "Economic Policy in Egypt: Breakdown in Reform Resistance," International Journal of Middle East Studies 25(3): 411.
32. Farah. 2009. p. 41.
33. Lofgren. 1993. p. 411.
34. Farah. 2009. pp. 41–42.
35. Mahmud A. Faksh. 1992. "Egypt and the Gulf Crisis: The Role of Leadership under Mubarak," Journal of Third World Studies 9(1): 50–51.
36. Khalid Ikram. 2006. The Egyptian Economy 1952–2000 (London: Routledge Press), p. 61.
37. Ibid.
38. Egypt's economic reform could be identified in three generations. In the first generation (1991–98), the economy was stabilized, and one-third of the state-owned enterprises were privatized. The second generation of reform (1998–2004) focused on trade and institutional measures. The third generation of reform (2004–present) witnessed the accelerated implementation of liberal economic policies and the accelerated pace of privatization.

For more information, see Sufyan Alissa. 2007. "The Political Economy of Reform in Egypt: Understanding the Role of Institutions." The Carnegie Papers. Carnegie Endowment for International Peace. pp. 4–5. At http://carnegieendowment.org/files/cmec5_alissa_egypt_final.pdf, accessed January 24, 2011.

39. Cited in Raymond Hinnebush. 1993. "The Politics of Economic Reform in Egypt," Third World Quarterly 14(1): 164.
40. Ray Bush. 2009. "The Land and the People," in Egypt: The Moment of Change, ed. Rabab El-Mahdi and Philip Marfleet (London: Zed Books), p. 58.
41. Ibid.
42. Joel Beinin and Hossam el-Hamalawy. 2007. "Textile Workers Confront the New Economic Order." Middle East Report Online, March 25. At http://www.merip.org/mero/mero032507, accessed June 10, 2012.
43. Ayubi. 1995. p. 407.
44. Kienle. 2001. p. 5.
45. Stephen King. 2009. The New Authoritarianism in the Middle East and North Africa (Bloomington: Indiana University Press), pp. 4–5.
46. Adly. 2009. pp. 14–15.
47. Bellin. 2002. p. 149.
48. Ibid. pp. 162–66.
49. Ziya Onis and Umut Turem. 2002. "Entrepreneurs, Democracy and Citizenship in Turkey," Comparative Politics 34(4): 439–56.
50. Michael Shafer. 1997. "The Political Economy of Sectors and Sectoral Change: Korea Then and Now," in Business and the State in Developing Countries, ed. Sylvia Maxfield and Ben Ross Schneider (Ithaca, NY: Cornell University Press), p. 112.
51. Jon Moran. 1999. "Patterns of Corruption and Development in East Asia," Third World Quarterly 20(3): 571.
52. Beatrice Hibou. 2004. "Fiscal Trajectories in Morocco and Tunisia," in Networks of Privilege in the Middle East: The Politics of Economic Reform Revisited, ed. Steven Heydemann (New York: Palgrave Macmillan), p. 215.
53. Hazem Beblawi. 1987. "The Rentier State in the Arab World," Arab Studies Quarterly 9(4): 383–98; Michael Ross. 2001. "Does Oil Hinder Democracy," World Politics 53(3): 326–61.
54. Adam Hanieh. 2011. Capitalism and Class in the Gulf Arab States (New York: Palgrave Macmillan), pp. 66–67.
55. Beblawi. 1987. p. 388.
56. Ross. 2001. p. 332.
57. Beblawi. 1987. p. 387.
58. Soliman. 2011. p. 141.
59. Margaret Levi. 1988. Of Rule and Revenue (Berkeley: University of California Press).
60. Soliman. 2011. p. 113–14.
61. Ibid. p. 127.

62. Bellin. 2002.
63. Beblawi. 1987.
64. Soliman. 2011.
65. Moran. 1999.
66. Hibou. 2004.
67. Carl H. Lande. 1977. "Introduction: The Dyadic Basis of Clientelism" in Friends, Followers and Faction: A Reader in Political Clientelism, ed. Steffen W. Schmidt, James C. Scott, Carle Lande and Laura Guasti (Berkley: University of California Press), p. xx.
68. James C. Scott. 1972. "Patron-Client Politics and Political Change in Southeast Asia," The American Political Science Review 66(1): 92.
69. Ibid. p. 93.
70. Jonathan Fox. 1994. "The Difficult Transition from Clientelism to Citizenship: Lessons from Mexico," World Politics 46(2): 153.
71. Samuel Huntington. 1991. The Third Wave: Democratization in the Late Twentieth Century (Norman: University of Oklahoma Press), pp. 178–79.
72. Brownlee. 2007. p. 6.
73. Juan Linz. 1964. "An Authoritarian Regime Spain," in Cleavages, Ideologies and Party Systems: Contribution to Comparative Political Sociology, ed. Erik Allardt and Yrjo Littunen (Helsinki: Transactions of the Westermarck Society), p. 297.
74. Huntington. 1991. pp. 174–75.
75. Blaydes. 2011. p. 54.
76. Kassem. 1999. p. 1.
77. Jennifer Gandhi and Adam Przeworski. 2006. "Cooperation, Cooptation and Rebellion under Dictatorships," Economics and Politics 18(1): 14.
78. Ellen Lust-Okar. 2009. "Democratization by Elections? Competitive Clientelism in the Middle East," Journal of Democracy 20(3): 124.
79. Brownlee. 2007. p. 156.
80. Philippe Schmitter. 1974. "Still the Century of Corporatism?," The Review of Politics 36(1): 85–131.
81. Robert Bianchi. 1990. "Interest Groups and Politics in Mubarak's Egypt," in The Political Economy of Contemporary Egypt, ed. Ibrahim M. Oweiss (Washington, DC: Center for Contemporary Arab Studies George Town University), p. 214.
82. Ibid. p. 215.
83. Ninette Fahmy. 2002. The Politics of Egypt: State-Society Relationship (London: Routledge), p. 105.
84. Sfakianakis. 2004. p. 84.
85. Jeffrey Winters. 2012. Oligarchy (Cambridge: Cambridge University Press), pp. 158–61.
86. Marleen Dieleman. 2007. The Rhythm of Strategy: A Corporate Biography of the Salim Group of Indonesia (Amsterdam: Amsterdam University Press), pp. 46–47.
87. Winters. 2012. p. 161.

88. Moran. 1999. p. 572.
89. Bassam Haddad. 2012. Business Networks in Syria: The Political Economy of Authoritarian Resilience (Stanford, CA: Stanford University Press), pp. 43–44.
90. Ibid. p. 87.
91. Gandhi and Przeworski. 2006. p. 22.
92. Fox. 1994. pp. 157–58.
93. Paul Klebnikov. 2001. Godfather of the Kremlin: The Decline of Russia in the Age of Gangster Capitalism (Orlando: Harcourt), p. 212.
94. Yasmeen Mohiuddin. 2007. "Boris Berezovsky: Russia's First Billionaire and Political Maverick Still Has It in for Vladimir Putin," International Journal 62(3): 683.
95. Peter Rutland. 2009. "The Oligarchs and Economic Development," in After Putin's Russia: Past Imperfect, Future Uncertain, ed. Stephen Wegren and Dale Herspring (Lanham: Rowman and Littlefield), pp. 163–64.
96. The Telegraph, March 24, 2013.
97. Mohiuddin. 2007. p. 684.
98. Karl Fields. 1997. "Strong States and Business Organization in Korea and Taiwan" in Business and the State in Developing Countries, ed. Sylvia Maxfield and Ben Ross Schneider (Ithaca, NY: Cornell University Press), p. 128.
99. Shafer. 1997. p. 112.
100. Eva Bellin. 2000. Contingent Democrats: Industrialists, Labor and Democratization in Late-Developing Countries. World Politics 52(2): 192.
101. Ibid. p. 191.
102. Scott. 1972. p. 95.
103. Ellen Lust-Okar. 2004. "Divided They Rule: The Management and Manipulation of Political Opposition," Journal of Democracy 36(2): 173.
104. Sydney Tarrow. 1998. Power in Movement: Social Movement and Contentious Politics (Cambridge: Cambridge University Press), pp. 149–50.
105. Lust-Okar. 2004. p. 162.
106. Dina Shehata. 2010. Islamists and Secularists in Egypt: Opposition, Conflict, and Cooperation (London: Routledge), pp. 2–3.
107. Fahmy. 2002. p. 171.
108. Ibid.
109. Kienle. 2001.
110. King. 2009.
111. Adly. 2009.
112. Bellin. 2002.
113. Kassem. 1999.
114. Blaydes. 2011.
115. Brownlee. 2007.
116. Sfakianakis. 2004.
117. Ibid.
118. Lust-Okar. 2004.

Chapter 2

1. Kenneth Cuno. 1980. "The Origins of Private Ownership of Land in Egypt: A Reappraisal," International Journal of Middle East Studies 12(3): 262; Saad Eddin Ibrahim. 2002. Egypt, Islam and Democracy (Cairo: American University in Cairo Press), p. 111.
2. Ibrahim. 2002. pp. 111–12.
3. Yahya Sadwoski. 1991. Businessmen and Bureaucrats in the development of Egyptian Agriculture (Washington, DC: Brookings Institution), pp. 96–97.
4. Samia Saeid Imam. 1986. Who Owns Egypt? An Analytical Study about the Social Origin of the Open-Door Economic Elite in Egyptian Society from 1974 to 1980 (in Arabic; Cairo: Dar El Mostakabal El Arabi), p. 38.
5. Ibrahim. 2002. p. 114.
6. Robert Tignor. 1980. "Dependency Theory and Egyptian Capitalism, 1920–1950," African Economic History 9: 108–9.
7. Robert Tignor. 1987. "British Textile Companies and the Egyptian Economy," Business and Economic History 16: 61.
8. Tignor. 1980. pp. 110–14.
9. Ibrahim. 2002. p. 116.
10. Nadia Farah. 2009. Egypt's Political Economy: Power Relations in Development (Cairo: American University in Cairo Press), pp. 30–31.
11. Ibid. p. 32.
12. Ibrahim. 2002. pp. 121–22.
13. Moheb Zaki. 1999. Egyptian Business Elites: Their Visions and Investment Behavior (Cairo: Konrad Adenauer Stiftung and the Arab Center for Development and Future Research), p. 60.
14. Malak Zaalouk. 1989. Power, Class and Foreign Capital in Egypt: The Rise of the New Bourgeoisie (London: Zed Books), p. 25.
15. Ibid. pp. 62–63.
16. Ibid. p. 34.
17. Anowar Abdel Malek. 1968. Egypt Military Society (New York: Random House), p. 4.
18. Cited in Zaalouk. 1989. p. 63.
19. Ibid.
20. Ibid. p. 35.
21. Zaki. 1999. p. 66.
22. Zaalouk. 1989. p. 35.
23. Zaki. 1999. p. 74.
24. Zaalouk. 1989. p. 42.
25. Malak Zaalouk (1989) called the new class that emerged in the 1960s "the state bourgeoisie." It comprises the upper stratum of the bureaucratic and managerial elites, high-ranking civil servants, army officers and directors, and managers of public-sector companies. Samia Saeid Imam (1986) used the term bureaucratic bourgeoisie to refer to the elements that held positions

in the state apparatus or the public sector and benefited from the social and economic changes during the 1960s.

26. Zaalouk. 1989. pp. 40–41.
27. Imam. 1986. p. 97.
28. Raymond Baker. 1990. Sadat and After: Struggle for Egypt's Political Soul (Cambridge, MA: Harvard University Press), p. 19.
29. Ibid. pp. 20–21.
30. John Waterbury. 1983. The Egypt of Nasser and Sadat: The Political Economy of Two Regimes (New Jersey: Princeton University Press), p. 182.
31. Yahya Sadwoski. 1991. Businessmen and Bureaucrats in the Development of Egyptian Agriculture (Washington, DC: Brookings Institution), p. 112.
32. Maisa El Gamal. 1992. "Egypt's Ministerial Elite, 1971–1981" (PhD dissertation, Birkbeck College, University of London), p. 196.
33. Waterbury. 1983. p. 182.
34. Ibid. p. 210.
35. Farah. 2009. p. 37.
36. Zaki. 1999. p. 73.
37. Cited in Waterbury. 1983. pp. 127–28.
38. Farah. 2009. p. 38.
39. Marvin G Weinbaum. 1985. "Egypt's Infitah and the Politics of US Economic Assistance," Middle Eastern Studies 21(2): 210–14.
40. Ibid. p. 214.
41. Steven Cook. 2005. "The Right Way to Promote Arab Reform," Foreign Affairs 84(2): 95.
42. Waterbury. 1983. p. 128.
43. Raymond Hinnebush. 1985. Egyptian Politics under Sadat: The Post-Populist Development of an Authoritarian-Modernizing State (Cambridge: Cambridge University Press), pp. 272–73.
44. Imam. 1986. p. 138.
45. Zaalouk. 1989. pp. 119–20.
46. Ibid. pp. 121–22.
47. Other parasitic activities that the Infitah bourgeoisie engaged in included shipping operations, contracting, real estate speculation, trade in foreign goods, and brokerage.
48. Imam. 1986. p. 131.
49. Ibid. pp. 137–38.
50. Zaalouk. 1989. p. 132.
51. Imam. 1986. p. 141.
52. Waterbury. 1983. p. 152.
53. Zaalouk. 1989. pp. 6–9.
54. Ibid. p. 125.
55. Zaki. 1999. pp. 85–86.
56. Marie-Christine Aulas. 1982. "Sadat's Egypt: A Balance Sheet," Middle East Report 107: 14.
57. Imam. 1986. p. 132.

58. El-Gamal. 1992. p. 197.
59. Waterbury. 1983. p. 183.
60. Clement Henry Moore. 1994. Images of Development: Egyptian Engineers in Search of Industry (Cairo: American University in Cairo Press), p. 124.
61. Hinnebush. 1985. pp. 273–74.
62. Ibid. p. 280.
63. Samer Soliman. 2011. The Autumn of Dictatorship: Fiscal Crises and Political Change in Egypt under Mubarak (Stanford, CA: Stanford University Press), p. 38.
64. Maye Kassem. 1999. In the Guise of Democracy: Governance in Contemporary Egypt (London: Ithaca Press), p. 78.
65. Ibid.
66. Nazih Ayubi. 1991. Political Islam: Religion and Politics in the Arab World (London: Routledge), p. 191.
67. Ashraf El Saad, interview by author, London, October 6, 2009.
68. Robert Springborg. 1989. Mubarak's Egypt: Fragmentation of the Political Order (Boulder: Westview), p. 47.
69. Sami Zubaida. 1990. "The Politics of the Islamic Investment Companies in Egypt," British Journal of Middle Eastern Studies 17(2): 153.
70. Ashraf El Saad, interview by author, London, October 6, 2009.
71. Zubaida. 1990. p. 152.
72. Springborg. 1989. pp. 47–48.
73. Ayubi. 1991. p. 190.
74. Springborg. 1989. p. 53.
75. Ashraf El Saad, interview by author, London, October 6, 2009.
76. Springborg. 1989. p. 57.
77. Ibid. p. 52.
78. Ashraf El Saad, interview by author, London, October 6, 2009.
79. Ayubi. 1991. p. 194.
80. Denis Sullivan. 1994. Private Voluntary Organizations in Egypt: Islamic Development, Private Initiative and State Control (Gainesville: University Press of Florida), pp. 63–64.
81. Springborg. 1989. pp. 81–82.
82. Ibid. p. 82.
83. Robert Bianchi. 1989. Unruly Corporatism: Associational Life in Twentieth-Century Egypt (Oxford: Oxford University Press), p. 162.
84. Ibid. p. 165.
85. Eberhard Kienle. 2001. A Grand Delusion: Democracy and Economic Reform in Egypt (London: I. B. Tauris), p. 36.
86. Ibid.
87. Nahed Ezz-El Din. 2003. The Workers and the Businessmen: The Transformation of Political Opportunities in Egypt (in Arabic; Cairo: El Ahram Center for Political and Strategic Studies), p. 26.
88. Maye Kassem. 2002. "Information and Production of Knowledge or Lobbying? Businessmen's Association, Federation of Labor Unions, and the

162 NOTES

Ministry of Manpower," in Institutional Reform and Economic Development in Egypt, ed. Noha El-Mikawy and Heba Handoussa (Cairo: American University in Cairo Press), p. 69.
89. Adel Gazarin, interview by author, Cairo, February 7, 2010.
90. Ninette Fahmy. 2002. The Politics of Egypt: State-Society Relationship (London: Routledge), pp. 173–74.
91. American Chamber of Commerce in Egypt. 2014. At http://www.amcham.org.eg/about_us/objdefault.asp, accessed March 27, 2014.
92. Springborg. 1989. p. 110.
93. Jadaliyya. December 23, 2011. At http://www.jadaliyya.com/pages/index/3732/the-army-and-the-economy-in-egypt, accessed March 26, 2014.
94. Springborg. 1989. p. 113.
95. Jadaliyya. December 23, 2011. At http://www.jadaliyya.com/pages/index/3732/the-army-and-the-economy-in-egypt, accessed March 26, 2014.
96. Springborg. 1989. p. 99.
97. Atef Said. 2008. "The Role of the Judges Club in Enhancing the Independence of the Judiciary and Spurring Political Reform," in Judges and Political Reform in Egypt, ed. Nathalie Bernard-Maugiran (Cairo: American University in Cairo Press), pp. 120–22.
98. Nathan J. Brown. 2012. "Egypt's Judges in a Revolutionary Age." The Carnegie Papers. Carnegie Endowment for International Peace. p. 4. At http://carnegieendowment.org/2012/02/22/egypt-s-judges-in-revolutionary-age/9sri, accessed March 27, 2014.
99. Mohamed Kamel, interview by author, Cairo, June 10, 2010.
100. Soliman. 2011. p. 44.
101. Hans Lofgren. 1993. "Economic Policy in Egypt: Breakdown in Reform Resistance," International Journal of Middle East Studies 25(3): 408.
102. Soliman. 2011. p. 44.
103. Gouda Abdel-Khalek and Karima Korayem. 2001. "Fiscal Policy Measures in Egypt: Public Debt and Food Subsidy," Cairo Papers in Social Science 23(1): 10.

Chapter 3

1. Eggers Andrew and Jens Hainmueller. 2009. "MPs for Sale? Returns to Office in Postwar British Politics," American Political Science Review 103(4): 1–21.
2. Maria Faccio. 2006. "Politically Connected Firms," American Economic Review 96(1): 369–86.
3. Maye Kassem. 1999. In the Guise of Democracy: Governance in Contemporary Egypt (London: Ithaca Press).
4. Lisa Blaydes. 2011. Elections and Distributive Politics in Mubarak's Egypt (Cambridge: Cambridge University Press).
5. Jason Brownlee. 2007. Authoritarianism in an Age of Democratization (Cambridge: Cambridge University Press).

6. Hazem Kandil. 2012. Soldiers, Spies and Statesmen: Egypt's Road to Revolt (London: Verso), p. 211.

7. Unless otherwise specified, information provided in this section is from intensive interviews by the author with Ibrahim Kamel on June 16, 23, and 27, 2010.

8. Kassem. 1999. p. 75.

9. Ibid. p. 87.

10. Cited in Kassem. 1999. p. 86.

11. This information is from a letter sent from Ibrahim Kamel to Mrs. Pola Hafez, the director of the legal department at Misr Bank, dated February 6, 2005.

12. This information is from a letter sent from Ibrahim Kamel to Dr. Mohamed Barakat, chairman of the board of trustees at Misr Bank, dated August 28, 2004.

13. More information about the irregularities at Cairo Bank, and how the loans were based on political decisions, will be discussed later in the section on loan MPs and in the case of Ramy Lakah.

14. All articles are quoted from the 1971 Egyptian constitution. 1999. The General Organization for Government Printing Offices.

15. Mona El-Ghobashy. 2012a. "The Dynamics of Elections under Mubarak," in The Journey to Tahrir: Revolution, Protest and Social Change in Egypt, ed. Jeannie Sowers and Chris Toensing (London: Verso), p. 138.

16. Kamel confessed in the interview that his wealth is based abroad, and he has no properties in his name in Egypt. The only few properties he has in Egypt are in the names of his wife and his son.

17. Other business tycoons were appointed to the board of the FGF—for example, Moataz El Alfi, Galal El Zorba, and Rashid Mohamed Rashid.

18. Mohamed Fahmy Menza. 2013. Patronage Politics in Egypt: The National Democratic Party and the Muslim Brotherhood in Cairo (London: Routledge), p. 108.

19. Ibid.

20. *Rose Al-Youssef,* June 26, 2008.

21. In Egypt, there are 19 companies working in the steel and iron industry. Two of them are owned by the public sector: the Egyptian Iron and Steel company in Helwan, established in 1955, and the Alexandria National Iron and Steel Company, Al Dekheila, established in 1982. The rest of the companies are owned by the private sector and include Kouta Steel Group, Suez Steel, Beshai Steel, Aswan for Iron, and the Arab Steel Factory, which account for around 26 percent of the market.

22. Shares of the company are owned by different banks and companies, which include the Alexandria Bank, the Arab Investment Company, Misr Insurance Companies, Misr Bank, National Bank, the Egyptian General Petroleum Corporation, Cairo Bank, the African Bank for Development, the Japanese Group, the International Finance Corporation, and so on.

23. Abu El Ezz El Hariry. 2002. Interpellation submitted to the People's Assembly about the monopoly of Ahmed Ezz to the Steel Industry.

24. Ibid. A copy of this letter has been obtained from opposition parliamentarian Abu El Ezz El Hariry. The letter was included among the documents that El Hariry submitted in his interpellation.

25. Abu El Ezz El Hariry, interview by author, Cairo, April 24, 2010.

26. Abu El Ezz El Hariry. 2002. Interpellation submitted to the People's Assembly about the monopoly of Ahmed Ezz to the Steel Industry.

27. It is worth mentioning that the selling of Al Dekheila was not part of the privatization program that was introduced by the government in the early 1990s. In other words, Al Dekheila was not listed among the companies to be privatized; however, as Abu El Ezz El Hariry commented on Ezz's acquisition of Al Dekheila, "Al Dekheila was neither privatized nor sold; it was stolen by Ezz." Abu El Ezz El Hariry, interview by author, Cairo, April 24, 2010.

28. Abu El Ezz El Hariry, interview by author, Cairo, April 24, 2010.

29. This information is available in a letter sent to the minister of economy by one of the prominent steel producers, Gamil Beshai. The letter is dated June 9, 2001. Mr. Beshai provided me with a copy of the letter.

30. *Al-Gomhuriya*, March 30, 2000.

31. *Akhbar Al-Youm*, June 16, 2001; cited in *Al-Wafd*, June 30, 2001.

32. *Al-Masry Al-Youm*, May 24, 2008.

33. This point about the appointment of the prosecutor general by the president of the republic will be discussed later in the case of Ramy Lakah.

34. Abdalla Shehata, interview by author, Cairo, May 15, 2010.

35. US Department of Justice. 2008. Report of the Attorney General to the Congress of the United States on the Administration of the Foreign Agents Registration Act. At http://www.fara.gov/reports/June30-2008.pdf, accessed August 7, 2011.

36. Joshua Stacher. 2012. Adaptable Autocrats: Regime Power in Egypt and Syria (Cairo: American University in Cairo Press), p. 106.

37. Abdalla Shehata, interview by author, Cairo, May 15, 2010.

38. Eberhard Kinele. 2001. A Grand Delusion: Democracy and Economic Reform in Egypt (London: I. B. Tauris), p. 59.

39. Kandil. 2012. p. 165.

40. Safinaz El Tarouty. 2004. "Institutionalization and Reform: The Case of the National Democratic Party in Egypt" (master's thesis, American University in Cairo), p. 38.

41. Mohamed Kamel, interview by author, Cairo, June 10, 2010.

42. Samer Soliman. 2011. The Autumn of Dictatorship: Fiscal Crises and Political Change in Egypt under Mubarak (Stanford, CA: Stanford University Press), pp. 146–47.

43. For more information about empirical figures on the monopolistic practices of Ezz, see Abdel Khalek Farouk. 2011. The Economics of Corruption in Egypt (in Arabic; Cairo: El Sherouk El Dawaliya).

44. Zeinab Abdalla. 2009. "Steel Market in Egypt: A Case of Power Abuse?" (Paper presented at the Middle East Studies Association, Boston).

45. *Al-Masry Al-Youm*, June 20, 2008.

46. Ibid.

47. *Al-Masry Al-Youm*, March 25, 2011.

48. Cited in Stacher. 2012. pp. 8–9.

49. *Ahram Online*, August 7, 2014. At http://english.ahram.org.eg/NewsContent/3/12/107956/Business/Economy/Mubarakera-Egyptian-steel-tycoon-Ahmed-Ezz-release.aspx, accessed September 8, 2014.

50. Khalid Ikram. 2006. The Egyptian Economy 1952–2000 (London: Routledge), p. 182; Stephan Roll. 2010. "Finance Matters! The Influence of Financial Sector Reforms on the Development of Entrepreneurial Elite in Egypt," Mediterranean Politics 15(3): 352.

51. *Al-Masry Al-Youm*, July 29, 2007.

52. *Al-Ahram Weekly*, June 7–13, 2001.

53. Ninette Fahmy. 2007. "Closing Up the Door: The Egyptian State and the Politico-Economic Entrepreneur: The Case of Nuwwab al-Qurud—Loans MPS," *L'Egypte Contemporaine* 485: 21–22; *Al-Mosawer*, May 11, 2007.

54. Osama El Karam. 1997. The Pretty Woman of the Bank and the Minister: How to Steal One Billion from the Banks (in Arabic; Cairo: Center for Arab Civilization), p. 17.

55. Tawfik Abdo Ismail is a businessman and was a former minister in two cabinets during the Nasser and Sadat regimes.

56. El Karam. 1997. pp. 17–18.

57. Ibid. p. 146.

58. These banks are Al Nile Bank, Al Dakahlia Bank, Al Mohandess Bank, Crédit Lyonnais, Commercial Alexandria Bank, Cairo Bank, Feisal Bank, Cairo-Barclays Bank.

59. Abdel Khalek Farouk. 2006. The Corruption in Egypt (in Arabic; Cairo: El Arabi), p. 50.

60. According to Article 99 of the 1971 constitution, "Except in cases of flagrante delicto, no member of the People's Assembly shall be subject to a criminal prosecution without the permission of the Assembly. If the Assembly is not in session, the permission of the Speaker of the Assembly must be taken. The Assembly must be notified of the measures taken in its first subsequent session."

61. Abdel Khalek Farouk. 2006. p. 49.

62. Fahmy. 2007. p. 32.

63. Ruling of the Supreme Security Court. July 31, 2002. The Case of Loan MPs.

64. *Al-Mosawer*, May 11, 2007.

65. Fahmy. 2007. pp. 34–35.

66. The amendment of this law enabled similar cases to reconcile with the banks in the future.

67. Fahmy. 2007. p. 35.

68. *Al-Masry Al-Youm*, January 30, 2005.

69. Ahmed El Baradei, interview by author, Cairo, May 25, 2010.
70. Hassan Hussein, interview by author, Cairo, June 16, 2010.
71. Ahmed El Baradei, interview by author, Cairo, May 25, 2010.
72. Hassan Hussein, interview by author, Cairo, June 16, 2010.
73. For instance, several cases of reconciliation proved that the banks got only half of the debts from businessmen. Money was paid back through installments over a number of years. For more information, see *Al-Destour*, May 13, 2009.
74. Peter Evans. 1989. "Predatory, Developmental, and Other Apparatuses: A Comparative Political Economy Perspective on the Third World State," Sociological Forum 4(4): 561–87.
75. Stephan Roll. 2010. p. 363.
76. Hassan Hussein, interview by author, Cairo, June 16, 2010.
77. Ayman Nour, interview by author, Cairo, December 17, 2009.
78. Ahmed El Baradei, interview by author, Cairo, May 25, 2010. For instance, it was common for the former head of Cairo Bank, Mohamed Abu El Fatah, during the 1990s to get political orders by phone from one of the ministers to give loans to businessmen without guarantees. Abu El Fatah never rejected any of the minister's orders because he knew that these businessmen were close to the regime. In return, this minister helped Abu El Fatah renew his contract in the bank four consecutive times after he reached the age of retirement. For more information, see *Al Ahrar*, February 13, 2003.
79. Egyptian Organization for Human Rights. "An Appeal to the President of the Republic: Those Responsible for the Events of Al-Kosheh Must Pay the Price." At http://www.derechos.org/human-rights/mena/eohr/price.html, accessed March 27, 2014.
80. Nicola Pratt. 2000/2001. "Maintaining the Moral Economy: Egyptian State-Labor Relations in an Era of Economic Liberalization," Arabic Studies Journal 8(2)/9(1): 81–84.
81. Ramy Lakah, interview by author, London, October 16, 2010.
82. Adel Hamouda. 2005. Those Who Fled with Billions from Egypt and the Puzzle of Ramy Lakah and Mahmoud Whaba: The Secret Files of the Famous Businessmen Who Fled the Country (in Arabic; Cairo: Dar El Forsan), p. 115.
83. *Al-Ahram Weekly*, March 30–April 5, 2000.
84. Hamouda. 2005. p. 115.
85. Ramy Lakah, interview by author, London, October 16, 2010.
86. *Al-Akhbar*, January 10, 2003; *Al-Masry Al-Youm*, December 8, 2008.
87. Mohamed Kamel, interview by author, Cairo, June 10, 2010.
88. Abdallah Khalil. 2008. "The General Prosecutor between the Judicial and Executive Authorities," in Judges and Political Reform in Egypt, ed. Nathalie Bernard-Maugiran (Cairo: American University in Cairo Press), pp. 63–64.
89. Ahmed El Baradei, interview by author, Cairo, May 25, 2010. For more information about Lakah's reconciliation with the banks, see *Al-Masry Al-Youm*, March 13, 2010; *Al-Masry Al-Youm*, March 14, 2010.

90. *Al-Masry Al-Youm*, March 14, 2010.
91. Anwar Esmat El Sadat, interview by author, Cairo, July 26, 2010.
92. *Al-Ahram Weekly*, November 24–30, 2011.
93. Anwar Esmat El Sadat, interview by author, Cairo, July 26, 2010. It is worth mentioning that NDP members are not allowed to present interpellations.
94. Ibid.
95. *Al-Ahram Weekly*, April 20–26, 2006.
96. *Al-Ahram Weekly*, March 23–29, 2006.
97. Anwar Esmat El Sadat, interview by author, Cairo, July 26, 2010.
98. Anwar Esmat El Sadat. 2006. Interpellation submitted to the People's Assembly about the monopolization of the Red Sea ports. When Sadat submitted this interpellation to parliament, he did not mention Omar Tantawi's name; otherwise, the steering office of the parliament would have refused to send the interpellation for discussion in parliament. But during the discussion of the interpellation, El Sadat mentioned Tantawi's name.
99. Anwar Esmat El Sadat, interview by author, Cairo, July 26, 2010.
100. Ibid.
101. Ibid.
102. Ibid.
103. Lisa Blaydes. 2006. "Electoral Budget Cycles under Authoritarianism: Economic Opportunism in Mubarak's Egypt" (Paper presented at the annual meeting of the Midwest Political Association, Chicago).
104. Other NDP parliamentary businessmen have been involved in corruption in buying state-owned lands—for example, Ahmed Ezz, Hisham Talaat Moustafa, and Abdel Wahab Kouta.
105. Eric Gobe. 1999. Les Hommes D'affaires Egyptiens: Démocratisation et Secteur Privé dans l'Egypte de L'infitah (Paris: Karthala), p. 81.
106. According to the 1971 constitution, in the Consultative Assembly, one-third of the seats are filled by presidential appointment. It is common for the president to appoint a number of businessmen in the seats filled by appointment. But in the People's Assembly, there are 454 seats. Ten seats are filled by appointment and the rest by election. In the ten seats filled by appointment, it is common for the president to appoint intellectuals, women, and Copts rather than businessmen. The fact that Mubarak appointed businessman Mohamed Abul-Enein suggests that this was a special favor to him.
107. Gamal Zahran. 2009. Interpellation submitted to the People's Assembly about the corruption in selling state-owned lands.
108. *Al-Ahram Daily*, March 30, 2005; *Al-Ahram Daily*, April 12, 2001.
109. Mohamed Kamel, interview by author, Cairo, June 10, 2010.
110. *Ahram Online*, April 19, 2011. At http://english.ahram.org.eg/NewsContent/1/64/10293/Egypt/Politics-/Bosses,-enforcers-and-thugs-in-Egypts-Battle-of-th.aspx, accessed March 8, 2012.
111. Ibid. In October 2012, the criminal court acquitted the 24 defendants in the Battle of the Camel, including Abul-Enein. The court found the evidence insufficient to convict the accused. However, the activists who played a role

in the protests of the Twenty-Fifth of January Revolution blamed the then prosecutor general, Mahmoud Abdel Meguid, who is considered reminiscent of the old regime, for the weak evidence presented by the prosecution in the case. In May 2013, the court of cassation rejected the prosecution appeal to the case of the Battle of the Camel. It is argued that the refusal was due to the failure of the prosecution to submit the appeal in time.

112. *Al-Youm Al-Sabae*, December 11, 2011.
113. *Al-Masry Al-Youm*, May 11, 2012; *Akhbarek.net*, May 11, 2012. At http://www.akhbarak.net/ncws/2012/05/11/872530/articles/8111446, accessed July 2, 2014.
114. Cited in Al-*Wafd*, June 29, 2012.
115. *Al-Gornal.net*, September 8, 2012. At http://elgornal.net/news/news.aspx?id=944452, accessed August 8, 2014.
116. *Al-Youm Al-Sabae*, November 20, 2012; *Elgornal.net*, September 8, 2012. At http://elgornal.net/news/news.aspx?id=944452, accessed August 8, 2014.
117. *Al-Wafd*, September 2, 2012.
118. *Al-Youm Al-Sabae*, March 13, 2014.
119. *Al-Sherouk*, June 30, 2014.
120. *Rose Al-Youssef Weekly Magazine*, June 21, 2014.
121. *Al-Masry Al-Youm*, June 25, 2014.
122. Alaa-Al Din Arafat. 2009. The Mubarak Leadership and Future of Democracy in Egypt (New York: Palgrave Macmillan), p. 70.
123. Menza. 2013. p. 135.
124. Lisa Blaydes and Safinaz El Tarouty. 2011. "La Concurrence Interne Au Parti National Democrate Egyptien," in Fabrique Des Elections, eds. Florian Kohstall and Frédéric Vairel (Cairo: CEDEJ), pp. 83–84.
125. Ibid. pp. 80–81.

Chapter 4

1. John Sfakianakis. 2004. "The Whales of the Nile: Networks, Businessmen, and Bureaucrats during the Era of Privatization in Egypt," in Networks of Privilege in the Middle East: The Politics of Economic Reform Revisited, ed. Steven Heydemann (New York: Palgrave Macmillan), pp. 77–100.
2. Amr Adly. 2011. "Mubarak (1990–2011): The State of Corruption." Arab Reform Initiative: Thematic Studies. At http://www.arab-reform.net/sites/default/files/Mubarak_1990-2011_The_State_of_Corruption.pdf, accessed March 10, 2012.
3. *Al-Usbu'*, March 2, 1998.
4. Ibid.
5. Eric Gobe. 2007. "Secteur Prive et Pouvoir Politique en Egypte: Entre Réformes Economiques, Logiques rentières et Autoritarisme Néopatrimonial." in États et Sociétés de l'Orient Arabe en quête d'avenir 1945–2005, ed. Gérard D. Khoury and Nadine Méouchy (Paris: Geuthner), p. 256.
6. Ibrahim Soliman will be discussed later in this chapter.

7. *Egyptian Gazette*, May 23, 2011.

8. *Al-Masry Al-Youm*, January 21, 2013.

9. Timothy Mitchell. 2002. Rule of Experts: Egypt, Techno-Politics, Modernity (Berkeley: University of California Press), pp. 274–75.

10. Mamoun Fandy. 2007. (Un)Civil War of World: Media and Politics in the Arab World (Westport, Connecticut: Praeger Security International), pp. 27–29.

11. *Al-Ahram Weekly*, November 7–13, 2002.

12. Ahmed Osman. 2004. "Rude Awakening: Dream Drops Top Talkers," Transnational Broadcasting Journal. Spring/summer. At http://www.tbsjournal .com/Archives/Spring04/dream.htm, accessed September 8, 2011.

13. Ibid.

14. *Al-Ahram Weekly*, November 7–13, 2002.

15. *Al-Ahram Weekly*, June 17–23, 2004.

16. Cited in Fandy. 2007. p. 27.

17. Charles Levinson. 2005. "Plus ca Change: The Role of the Media in Egypt's First Contested Presidential Elections," Transnational Broadcasting Journal. Fall. At http://www.tbsjournal.com/Archives/Fall05/Levinson.html, accessed August 9, 2012.

18. *Al-Masry Al-Youm*, February 2, 2011; Ursula Lindsey. 2012. "Revolution and Counter-Revolution in the Egyptian Media," in The Journey to Tahrir: Revolution, Protest, and Social Change in Egypt, ed. Jeannie Sowers and Chris Toensing (London: Verso), p. 59.

19. Ursula Lindsey. 2012. pp. 59–60.

20. *Al-Youm Al-Sabae*, February 6, 2013.

21. All articles are quoted from the 1971 constitution.

22. Toby Mendel. 2011. "Political and Media Transitions in Egypt: A Snapshot of Media Policy and Regulatory Environment." Internews, pp. 10–11. At http://www.internews.org/sites/default/files/resources/Internews_Egypt _MediaLawReview_Aug11.pdf, accessed April 9, 2012.

23. Ibid. p. 11.

24. *Al-Wafd*, December 13, 2011.

25. *Al-Wafd*, July 21, 2011.

26. Alaa El Aswany, interview by author, August 20, 2010.

27. *Al-Emarat Al-Youm*, October 6, 2010.

28. Tim Besley and Andrea Prat. 2006. "Handcuffs for the Grabbing Hand? Media Capture and Government Accountability," American Economic Review 96(3): 720–36.

29. Eberhard Kienle. 2001. A Grand Delusion: Democracy and Economic Reform in Egypt (London: I. B. Tauris), p. 158.

30. *Al-Ahram Weekly*, April 4–10, 2002.

31. *Al-Youm Al-Sabae*, October 21, 2008.

32. *Al-Ahram Weekly*, April 4–10, 2002.

33. Sfakianakis. 2004. p. 89.

34. *Al-Alam Al-Youm*, September 25, 2006; *Al-Youm Al-Sabae*, October 21, 2008.

35. Eberhard Kienle. 2004. "Reconciling Privilege and Reform: Fiscal Policy in Egypt, 1991–2000," in Networks of Privilege in the Middle East: The Politics of Economic Reform Revisited, ed. Steven Heydemann (New York: Palgrave Macmillan), p. 288.

36. Al-Youm Al-Sabae, October 12, 2008.

37. Margaret Levi. 1988. Of Rule and Revenue (Berkeley: University of California Press).

38. Al-Alam Al-Youm, September 25, 2006; Al-Youm Al-Sabae, October 21, 2008; Al-Youm Al-Sabae, June 4, 2009.

39. Al-Ahram Weekly, September 20–26, 2007; Rocky Mountain News, July 26, 2008.

40. Al-Masry Al-Youm, July 17, 2006.

41. Rose Al-Youssef, May 15, 2010; Rocky Mountain News, July 26, 2008.

42. Diane Singerman. 1995. Avenues of Participation: Family, Politics, and Networks in Urban Quarters of Cairo (Princeton, NJ: Princeton University Press).

43. Financial Times, March 26, 2009; Al-Ahram Weekly, July 22–28, 1999.

44. Al-Ahram Daily, June 23, 2003.

45. Al-Akhbar, May 14, 2010.

46. Kienle. 2004. p. 287.

47. Ibid. p. 290.

48. Sout Al-Oma, September 21, 2001; Sout Al-Oma, October 17, 2001; Sout Al-Oma, November 7, 2001.

49. Jadaliyya, November 18, 2011. At http://www.jadaliyya.com/pages/index/3182/al-sayed-al-badawi, accessed June 25, 2012.

50. Mohamed Hamas El Masry. 2012. "Journalism with Restraint: A Comparative Content Analysis of Independent, Government, and Opposition Newspapers in Pre-Revolution Egypt," Journal of Middle East Media 8(1): 1–34.

51. Kenneth Cooper. 2008. "Politics and Priorities: Inside the Egyptian Press," Arab Society and Media 6. At http://www.arabmediasociety.com/?article=689, accessed November 6, 2011.

52. Magdy El Galad. 2010. "I Will Vote For Gamal Mubarak," May 23. Available on YouTube at http://www.youtube.com/watch?v=7OVFWYf3Z28&NR=1, accessed August 20, 2013.

53. Oxford Business Group, May 18, 2007. At http://www.oxfordbusinessgroup.com/economic_updates/sawiris-assessment-otv-channel, accessed August 20, 2013.

54. Al Shark Al-Awsat, October 6, 2010.

55. Mona El-Ghobashy. 2010. "The Liquidation of Egypt's Illiberal Experiment." Middle East Report Online. December 29. At http://www.merip.org/mero/mero122910, accessed May 23, 2011.

56. Osama El Ghazaly Harb, interview by author, Cairo, April 6, 2010.

57. Information provided off the record by an Egyptian journalist who told me that State Security instructed Sawiris not to join the party.

58. *Al-Masry Al-Youm*, July 27, 2012. The author of this article, Alaa El Aswany, collected a number of quotes from television interviews with Naguib Sawiris to show Naguib's transformation from being supportive of Mubarak before the outbreak of the revolution to being an opponent of Mubarak afterward.

59. Ibid.

60. Ibid.

61. *Al-Wasat*, April 7, 2011.

62. Cited in *Ahram Online*, May 4, 2012. At http://english.ahram.org.eg/NewsContent/3/12/66259/Business/Economy/My-family-is-targeted-by-Brotherhood-Egypt-busines.aspx.

63. *Al-Ahram Weekly*, March 7–13, 2013.

64. *Al Arabyia*, May 24, 2013.

65. *Al-Youm Al-Sabae*, July 12, 2013.

66. Sherif Kamel. 2004. "Evolution of Mobile Technology in Egypt" (Paper presented at the Information Resources Management Association International Conference, New Orleans, LA). At http://www.irma-international.org/viewtitle/32466, accessed June 10, 2011.

67. *Al-Ahram Weekly*, June 14–20, 2001.

68. *Al-Ahram Weekly*, April 4–10, 2002.

69. Andrew Dowell. 1999. "MisrFone Starts to Compete." *Business Monthly*, November. At http://www.amcham.org.eg/resources_publications/publications/business_monthly/issue.asp?sec=17&subsec=MisrFone%20starts%20to%20compete&im=11&iy=1999, accessed July 30, 2013.

70. *Jadaliyya*, November 18, 2011.

71. *Al-Masry Al-Youm*, January 25, 2010.

72. *Al-Ahram Weekly*, April 4–10, 2002.

73. Abu El Ezz El Hariry. 2004. Interpellation submitted to the People's Assembly about the monopoly in the telecommunications sector.

74. *Al-Ahram Weekly*, February 3–9, 2005.

75. *Al-Ahram Weekly*, April 4–10, 2002.

76. *Al-Ahram Weekly*, November 29–December 5, 2001.

77. Abdel Khalek Farouk. 2008. Petition of Indictment (in Arabic; Cairo: Yafa Center for Studies and Research), pp. 136, 156.

78. Ibid. p. 149.

79. *Al-Messa*, May 15, 2011.

80. Farouk. 2008. pp. 152–53; *Al-Karama*, October 31, 2006.

81. *Al-Wafd*, September 30, 2012.

82. *Al-Ahram Weekly*, December 25–31, 2003.

83. Abdel Khalek Farouk. 2011. The Economics of Corruption in Egypt (in Arabic; Cairo: El Sherouk El Dawaliya), pp. 195–96.

84. *Al-Wafd*, November 18, 2011.

85. Sumit K. Majundar. 1992. "Performance in the US Telecommunications Services Industry: An Analysis of the Impact of Deregulation," Telecommunications Policy 16(4): pp. 327–38.

86. Although Israel withdrew from Sinai on April 25, 1982, it did not withdraw from Taba until April 29, 1988, when an international arbitration committee ruled in Egypt's favor.
87. Wagih Siag, interview by author, London, October 16, 2009.
88. Ibid.
89. Ibid.
90. *Al-Masry Al-Youm*, August 9, 2009.
91. Wagih Siag, interview by author, London, October 16, 2009.
92. Ibid.
93. Wagih Siag waived his Egyptian nationality to be able to file a lawsuit against the Egyptian government before the International Arbitration Centre of the World Bank.
94. Wagih Siag, interview by author, London, October 16, 2009.
95. Karam Yehia. 2012. The Black Box: The Story of Hussein Salem (in Arabic; Cairo: Dar El Thakafa El Gadida), p. 84.
96. *Al-Ahram Weekly*, June 23–29, 2011.
97. Cited in Yehia. 2012. p. 116.
98. *Al-Ahram Weekly* May 26–June 1, 2011. The charges against the Mubarak family regarding the Sharm El Sheikh palaces have lapsed because the alleged crime took place more than ten years ago.
99. *Al-Masry Al-Youm*, March 6, 2011; Yehia. 2012. pp. 129–32.
100. Cited in Yehia. 2012. p. 132.
101. Ibid.
102. Ibid. pp. 133–34.
103. Ibid. p. 133.
104. Mostafa Ebeid. 2009. Normalization through Business: The Secrets of Businessmen's Relations with Israel (in Arabic; Cairo: Mirette for Publishing), p. 147.
105. Yehia. 2012. p. 114.
106. Adly. 2011. p. 13.
107. Ibid.
108. *Haaretz*, June 20, 2007.
109. *Ahram Online*, May 4, 2012. At http://english.ahram.org.eg/NewsContent/3/12/40805/Business/Economy/Fugitive-tycoon-Hussein-Salem-talks-Mubarak,-Israe.aspx, accessed May 15, 2013.
110. *Al-Ahram Weekly*, May 12–18, 2011.
111. *Al-Jarida Al-Kwaitia* cited in *Haaretz*, March 7, 2011; *Al-Ahram Weekly*, June 23–29, 2011.
112. *Ahram Online*, May 4, 2012. At http://english.ahram.org.eg/NewsContent/3/12/40805/Business/Economy/Fugitive-tycoon-Hussein-Salem-talks-Mubarak,-Israe.aspx, accessed May 15, 2013.
113. Peter Evans. 1989. "Predatory, Developmental, and Other Apparatuses: A Comparative Political Economy Perspective on the Third World State," Sociological Forum 4(4): 561–87.
114. Farouk Gouida. 2010. Raping a Homeland: The Crime of Looting the Lands of the State (in Arabic; Cairo: Dar El Sherouk), pp. 123–27.

115. *Rose Al-Youssef*, November 18, 2009.
116. Gouida. 2010. pp. 123–27.
117. Saad Khattab 2005. The Black Book about the Minister of Housing: Mohamed Ibrahim Soliman (in Arabic; Cairo: El Rawy), pp. 40–42.
118. *Al-Masry Al-Youm*, March 13, 2011.
119. One of the members of the El Mansour family, Mohamed Mansour, was appointed minister of transportation from 2005 to 2009.
120. Ahmed El Maghrabi was appointed minister of tourism (2004–9) and minister of housing (2009–11).
121. *Al-Ahram Weekly*, March 10–16, 2011.
122. Ibid.
123. *Al-Masry Al-Youm*, June 3, 2011.
124. *Al-Masry Al-Youm*, March 25, 2011.
125. El Badri Farghali. 2002. Interpellation submitted to the People's Assembly about the corruption of Minister of Housing Ibrahim Soliman. Attached to the interpellation is EnviroCivic's pamphlet, which stated the projects that it implemented from 1992–2000. According to the pamphlet, 98 percent of the projects were awarded through the Ministry of Housing.
126. Khattab. 2005. pp. 298–99.
127. William L. Megginson and Jeffry M. Netter. 2001. "From State to Market: A Survey of Empirical Studies on Privatization," Journal of Economic Literature 39(2): 321–89.

Chapter 5

1. Ellen Lust-Okar. 2004. "Divided They Rule: The Management and Manipulation of Political Opposition," Journal of Democracy 36(2): 139–56.
2. Holger Albrecht. 2010. "Political Opposition and Arab Authoritarianism: Some Conceptual Remarks," in Contentious Politics in the Middle East: Political Opposition under Authoritarianism, ed. Holger Albrecht (Gainesville: University Press of Florida), pp. 17–33.
3. All articles are quoted from the 1971 constitution.
4. Cited in David C. Kang. 2002. "Bad Loans to Good Friends: Money Politics and Developmental State in South Korea," International Organization 56(1):185–86.
5. Albrecht. 2010. pp. 21–23.
6. Omar Said El Ahl, interview by author, Cairo, August 26, 2010.
7. Eric Trager. 2012. "Trapped and Untrapped: Mubarak's Opponents on the Eve of His Oust" (PhD dissertation, University of Pennsylvania), p. 121.
8. In the 2000 parliament, the opposition parties (the liberal, the Nasserite, the Tagammu', and the Wafd) got 16 seats. Out of the 16 seats, the Wafd got 7 seats. In addition to the 16 seats won by the official opposition parties, the illegal Muslim Brothers organization got 17 seats. This means that the total number of opposition seats in parliament was 33 (including official opposition parties and Muslim Brothers). Parliament had 454 seats (444 elected

and 10 appointed). This suggests that out of the 161 votes that Nour got, perhaps 33 came from the opposition, and the rest (128 votes) must have come from NDP members.

9. Ayman Nour, interview by author, Cairo, December 17, 2009.
10. Morsi El Sheikh, interview by author, April 20, 2010.
11. *Al-Ahram Weekly*, March 15–21, 2001.
12. Ayman Nour, interview by author, Cairo, December 17, 2009.
13. Joshua Stacher. 2004. "Parties Over: The Demise of Egypt's Opposition Parties," British Journal of Middle Eastern Studies 31(2): 231–32.
14. Cited in Stacher. 2004. p. 232.
15. Ibid.
16. *Al-Youm Al-Sabae*, April 9, 2012.
17. Ibid.
18. Ninette Fahmy. 2002. The Politics of Egypt: State-Society Relationship (London: Routledge), p. 68.
19. Tamir Moustafa. 2007. The Struggle for Constitutional Power: Law, Politics and Economic Development in Egypt (Cambridge: Cambridge University Press), p. 94.
20. Maye Kassem. 1999. In the Guise of Democracy: Governance in Contemporary Egypt (London: Ithaca Press), p. 4.
21. Ibid.
22. Wael Nawara, interview by author, Cairo, April 13, 2010.
23. Morsi El Sheikh, interview by author, April 20, 2010.
24. Wael Nawara, interview by author, Cairo, April 13, 2010.
25. Eberhard Kienle. 2001. A Grand Delusion: Democracy and Economic Reform in Egypt (London: I. B. Tauris), p. 29.
26. Wael Nawara, interview by author, Cairo, April 13, 2010.
27. Cited in Moheb Zaki. 1999. Egyptian Business Elites: Their Visions and Investment Behavior (Cairo: Konrad Adenauer Stiftung and the Arab Center for Development and Future Research), p. 122.
28. *Al-Shark Al-Awsat*, July 19, 2004.
29. Ibrahim Eissa will be discussed in the following section on *El Sayyid El Badawi* and *Al-Destour* newspapers.
30. Wael Nawara, interview by author, Cairo, April 13, 2010. It should be noted that established political parties had the right to publish newspapers and periodicals without the prior consent of the Higher Press Council. But at the same time, Article 14 of Law 40 of 1977 empowers the PPC to stop a party's newspapers and activities if the committee deems it necessary in the national interest.
31. Wael Nawara, interview by author, Cairo, April 13, 2010.
32. Morsi El Sheikh, interview by author, Cairo, April 20, 2010.
33. Ibid.
34. Hisham Kassem, interview by author, Cairo, March 23, 2010.
35. Morsi El Sheikh, interview by author, Cairo, April 20, 2010.
36. Hisham Kassem, interview by author, Cairo, March 23, 2010.

37. Mona Makram Ebeid, interview by author, Cairo, June 11, 2010.
38. Yoram Meital. 2006. "The Struggle over Political Order in Egypt: The 2005 Elections," Middle East Journal 60(2): 266.
39. Wael Nawara, interview by author, Cairo, April 13, 2010.
40. Mona Makram Ebeid, interview by author, Cairo, June 11, 2010.
41. Ibid.
42. Wael Nawara, interview by author, Cairo, April 13, 2010.
43. Ibid.
44. Ray Bush and Jeremy Keenan. 2006. "North Africa: Power, Politics and Promise," Review of African Political Economy 33(108): 177. After the Twenty-Fifth of January Revolution, Nour submitted a petition to the prosecutor general for a retrial of his case. He argued that the witness had later changed his testimony and confessed that the then minister of interior, Habib El Adly, had ordered the witness to forge the party documents and that he was threatened with being jailed for the rest of his life if he did not forge the party documents. However, the Court of Cassation refused Nour's appeal.
45. Morsi El Sheikh, interview by author, Cairo, April 20, 2010. It should be noted that Morsi El Sheikh was among those who defected from Nour's wing and joined Moussa's wing; however, he soon returned to Nour's wing after realizing that Moussa's wing is run by State Security and does not oppose the regime.
46. Trager. 2012. p. 145.
47. Wael Nawara, interview by author, Cairo, April 13, 2010.
48. Cited in Trager. 2012. p. 152.
49. Al-Destour, June 4, 2010.
50. Al-Masry Al-Youm, June 13, 2010.
51. Wael Nawara. 2010. "Interview with Wael Nawara, Secretary General of the Ghad (Tomorrow) Party." The Carnegie Papers. Carnegie Endowment for International Peace. At http://egyptelections.carnegieendowment.org/2010/11/22/interview-with-wael-nawara-secretary-general-of-the-ghad-tomorrow-party, accessed March 9, 2012.
52. Nagui El Ghatrify, interview by author, July 8, 2010.
53. Mohamed Mansour Hassan, interview by author, April 18, 2010.
54. Ibid.
55. Jadaliyya, November 18, 2011. At http://www.jadaliyya.com/pages/index/3182/al-sayed-al-badawi, accessed June 25, 2012.
56. Ibrahim Eissa. 2010. The Book of the Destour: The Story of a Country and a Newspaper (in Arabic; Cairo: El Masry for Publishing), p. 19.
57. Al-Ahram Weekly, March 27–April 2, 2008; Al-Ahram Weekly, March 31–April 6, 2005.
58. Al-Ahram Weekly, March 27–April 2, 2008.
59. Al-Ahram Weekly, October 14–20, 2010.
60. Jaridat Al-Shaab Al-Jadid, January 8, 2013. At http://elshaab.org/thread.php?ID=45508, accessed June 14, 2013.
61. Jadaliyya, November 18, 2011.

62. *Al-Destour*, October 8, 2012.
63. Trager. 2012. p. 106.
64. Ministry of Health. "The Minister Decree 350 for Regulation of Tramadol." At http://www.eda.mohp.gov.eg/Download/Docs/Decree350.pdf, accessed March 26, 2014.
65. *Al-Destour*, October 8, 2012.
66. For more information about the division that happened in 2006 in the Wafd Party between Noaman Goma'a and Mahmoud Abaza, see *Al-Ahram Weekly*, March 2–8, 2006.
67. Eissa. 2010. p. 20.
68. Ibid. p. 24.
69. Ibid. pp. 25–26.
70. Ibid. p. 25.
71. Ibid.
72. Trager. 2012. p. 109.
73. *Al-Wafd*, September 7, 2011.
74. *Al-Masry Al-Youm* was known as a newspaper that did not cross the red line with the Mubarak family. For instance, in 2007, there was an attempt by business tycoon Hisham Talaat Moustafa to buy *Al-Destour* newspaper and *Sout Al-Oma,* another opposition newspaper, and he wanted to pay $8 million for this transaction. This means he wanted to buy both editors in chief, Ibrahim Eissa and Wael El Ebrashy. Moustafa said to Ibrahim Eissa, "I wanted to buy *Al-Destour* and *Sout Al-Oma* newspapers and do not want any politics in them. I only want the politics of *Al-Masry Al-Youm*. I want to give it as a present to my father [Mubarak]. However, Moustafa's offer was refused by both editors-in-chief." (See Eissa 2010, p. 17.)
75. *Al-Ahram Daily*, May 8, 2010.
76. Hesham Al-Awadi. 2005. "Mubarak and the Islamists: Why Did the Honeymoon End?," Middle East Journal 59(1): 63.
77. Ellen Lust-Okar. 2005. Structuring Conflict in the Arab World: Incumbents, Opponents, and Institutions (Cambridge: Cambridge University Press), p. 141.
78. Ibid.
79. Al-Awadi. 2005. p. 63.
80. Cited in Mona El-Ghobashy. 2005. "The Metamorphosis of the Egyptian Muslim Brothers," International Journal of Middle East Studies 37(3): 378.
81. For instance, in 1987, the MB won 54 of the 61 contested seats in the Engineers' Association; in 1988, they won all 12 seats in the Medical Doctors' Association; and in 1989, the Islamic list won a considerable number of seats in the Commercial Graduates Association. See Alaa-Al Din Arafat. 2009. The Mubarak Leadership and Future of Democracy in Egypt (New York: Palgrave Macmillan), p. 172.
82. Hesham Al-Awadi. 2004. In Pursuit of Legitimacy: The Muslim Brothers and Mubarak (London: Tauris Academic Studies), p. 161.
83. Cited in Al-Awadi 2005, p. 67.

84. Ibid. p. 73.
85. Ellen Lust-Okar. 2005. p. 148.
86. Maye Kassem. 1999. p. 58.
87. Ibid. p. 40.
88. Ibid. p. 59.
89. Sawasiya Center for Human Rights. 2008. "Report about the Military Trial of the Leaders of the Muslim Brothers" (in Arabic; Cairo: Sawasiya), pp. 78–79.
90. Mona El-Ghobashy. 2012a, "The Dynamics of Elections under Mubarak," in The Journey to Tahrir: Revolution, Protest and Social Change in Egypt, ed. Jeannie Sowers and Chris Toensing (London: Verso), p. 138.
91. Cited in Jason Brownlee. 2007. Authoritarianism in an Age of Democratization. Cambridge: Cambridge University Press, p. 136. Bracketed insertions by Brownlee.
92. Ruling of the Cairo Court of Appeals. December 24, 2000. The Case of Medhat El Haddad. The Court of Appeals ruled for a compensation of thirty thousand EGP for Medhat El Haddad, for the 1995 Consultative Assembly election, because of police irregularities, which eliminated his chance of winning.
93. Ruling of the Cairo Court of Appeals. February 13, 2001. The Case of Medhat El Haddad. The Court of Appeals ruled for a compensation of twenty thousand EGP for Medhat El Haddad, for the 1995 People's Assembly election, because of irregularities during the election by the Ministry of Interior, which invalidated the election.
94. Medhat El Haddad, interview by author, Cairo, April 15, 2010.
95. Ikhwan Online, September 26, 2005. At http://www.ikhwanonline.com/print .aspx?ArtID=14659&SecID=0, accessed October 15, 2013.
96. Alaa-Al Din Arafat. 2009. The Mubarak Leadership and Future of Democracy in Egypt. New York: Palgrave Macmillan, p. 172.
97. International Crisis Group. 2005. "Reforming Egypt: In Search of a Strategy." At http://www.crisisgroup.org/~/media/Files/Middle%20East%20North%20 Africa/North%20Africa/Egypt/Reforming%20Egypt%20In%20Search %20of%20a%20Strategy.pdf, accessed July 9, 2012.
98. Arafat. 2009. p. 172. The Kefaya movement will be discussed in the following section.
99. Ibid. pp. 172–73.
100. Al-Shark Al-Awsat, May 5, 2005.
101. International Crisis Group. 2005.
102. Medhat El Haddad, interview by author, Cairo, April 15, 2010.
103. Samer Shehata and Joshua Stacher. 2012. "The Muslim Brothers in Mubarak's Last Decade," in The Journey to Tahrir: Revolution, Protest and Social Change in Egypt, ed. Jeannie Sowers and Chris Toensing (London: Verso), p. 160.
104. Issand El Amrani. 2012. "Controlled Reform in Egypt: Neither Reformist nor Controlled," in The Journey to Tahrir: Revolution, Protest and Social

Change in Egypt, ed. Jeannie Sowers and Chris Toensing (London: Verso), p. 156.
105. Ibid. 2012. p. 157.
106. Medhat El Haddad, interview by author, Cairo, April 15, 2010.
107. Shehata and Stacher. 2012. p. 169.
108. *Al-Ahram Weekly*, December 27–January 2, 2008.
109. Sawasiya. 2008. pp. 64–65.
110. Shehata and Stacher. 2012. p. 173.
111. *Al-Ahram-Weekly*, July 23–29, 2009.
112. Mohamed Bishr, interview by author, Cairo, March 13, 2010.
113. El Haddad referred to verses of the Quran to confirm that his words were coming from Islam. Surat Al Goma'a, verse 10: "And when the prayer has been concluded, disperse within the land and seek from the bounty of Allah, and remember Allah often that you may succeed." Surat Al Omran, verse 104: "And let there be [arising] from you a nation inviting to [all that is] good, enjoining what is right and forbidding what is wrong, and those will be the successful ones."
114. Medhat El Haddad, interview by author, Cairo, April 15, 2010.
115. Ibid.
116. For instance, in the 2010 parliamentary election, only one seat was won by an MB candidate who did not abide by the MB decision to boycott the run-off election.
117. *Al-Ahram Daily*, December 24, 2010. This information is from an article written for *Al-Ahram* by Ahmed Ezz. For instance, in the Shubra Al-Kheima constituency in Qalyoubia Governorate, the MB candidate Mohamed El Beltagui could not get the majority of votes (50 percent + 1) in the first round against the two NDP candidates, Magahed Nassar and Hani Tawfik. This is because the votes had been divided among the candidates. Both NDP candidates got 26,434 votes, while the MB candidate got 9,798 votes. Then, in the second round, the votes of the NDP candidates (two or three) would unite against the MB candidate.
118. Hani Enan, interview by author, Cairo, March 22, 2010.
119. Ibid.
120. *Al-Youm Al-Sabae*, January 2, 2009.
121. *Al-Masry Al-Youm*, September 13, 2009.
122. Hani Enan, interview by author, Cairo, March 22, 2010.
123. Neha Sahgal. 2008. "Divided We Stand, but United We Oppose: Opposition Alliances in Egypt and Pakistan" (PhD dissertation, University of Maryland), p. 163.
124. Amr Hamzawy and Nathan J. Brown. 2010. "The Egyptian Muslim Brotherhood: Islamist Participation in a Closing Political Environment." The Carnegie Papers. Carnegie Endowment for International Peace. At http://carnegieendowment.org/files/muslim_bros_participation.pdf, accessed July 11, 2011.
125. *Islam Online*, December 10, 2006. At http://www.onislam.net/arabic/newsanalysis/3001-3001/82448-2006-12-10%2014-41-41.html, accessed June 10, 2013.

126. Cited in *Al-Ahram Daily*, May 14, 2005.
127. Albrecht. 2010.
128. Lust-Okar. 2004.

Conclusion

1. Barrington Moore. 1966. Social Origins of Dictatorship and Democracy (Boston: Beacon); Charles Moraz. 1968. The Triumph of the Middle Class (New York: Anchor); Eric Hobsbawm. 1969. Industry and Empire (Harmondsworth: Penguin).
2. Amr Adly. 2009. "Politically-Embedded Cronyism: The Case of Egypt," Business and Politics 11(4): 1–28.
3. John Sfakianakis. 2004. "The Whales of the Nile: Networks, Businessmen, and Bureaucrats during the Era of Privatization in Egypt," in Networks of Privilege in the Middle East: The Politics of Economic Reform Revisited, ed. Steven Heydemann (New York: Palgrave Macmillan), pp. 77–100.
4. Eva Bellin. 2002. Stalled Democracy: Capital, Labor, and the Paradox of State-Sponsored Development (Ithaca, NY: Cornell University Press).
5. Peter Evans. 1989. "Predatory, Developmental, and Other Apparatuses: A Comparative Political Economy Perspective on the Third World State," Sociological Forum 4(4): 561–87; Margaret Levi. 1988. Of Rule and Revenue (Berkeley: University of California Press).
6. Evans. 1989.
7. Levi. 1988.
8. Ellen Lust-Okar. 2004. "Divided They Rule: The Management and Manipulation of Political Opposition," Journal of Democracy 36(2): 159–79.
9. It should be noted that in April 2011, a court ruling dissolved the NDP.
10. Stephan Roll. 2013. "Egypt's Business Elite after Mubarak: A Powerful Player between Generals and Brotherhood." SWP Research Paper. Stiftung Wissenschaft und Politik German Institute for International and Security Affairs. At http://www.swp-berlin.org/fileadmin/contents/products/research_papers/2013_RP08_rll.pdf, accessed March 22, 2014.
11. *Ahram Online*, December 1, 2011. At http://english.ahram.org.eg/News Content/33/104/28221/Elections-/Political-Parties/AlAdl.aspx; Roll. 2013.
12. *Al Wafd*, October 27, 2011.
13. Roll. 2013.
14. *Al-Wafd*, May 29, 2012.
15. The National Salvation Front alliance includes the Constitution Party, cofounded by opposition leader Mohamed El-Baradei, the Egyptian Popular Current, the April 6 Youth Movement, the Egyptian Social Democratic Party, the Socialist Popular Alliance Party, the Kefaya movement, and others.
16. *Egypt Independent*, July 25, 2013. At http://www.egyptindependent.com/news/special-report-how-muslim-brotherhood-lost-egypt, accessed December 12, 2014.
17. *Jadaliyya*, June 28, 2013. At http://www.jadaliyya.com/pages/index/12466/unpacking-anti-muslim-brotherhood-discourse, accessed February 17, 2014.

18. Roll. 2013.
19. *Al Nahar*, July 6, 2014. Information is based on an interview with retired General Sameh Seif El Yazal.
20. *New York Times*, June 27, 2013.
21. *Ahram Online*, June 27, 2013. At http://english.ahram.org.eg/NewsContent Print/3/0/75092/Business/0/CBC-owner-travel-ban-confirmed-after-Morsi -accusat.aspx, accessed June 16, 2014.
22. *New York Times*, July 24, 2013.
23. *Daily News*, November 26, 2014. At http://www.dailyncwsegypt.com/ 2014/11/26/607-protesters-died-rabaa-al-adaweya-sit-committee-report, accessed March 6, 2014.
24. *Al-Ahram Weekly*, August 15, 2013.
25. *The Guardian*, November 24, 2013.
26. *Al Monitor*, April 7, 2014. At http://www.al-monitor.com/pulse/ru/contents/ articles/originals/2014/04/economic-crisis-egypt-influence-sisi-popularity .html#ixzz3U6UiFifp, accessed March 11, 2015.
27. *Gulf Business*, October 19, 2014. At http://gulfbusiness.com/2014/10/will-al -sisi-help-bring-egypt-back-track/#.VQCGQY5wvXA, accessed March 7, 2015.
28. *Ahram Online*, May 6, 2014. At http://english.ahram.org.eg/NewsContent/ 1/64/100653/Egypt/Politics-/Gulf-aid-to-Egypt-since-June-more-than -billion-E.aspx, accessed March 8, 2015.
29. Chérine Chams el-Dine. 2014. "Fragile Alliances in Egypt's Post-Revolutionary Order: The Military and Its Partners." SWP Research Paper. German Institute for International and Security Affairs. At http://www.ssoar .info/ssoar/handle/document/41083, accessed March 6, 2015.
30. Emad Shahin. 2014. "Lessons Not Learned: Trading Democracy for Neo-liberal Militarism in Egypt." Al Jazeera Center for Studies. At http:// studies.aljazeera.net/en/reports/2014/09/2014946275380514.htm, accessed March 3, 2015.
31. *Al Youm Al-Sabae*, May 13, 2014.
32. *Al Masry Al-Youm*, July 14, 2014.
33. Chams El Dine. 2014.
34. *Middle East Eye*. November 5, 2014. At http://www.middleeasteye.net/in -depth/features/sisi-s-economy-out-storm-how-long-1489867453, accessed March 10, 2015.
35. *Al-Ahram Weekly*, January 9, 2014.
36. *New York Times*, January 24, 2015.
37. *Radio Sawa*, February 2, 2015. At http://www.radiosawa.com/content/egypt -shimaa-elsabbagh/265763.html, accessed March 8, 2015.
38. Chams El Dine. 2014.

Bibliography

Books and Journal Articles

Abdallah Khalil. 2008. "The General Prosecutor between the Judicial and Executive Authorities." In *Judges and Political Reform in Egypt*, edited by Nathalie Bernard-Maugiran. Cairo: American University in Cairo Press: 59–70.

Abdel-Fattah Mady. 2013. "Popular Discontent, Revolution, and Democratization in Egypt in a Globalizing World." *Indiana Journal of Global Legal Studies* 20(1): 313–37.

Abdel Khalek Farouk. 2006. *The Corruption in Egypt* (in Arabic). Cairo: El Arabi.

———. 2008. *Petition of Indictment* (in Arabic). Cairo: Yafa Center for Studies and Research.

———. 2011. *The Economics of Corruption in Egypt* (in Arabic). Cairo: El Sherouk El Dawaliya.

Adam Hanieh. 2011. *Capitalism and Class in the Gulf Arab States*. New York: Palgrave Macmillan.

Adel Hamouda. 2005. *Those Who Fled with Billions from Egypt, and the Puzzle of Ramy Lakah and Mahmoud Whaba: The Secret Files of the Famous Businessmen Who Fled the Country* (in Arabic). Cairo: Dar El Forsan.

Ahmed Osman. 2004, "Rude Awakening: Dream Drops Top Talkers." *Transnational Broadcasting Journal*. Spring/summer. At http://www.tbsjournal.com/Archives/Spring04/dream.htm, accessed September 8, 2011.

Alaa-Al Din Arafat. 2009. *The Mubarak Leadership and Future of Democracy in Egypt*. New York: Palgrave Macmillan.

Amr Adly. 2009. "Politically-Embedded Cronyism: The Case of Egypt." *Business and Politics* 11(4): 1–28.

———. 2011. "Mubarak (1990–2011): The State of Corruption." Arab Reform Initiative: Thematic Studies. At http://www.arab-reform.net/sites/default/files/Mubarak_1990-2011_The_State_of_Corruption.pdf, accessed March 10, 2012.

Amr Hamzawy and Nathan J. Brown. 2010. "The Egyptian Muslim Brotherhood: Islamist Participation in a Closing Political Environment." *The Carnegie Papers*. Carnegie Endowment for International Peace. At http://carnegieendowment.org/files/muslim_bros_participation.pdf, accessed July 11, 2011.

Andrew Dowell. 1999. "MisrFone Starts to Compete." *Business Monthly*, November. At http://www.amcham.org.eg/resources_publications/publications/business_monthly/issue.asp?sec=17&subsec=MisrFone%20starts%20to%20compete&im=11&iy=1999, accessed July 30, 2013.

Anowar Abdel Malek. 1968. *Egypt Military Society*. New York: Random House.

Atef Said. 2008. "The Role of the Judges Club in Enhancing the Independence of the Judiciary and Spurring Political Reform." In *Judges and Political Reform in Egypt*, edited by Nathalie Bernard-Maugiran. Cairo: American University in Cairo Press: 111–32.

Barrington Moore. 1966. *Social Origins of Dictatorship and Democracy*. Boston: Beacon.

Bassam Haddad. 2012. *Business Networks in Syria: The Political Economy of Authoritarian Resilience*. Stanford, CA: Stanford University Press.

Beatrice Hibou. 2004. "Fiscal Trajectories in Morocco and Tunisia." In *Networks of Privilege in the Middle East: The Politics of Economic Reform Revisited*, edited by Steven Heydemann. New York: Palgrave Macmillan: 201–22.

Carl H. Lande. 1977. "Introduction: The Dyadic Basis of Clientelism." In *Friends, Followers and Faction: A Reader in Political Clientelism*, edited by Steffen W. Schmidt, James C. Scott, Carle Lande, and Laura Guasti. Berkley: University of California Press: xiii–xxxii.

Charles Levinson. 2005, "Plus ca Change: The Role of the Media in Egypt's First Contested Presidential Elections." *Transnational Broadcasting Journal*. Fall. At http://www.tbsjournal.com/Archives/Fall05/Levinson.html, accessed August 9, 2012.

Charles Moraz. 1968. *The Triumph of the Middle Class*. New York: Anchor.

Chérine Chams el-Dine. 2014. "Fragile Alliances in Egypt's Post-Revolutionary Order: The Military and Its Partners." *SWP Research Paper*. German Institute for International and Security Affairs. At http://www.ssoar.info/ssoar/handle/document/41083, accessed March 6, 2015.

Clement Henry Moore. 1994. *Images of Development: Egyptian Engineers in Search of Industry*. Cairo: American University in Cairo Press.

David C. Kang. 2002. "Bad Loans to Good Friends: Money Politics and Developmental State in South Korea." *International Organization* 56(1): 177–207.

Denis Sullivan. 1994. *Private Voluntary Organizations in Egypt: Islamic Development, Private Initiative and State Control*. Gainesville: University Press of Florida.

Diane Singerman. 1995. *Avenues of Participation: Family, Politics, and Networks in Urban Quarters of Cairo*. Princeton, NJ: Princeton University Press.

Dina Shehata. 2010. *Islamists and Secularist in Egypt: Opposition, Conflict, and Cooperation*. London: Routledge.

Eberhard Kienle. 2001. *A Grand Delusion: Democracy and Economic Reform in Egypt*. London: I. B. Tauris.

———. 2004. "Reconciling Privilege and Reform: Fiscal Policy in Egypt, 1991–2000." In *Networks of Privilege in the Middle East: The Politics of Economic Reform Revisited*, edited by Steven Heydemann. New York: Palgrave Macmillan: 281–96.

Eggers Andrew and Jens Hainmueller. 2009. "MPs for Sale? Returns to Office in Postwar British Politics." *American Political Science Review* 103(4): 1–21.

Ellen Lust-Okar. 2004. "Divided They Rule: The Management and Manipulation of Political Opposition." *Journal of Democracy* 36(2): 139–56.

———. 2005. *Structuring Conflict in the Arab World: Incumbents, Opponents, and Institutions.* Cambridge: Cambridge University Press.

———. 2009. "Democratization by Elections? Competitive Clientelism in the Middle East." *Journal of Democracy* 20(3): 122–35.

Emad Shahin. 2013. "The Egyptian Revolution: the Power of Mass Mobilization and the Spirit of Tahrir Square." In *Revolution, Revolt, and Reform in North Africa: The Arab Spring and Beyond,* edited by Ricardo Rene Laremont. London: Routledge: 53–74.

———. 2014. "Lessons Not Learned: Trading Democracy for Neoliberal Militarism in Egypt." *Al Jazeera Center for Studies.* At http://studies.aljazeera.net/en/reports/2014/09/2014946275380514.htm, accessed March 3, 2015.

Eric Gobe. 1999. *Les Hommes D'affaires Egyptiens: Démocratisation et Secteur Privé dans l'Egypte de L'infitah.* Paris: Karthala.

———. 2007. "Secteur Prive et Pouvoir Politique en Egypte: Entre Réformes Economiques, Logiques rentières et Autoritarisme Néo-patrimonial," In *États et Sociétés de l'Orient Arabe en quête d'avenir 1945–2005,* edited by Gérard D. Khoury and Nadine Méouchy. Paris: Geuthner: 253–65.

Eric Hobsbawm. 1969. *Industry and Empire.* Harmondsworth: Penguin.

Eva Bellin. 2000. "Contingent Democrats: Industrialists, Labor and Democratization in Late-Developing Countries." *World Politics* 52(2): 175–205.

———. 2002. *Stalled Democracy: Capital, Labor, and the Paradox of State-Sponsored Development.* Ithaca, NY: Cornell University Press.

Farouk Gouida. 2010. *Raping a Homeland: The Crime of Looting the Lands of the State* (in Arabic). Cairo: Dar El Sherouk.

Gouda Abdel-Khalek and Karima Korayem. 2001. "Fiscal Policy Measures in Egypt: Public Debt and Food Subsidy." *Cairo Papers in Social Science* 23(1).

Hans Lofgren. 1993. "Economic Policy in Egypt: Breakdown in Reform Resistance." *International Journal of Middle East Studies* 25(3):407–21.

Hazem Beblawi. 1987. "The Rentier State in the Arab World." *Arab Studies Quarterly* 9(4): 383–98.

Hazem Kandil. 2012. *Soldiers, Spies and Statesmen: Egypt's Road to Revolt.* London: Verso.

Hesham Al-Awadi. 2004. *In Pursuit of Legitimacy: The Muslim Brothers and Mubarak.* London: Tauris Academic Studies.

———. 2005. "Mubarak and the Islamists: Why Did the Honeymoon End?" *Middle East Journal* 59(1): 62–80.

Holger Albrecht. 2010. "Political Opposition and Arab Authoritarianism: Some Conceptual Remarks." In *Contentious Politics in the Middle East: Political Opposition under Authoritarianism,* edited by Holger Albrecht. Gainesville: University Press of Florida: 17–33.

Hossam el-Hamalawy. 2011. "Jan 25: The Workers, Middle Class, Military Junta and the Permanent Revolution." Arabawy blog, February 12, 2011. At http://www.arabawy.org/2011/02/12/permanent-revolution, accessed January 10, 2012.

Ibrahim Eissa. 2010. *The Book of the Destour: The Story of a Country and a Newspaper* (in Arabic). Cairo: El Masry for Publishing.

International Crisis Group. 2005. "Reforming Egypt: In Search of a Strategy." At http://www.crisisgroup.org/~/media/Files/Middle%20East%20North%20 Africa/North%20Africa/Egypt/Reforming%20Egypt%20In%20Search%20of %20a%20Strategy.pdf, accessed July 9, 2012.

Issandr El Amrani. 2012. "Controlled Reform in Egypt: Neither Reformist nor Controlled." In *The Journey to Tahrir: Revolution, Protest and Social Change in Egypt*, edited by Jeannie Sowers and Chris Toensing. London: Verso: 149–59.

James C. Scott. 1972. "Patron-Client Politics and Political Change in Southeast Asia." *The American Political Science Review* 66(1): 91–113.

Jane Kinninmont. 2012. "Bread, Dignity and Social Justice: The Political Economy of Egypt's Transition." *Chatham House*. Briefing Paper. At http://www .chathamhouse.org/sites/default/files/public/Research/Middle%20East/bp0412 _kinninmont.pdf, accessed March 20, 2014.

Jason Brownlee. 2007. *Authoritarianism in an Age of Democratization*. Cambridge: Cambridge University Press.

Jeffrey Winters. 2012. *Oligarchy*. Cambridge: Cambridge University Press.

Jennifer Gandhi and Adam Przeworski. 2006. "Cooperation, Cooptation and Rebellion under Dictatorships." *Economics and Politics* 18(1): 1–26.

Joel Beinin and Hossam el-Hamalawy. 2007. "Textile Workers Confront the New Economic Order." Middle East Report Online. March 25. At http://www.merip .org/mero/mero032507, accessed June 10, 2012.

John Sfakianakis. 2004. "The Whales of the Nile: Networks, Businessmen, and Bureaucrats during the Era of Privatization in Egypt." In *Networks of Privilege in the Middle East: The Politics of Economic Reform Revisited*, edited by Steven Heydemann. New York: Palgrave Macmillan: 77–100.

John Waterbury. 1983. *The Egypt of Nasser and Sadat: The Political Economy of Two Regimes*. New Jersey: Princeton University Press.

Jonathan Fox. 1994. "The Difficult Transition from Clientelism to Citizenship: Lessons from Mexico." *World Politics* 46(2): 151–84.

Jon Moran. 1999. "Patterns of Corruption and Development in East Asia." *Third World Quarterly* 20(3): 569–87.

Joshua Stacher. 2004. "Parties Over: The Demise of Egypt's Opposition Parties." *British Journal of Middle Eastern Studies* 31(2): 215–34.

———. 2012. *Adaptable Autocrats: Regime Power in Egypt and Syria*. Cairo: American University in Cairo Press.

Juan Linz. 1964. "An Authoritarian Regime: Spain." In *Cleavages, Ideologies and Party Systems: Contribution to Comparative Political Sociology*, edited by Erik Allardt and Yrjo Littunen. Helsinki: Transactions of the Westermarck Society: 291–341.

Karam Yehia. 2012. *The Black Box: The Story of Hussein Salem* (in Arabic). Cairo: Dar El Thakafa El Gadida.

Karl Fields. 1997. "Strong States and Business Organization in Korea and Taiwan." In *Business and the State in Developing Countries*, edited by Sylvia Maxfield and Ben Ross Schneider. Ithaca, NY: Cornell University Press: 121–51.

Kenneth Cooper. 2008. "Politics and Priorities: Inside the Egyptian Press." *Arab Society and Media* 6. At http://www.arabmediasociety.com/?article=689, accessed November 6, 2011.

Kenneth Cuno. 1980. "The Origins of Private Ownership of Land in Egypt: A Reappraisal." *International Journal of Middle East Studies* 12(3): 245–75.

Khalid Ikram. 2006. *The Egyptian Economy 1952–2000.* London: Routledge.

Lisa Blaydes. 2011. *Elections and Distributive Politics in Mubarak's Egypt.* Cambridge: Cambridge University Press.

Lisa Blaydes and Safinaz El Tarouty. 2011. "La Concurrence Interne Au Parti National Democrate Egyptien." In *Fabrique Des Elections,* edited by Florian Kohstall and Frédéric Vairel. Cairo: CEDEJ: 69–94.

Mahmud A. Faksh. 1992. "Egypt and the Gulf Crisis: The Role of Leadership under Mubarak." *Journal of Third World Studies* 9(1): 40–58.

Malak Zaalouk. 1989. *Power, Class and Foreign Capital in Egypt: The Rise of the New Bourgeoisie.* London: Zed Books.

Mamoun Fandy. 2007. *(Un)Civil War of Words: Media and Politics in the Arab World.* Westport, Connecticut: Praeger Security International.

Margaret Levi. 1988. *Of Rule and Revenue.* Berkeley: University of California Press.

Maria Faccio. 2006. "Politically Connected Firms." *American Economic Review* 96(1): 369–86.

Marie-Christine Aulas. 1982. "Sadat's Egypt: A Balance Sheet." *Middle East Report* 107: 6–18, 30–31.

Marleen Dieleman. 2007. *The Rhythm of Strategy: A Corporate Biography of the Salim Group of Indonesia.* Amsterdam: Amsterdam University Press.

Marvin G Weinbaum. 1985. "Egypt's *Infitah* and the Politics of US Economic Assistance." *Middle Eastern Studies* 21(2): 206–22.

Maye Kassem. 1999. *In the Guise of Democracy: Governance in Contemporary Egypt.* London: Ithaca Press.

———. 2002. "Information and Production of Knowledge or Lobbying? Businessmen's Association, Federation of Labor Unions, and the Ministry of Manpower." In *Institutional Reform and Economic Development in Egypt,* edited by Noha El-Mikawy and Heba Handoussa. Cairo: American University in Cairo Press: 61–78.

Michael Ross. 2001. "Does Oil Hinder Democracy." *World Politics* 53(3): 325–61.

Michael Shafer. 1997. "The Political Economy of Sectors and Sectoral Change: Korea Then and Now." In *Business and the State in Developing Countries,* edited by Sylvia Maxfield and Ben Ross Schneider. Ithaca, NY: Cornell University Press: 88–121.

Mohamed Fahmy Menza. 2013. *Patronage Politics in Egypt: The National Democratic Party and the Muslim Brotherhood in Cairo.* London: Routledge.

Mohamed Hamas El Masry. 2012. "Journalism with Restraint: A Comparative Content Analysis of Independent, Government, and Opposition Newspapers in Pre-Revolution Egypt." *Journal of Middle East Media* 8(1): 1–34.

Moheb Zaki. 1999. *Egyptian Business Elites: Their Visions and Investment Behavior.* Cairo: Konrad Adenauer Stiftung and the Arab Center for Development and Future Research.

Mona El-Ghobashy. 2005. "The Metamorphosis of the Egyptian Muslim Brothers." *International Journal of Middle East Studies* 37(3): 373–95.

———. 2010. "The Liquidation of Egypt's Illiberal Experiment." *Middle East Report Online.* December 29. At http://www.merip.org/mero/mero122910, accessed May 23, 2011.

———. 2012a. "The Dynamics of Elections under Mubarak." In *The Journey to Tahrir: Revolution, Protest and Social Change in Egypt,* edited by Jeannie Sowers and Chris Toensing. London: Verso: 132–48.

———. 2012b. "The Praxis of the Egyptian Revolution." In *The Journey to Tahrir: Revolution, Protest and Social Change in Egypt,* edited by Jeannie Sowers and Chris Toensing. London: Verso: 21–40.

Mostafa Ebeid. 2009. *Normalization through Business: The Secrets of Businessmen's Relations with Israel* (in Arabic). Cairo: Mirette for Publishing.

Nadia Farah. 2009. *Egypt's Political Economy: Power Relations in Development.* Cairo: American University in Cairo Press.

Nahed Ezz-El Din. 2003. *The Workers and the Businessmen: The Transformation of Political Opportunities in Egypt* (in Arabic). Cairo: Al-Ahram Center for Political and Strategic Studies.

Nathan J. Brown. 2012. "Egypt's Judges in a Revolutionary Age." *The Carnegie Papers.* Carnegie Endowment for International Peace. At http://carnegieendowment.org/2012/02/22/egypt-s-judges-in-revolutionary-age/9sri, accessed March 27, 2014.

Nazih Ayubi. 1991. *Political Islam: Religion and Politics in the Arab World.* London: Routledge.

———. 1995. *Over-Stating the Arab State: Politics and Society in the Middle East.* London: I. B. Tauris.

Nicola Pratt. 2000/2001. "Maintaining the Moral Economy: Egyptian State-Labor Relations in an Era of Economic Liberalization." *Arabic Studies Journal* 8(2)/9(1): 111–29.

Ninette Fahmy. 2002. *The Politics of Egypt: State-Society Relationship.* London: Routledge.

———. 2007. "Closing Up the Door: The Egyptian State and the Politico-Economic Entrepreneur: The Case of Nuwwab al-Qurud—Loans MPS." *L'Egypte Contemporaine* 485: 13–37.

Osama El Karam. 1997. *The Pretty Woman of the Bank and the Minister: How to Steal One Billion from the Banks* (in Arabic). Cairo: Center for Arab Civilization.

Oxford Business Group. May 18, 2007. At http://www.oxfordbusinessgroup.com/economic_updates/sawiris-assessment-otv-channel, accessed August 20, 2013.

Paul Klebnikov. 2001. *Godfather of the Kremlin: The Decline of Russia in the Age of Gangster Capitalism.* Orlando: Harcourt.

Peter Evans. 1989. "Predatory, Developmental, and Other Apparatuses: A Comparative Political Economy Perspective on the Third World State." *Sociological Forum* 4(4): 561–87.

Peter Rutland. 2009. "The Oligarchs and Economic Development." In *After Putin's Russia: Past Imperfect, Future Uncertain,* edited by Stephen Wegren and Dale Herspring. Lanham: Rowman and Littlefield: 159–82.

Philippe Schmitter. 1974. "Still the Century of Corporatism?" *The Review of Politics* 36(1): 85–131.

Ray Bush. 2007. "Politics, Power and Poverty: Twenty Years of Agriculture Reform and Market Liberalization in Egypt." *Third World Quarterly* 28(8): 1599–615.

———. 2009. "The Land and the People." In *Egypt the Moment of Change,* edited by Rabab El-Mahdi and Philip Marfleet. London: Zed Books: 51–67.

———. 2012. "Marginality or Abjection? The Political Economy of Poverty Production in Egypt." In *Marginality and Exclusion in Egypt,* edited by Ray Bush and Habib Ayeb. Cairo: American University in Cairo Press: 55–71.

Ray Bush and Jeremy Keenan. 2006. "North Africa: Power, Politics and Promise." *Review of African Political Economy* 33(108): 175–84.

Raymond Baker. 1990. *Sadat and After: Struggle for Egypt's Political Soul.* Cambridge, MA: Harvard University Press.

Raymond Hinnebusch. 1985. *Egyptian Politics under Sadat: The Post-Populist Development of an Authoritarian-Modernizing State.* Cambridge: Cambridge University Press.

———. 1993. "The Politics of Economic Reform in Egypt." *Third World Quarterly* 14(1): 159–71.

Robert Bianchi. 1989. *Unruly Corporatism: Associational Life in Twentieth-Century Egypt.* Oxford: Oxford University Press.

———. 1990. "Interest Groups and Politics in Mubarak's Egypt." In *The Political Economy of Contemporary Egypt,* edited by Ibrahim M. Oweiss. Washington, DC: Center for Contemporary Arab Studies at Georgetown University.

Robert Springborg. 1989. *Mubarak's Egypt: Fragmentation of the Political Order.* Boulder: Westview.

Robert Tignor. 1980. "Dependency Theory and Egyptian Capitalism, 1920–1950." *African Economic History* 9: 101–18.

———. 1987. "British Textile Companies and the Egyptian Economy." *Business and Economic History* 16: 53–67.

Robert Yin. 1984. *Case Study Research: Design and Methods.* Beverly Hills, CA: Sage.

Saad Eddin Ibrahim. 2002. *Egypt, Islam and Democracy.* Cairo: American University in Cairo Press.

Saad Khattab. 2005. *The Black Book about the Minister of Housing: Mohamed Ibrahim Soliman* (in Arabic). Cairo: El Rawy.

Samer Shehata and Joshua Stacher. 2012. "The Muslim Brothers in Mubarak's Last Decade." In *The Journey to Tahrir: Revolution, Protest and Social Change in Egypt,* edited by Jeannie Sowers and Chris Toensing. London: Verso: 160–77.

Samer Soliman. 2011. *The Autumn of Dictatorship: Fiscal Crises and Political Change in Egypt under Mubarak.* Stanford, CA: Stanford University Press.

Samia Saeid Imam. 1986. *Who Owns Egypt? An Analytical Study about the Social Origin of the Open-Door Economic Elite in Egyptian Society from 1974 to 1980* (in Arabic). Cairo: Dar El Mostakabal El Arabi.

Sami Zubaida. 1990. "The Politics of the Islamic Investment Companies in Egypt." *British Journal of Middle Eastern Studies* 17(2): 152–61.

Samuel Huntington. 1991. *The Third Wave: Democratization in the Late Twentieth Century*. Norman: University of Oklahoma Press.

Sawasiya Center for Human Rights. 2008. "Report about the Military Trial of the Leaders of the Muslim Brothers" (in Arabic). Cairo: Sawasiya.

Stephan Roll. 2010. "Finance Matters! The Influence of Financial Sector Reforms on the Development of Entrepreneurial Elite in Egypt." *Mediterranean Politics* 15(3): 349–70.

———. 2013. "Egypt's Business Elite after Mubarak: A Powerful Player between Generals and Brotherhood." *SWP Research Paper*. German Institute for International and Security Affairs. At http://www.swp-berlin.org/fileadmin/contents/products/research_papers/2013_RP08_rll.pdf, accessed March 22, 2014.

Stephen King. 2009. *The New Authoritarianism in the Middle East and North Africa*. Bloomington: Indiana University Press.

Steven Cook. 2005. "The Right Way to Promote Arab Reform." *Foreign Affairs* 84(2): 91–102.

Sufyan Alissa. 2007. "The Political Economy of Reform in Egypt: Understanding the Role of Institutions." *The Carnegie Papers*. Carnegie Endowment for International Peace. At http://carnegieendowment.org/files/cmec5_alissa_egypt_final.pdf, accessed January 24, 2011.

Sumit K. Majundar. 1992. "Performance in the US Telecommunications Services Industry: An Analysis of the Impact of Deregulation." *Telecommunications Policy* 16(4): 327–38.

Sydney Tarrow. 1998. *Power in Movement: Social Movement and Contentious Politics*. Cambridge: Cambridge University Press.

Tamir Moustafa. 2007. *The Struggle for Constitutional Power: Law, Politics and Economic Development in Egypt* Cambridge: Cambridge University Press.

Tim Besley and Andrea Prat. 2006. "Handcuffs for the Grabbing Hand? Media Capture and Government Accountability." *American Economic Review* 96(3): 720–36.

Timothy Mitchell. 2002. *Rule of Experts: Egypt, Techno-Politics, Modernity*. Berkeley: University of California Press.

Toby Mendel. 2011. "Political and Media Transitions in Egypt: A Snapshot of Media Policy and Regulatory Environment." *Internews*. At http://www.internews.org/sites/default/files/resources/Internews_Egypt_MediaLawReview_Aug11.pdf, accessed April 9, 2012.

Ursula Lindsey. 2012. "Revolution and Counter-Revolution in the Egyptian Media." In *The Journey to Tahrir, Revolution, Protest, and Social Change in Egypt*, edited by Jeannie Sowers and Chris Toensing. London: Verso: 107–17.

Wael Nawara. 2010. "Interview with Wael Nawara, Secretary General of the Ghad (Tomorrow) Party." *The Carnegie Papers*. Carnegie Endowment for International Peace. At http://egyptelections.carnegieendowment.org/2010/11/22/interview-with-wael-nawara-secretary-general-of-the-ghad-tomorrow-party, accessed March 9, 2012.

William L. Megginson and Jeffry M. Netter. 2001. "From State to Market: A Survey of Empirical Studies on Privatization." *Journal of Economic Literature* 39(2): 321–89.

Yahya Sadwoski. 1991. *Businessmen and Bureaucrats in the Development of Egyptian Agriculture*. Washington, DC: Brookings Institution.

Yasmeen Mohiuddin. 2007. "Boris Berezovsky: Russia's First Billionaire and Political Maverick Still Has It in for Vladimir Putin." *International Journal* 62(3): 681–88.

Yoram Meital. 2006. "The Struggle over Political Order in Egypt: The 2005 Elections." *Middle East Journal* 60(2): 257–79.

Ziya Onis and Umut Turem. 2002. "Entrepreneurs, Democracy and Citizenship in Turkey." *Comparative Politics* 34(4): 439–56.

Conference Papers

Lisa Blaydes. 2006. "Electoral Budget Cycles under Authoritarianism: Economic Opportunism in Mubarak's Egypt." Paper presented at the annual meeting of the Midwest Political Association, Chicago.

Sherif Kamel. 2004. "Evolution of Mobile Technology in Egypt." Paper presented at the Information Resources Management Association International Conference, New Orleans. At http://www.irma-international.org/viewtitle/32466, accessed June 10, 2011.

Zeinab Abdalla. 2009. "Steel Market in Egypt: A Case of Power Abuse?" Paper presented at the Middle East Studies Association, Boston.

Interpellations

Abu El Ezz El Hariry. 2002. Interpellation submitted to the People's Assembly about the monopoly of Ahmed Ezz to the Steel Industry.

———. 2004. Interpellation submitted to the People's Assembly about the monopoly in the telecommunications sector.

Anwar Esmat El Sadat. 2006. Interpellation submitted to the People's Assembly about the monopolization of the Red Sea ports.

El Badri Farghali. 2002. Interpellation submitted to the People's Assembly about the corruption of Minister of Housing Ibrahim Soliman.

Gamal Zahran. 2009. Interpellation submitted to the People's Assembly about the corruption in selling state-owned lands.

Interviews

Abdalla Shehata, professor of economics, Cairo University, May 15, 2010—Cairo.

Abdel Alim Dawood, member of parliament, the Wafd Party, March 15, 2010—Cairo.

Abdel Khalek Farouk, economist, May 18, 2010—Cairo.

Abdel Moneim Abu El Fotouh, former member of the Guidance Bureau of the Muslim Brothers (MB), February 28, 2010—Cairo.

Abu El Ezz El Hariry, opposition member of parliament and former member of the Tagammu' Party, April 24, 2010—Cairo.

Adel Gazarin, former head of the Egyptian Federation of Industry and the Egyptian Business Association, February 7 and 9, 2010—Cairo.

Ahmed Ayoub, journalist with *Al-Mossawar* Magazine, July 31, 2010—Cairo.

Ahmed El Baradei, former head of Cairo Bank, May 25, 2010—Cairo.

Ahmed Ezz, businessman, National Democratic Party (NDP) secretary, and head of the budget and planning committee of parliament, March 27, 2010—Cairo.

Ahmed Hussein Sabbour, former head of the Junior Egyptian Business Association, March 24, 2010—Cairo.

Alaa Abdel Moneim, independent member of parliament, March 4, 2010—Cairo.

Alaa El Aswany, author and political activist, August 20, 2010—Cairo.

Ali Fath El Bab, MB member of parliament, April 6, 2010—Cairo.

Ali Kamel, US Agency for International Development, July 27, 2010—Cairo.

Amr Assal, Development Authority chairman, February 28, 2010—Cairo.

Amr El Nasharti, businessman living abroad, October 29, 2009—London.

Amr El Shobaki, political activist, June 24, 2010—Cairo.

Anwar Esmat El Sadat, independent parliamentary businessman (nephew of President Sadat), July 26, 2010—Cairo.

Ashraf El Saad, businessman living abroad, October 6, 2009—London.

Ayman Nour, former president of the Ghad Party, December 17, 2009—Cairo.

Bahaa Raafat, businessman in the textile industry, March 9, 2010—Cairo.

El Badri Faraghli, senior member of the Tagammu' Party April 10, 2010—Cairo.

Essam El Haddad, businessman and brother of MB member Medhat El Haddad, April 15, 2010—Cairo.

Farid Ismail, MB member of parliament, March 24 and April 15, 2010—Cairo.

Fouad Sultan, former minister of tourism, May 10, 2010—Cairo.

Gamal Zahran, professor of political science, member of parliament, and head of the independent parliamentary bloc, April 12, 2010—Cairo.

Hamdin Sabahi, member of parliament and founder of the Karama Party, August 24, 2010—Cairo.

Hani Enan, businessman and sponsor of the Kefaya (Enough) movement, March 22, 2010–Cairo.

Hassan Hussein, former head of Bank Misr El Motahad, June 16, 2010—Cairo.

Hisham Kassem, newspaper publisher and former senior member of the Ghad Party, March 13, 2010—Cairo.

Hussein Sabbour, former head of the Egyptian Business Association, February 14, 2010—Cairo.

Ibrahim Darwish, constitutional expert and lawyer, March 2, 2010—Cairo.

Ibrahim El Essawy, professor of economics, May 12, 2010—Cairo.

Ibrahim Kamel, former member of parliament (joined parliament as an independent, then joined the NDP and then got dismissed from the party), June 16 and 23, 2010—Cairo.

Ismail Osman, NDP businessman (nephew of Osman Ahmed Osman), March 18, 2010—Cairo.

Kamal Ahmed, independent member of parliament, February 10, 2010—Cairo.

Kamal Beshai, businessman in the steel industry, April 8, 2010—Cairo.

Khaled Bahaa Raafat, businessman in the textile industry, March 16, 2010—Cairo.

Khaled El Mikati, businessman and former head of the Egyptian Junior Business Association, May 30, 2010—Cairo.

Khaled Khalil, businessman and member of the Egyptian Junior Business Association, June 2, 2010—Cairo.

Mamdouh Hamza, independent businessman and political activist, February 17 and May 2, 2010—Cairo.

Medhat El Haddad, MB businessman, March 24 and April 15, 2010—Cairo.

Mohamed Abdel Wahab, former minister of economy, June 8, 2010—Cairo.

Mohamed Bishr, member of the Guidance Bureau of the MB, March 13, 2010—Cairo.

Mohamed Kamel, lawyer and former member of parliament the Wafd Party, June 16, 2010—Cairo.

Mohamed Kassem, independent businessman, May 31, 2010—Cairo.

Mohamed Mansour Hassan, businessman and senior member of the Democratic Front Party, April 18, 2010—Cairo.

Mohamed Metwalli, independent businessman, April 2, 2010—Cairo.

Mohamed Youssef, secretary general of the Egyptian Business Association, May 16, 2010—Cairo.

Mona Makram Ebeid, former member of parliament and former senior member of the Ghad Party, June 11, 2010—Cairo.

Mounir Fakhry Abdel Nour, senior member of the Wafd Party, August 3, 2010—Cairo.

Morsi El Sheikh, former judge and senior member of the Ghad Party, April 20, 2010—Cairo.

Nagui El Ghatrify, ambassador and former senior member of the Ghad Party, July 8, 2010—Cairo.

Negad El Borai, human rights activist, July 6, 2010—Cairo.

Omar Said El Ahl, businessman and former senior member of the Ghad Party, August 26, 2010—Cairo.

Ossama El Ghazaly Harb, president of the Democratic Front Party, April 7, 2010—Cairo.

Ramy Lakah, businessman living abroad, October 16, 2009—London.
Reda Eissa, expert on the Egyptian taxation system, April 8, 2010—Cairo.
Saad El Husseiny, member of the Guidance Bureau of the MB and member of parliament, March 13, 2010—Cairo.
Saad Khairat El Shatter, son of MB member and businessman Khairat El Shatter, February 3, 2010—Cairo.
Talaat Esmat El Sadat, lawyer and independent member of parliament (nephew of President Sadat), July 15, 2010—Cairo.
Tarek El Malt, senior member of the Wasat Party, August 19, 2010—Cairo.
Wael Nawara, senior member of the Ghad Party, April 13, 2010—Cairo.
Wagdy Robat, senior banker, May 26, 2010—Cairo.
Wagih Siag, businessman living abroad, October 16, 2009—London.

Official Documents

1971 Egyptian Constitution. 1999. The General Organization for Government Printing Offices.
Ruling of the Cairo Court of Appeals. December 24, 2000. The Case of Medhat El Haddad.
Ruling of the Cairo Court of Appeals. February 13, 2001. The Case of Medhat El Haddad.
Ruling of the Supreme Security Court. July 31, 2002. The Case of Loan MPs.
US Department of Justice. 2008. Report of the Attorney General to the Congress of the United States on the Administration of the Foreign Agents Registration Act. At http://www.fara.gov/reports/June30-2008.pdf, accessed August 7, 2011.

PhD Dissertations and MA Theses

Eric Trager. 2012. "Trapped and Untrapped: Mubarak's Opponents on the Eve of His Oust." PhD dissertation, University of Pennsylvania.
Maisa El Gamal. 1992. "Egypt's Ministerial Elite, 1971–1981." PhD dissertation, Birkbeck College, University of London.
Neha Sahgal. 2008. "Divided We Stand, but United We Oppose: Opposition Alliances in Egypt and Pakistan." PhD dissertation, University of Maryland.
Safinaz El Tarouty. 2004. "Institutionalization and Reform: The Case of the National Democratic Party in Egypt." Master's thesis, American University in Cairo.

Web Sites

American Chamber of Commerce in Egypt. "About AMCHAM/History." At http://www.amcham.org.eg/about_us/objdefault.asp, accessed March 27, 2014.

Egyptian Organization for Human Rights. "An Appeal to the President of the Republic: Those Responsible for the Events of Al-Kosheh Must Pay the Price." At http://www.derechos.org/human-rights/mena/eohr/price.html, accessed March 27, 2014.

Magdy El Galad. "I Will Vote for Gamal Mubarak." May 23, 2010. Available on You-Tube. At http://www.youtube.com/watch?v=7OVFWYf3Z28&NR=1, accessed August 20, 2013.

Ministry of Health. "The Minister Decree 350 for Regulation of Tramadol." At http://www.eda.mohp.gov.eg/Download/Docs/Decree350.pdf, accessed March 26, 2014.

Index

Al or El (the article meaning the) is ignored in the alphabetizing of Arabic names; for example, El Baradei will be listed under *B*; El-Sadat will be listed under *S*.

CPSIA information can be obtained
at www.ICGtesting.com
Printed in the USA
LVOW02*0550310317
529164LV00007B/24/P